SOUTH

# GLOBAL SUSTAINABLE DEVELOPMENT IN THE TWENTY-FIRST CENTURY

# Global Sustainable Development in the Twenty-first Century

Edited by

Keekok Lee, Alan Holland and Desmond McNeill

Edinburgh University Press

Edinburgh University Press Ltd
22 George Square, Edinburgh

Typeset in Goudy Old Style
by Hewer Text Ltd, Edinburgh, and
printed and bound in Great Britain
by MPG Books Ltd, Bodmin

A CIP record for this book is
available from the British Library

ISBN 1 85331 241 X (paperback)

# Contents

CONTENTS

# *Preface*

This volume contains contributions from writers in diverse disciplines, such as environmental philosophy, sociology, social anthropology and development studies, as well as practitioners in developmental work. With one exception, all the contributions are original to the volume; a slightly different version of Mark Sagoff's paper appeared recently in *The Atlantic Monthly*. The editors hope that by drawing together strands of thought culled from so many different and varied sources, the volume will succeed in bringing out the complexities of the very notion of global sustainable development, including its contested nature. This collection also exposes some of the very real problems facing any attempt simultaneously to procure justice and to safeguard the environment in a world of rapid technological change, riven by inequalities of wealth and power, and driven in the main by economic growth. By so doing, this volume focuses on one of the crucial challenges, if not the main challenge, facing humankind in the twenty-first century.

The Commentaries preceding each chapter have been provided by Alan Holland.

The Editors

# Acknowledgements

The editors would like to thank all the contributors for their cheerful cooperation and patience as well as their expenditure of precious time and energy in making this volume a reality. The editors are also very grateful to Edinburgh University Press for seeing through a project which was initiated under a different aegis and also, in particular, to Nicola Carr for her forebearance and understanding in coping with the inevitable problems inherent in such an undertaking.

# Sustainable Development:
# The Contested Vision

The presiding deity for this volume has to be the god Janus, who gave his name to the month of January. He stands poised at the turn of the year, looking both backwards to what has been, and forwards to what is to come. In like fashion the contributors to this volume look first, and reflectively, at the particular social, political and environmental circumstances in which the concept of sustainable development was forged, and the set of problems which it sought to address. In this connection, attention naturally falls on what was undoubtedly one of the most influential texts of its time – the 'Brundtland Report.' This took its name from the then Norwegian prime minister, Gro Harlem Brundtland, who chaired the World Commission on Environment and Development which was responsible for producing the report. It is commonly agreed that the Brundtland Report broke the mould by replacing the confrontational and sometimes rancorous debates that had hitherto prevailed with a more constructive approach to environment and development issues. It offered people hope by purporting to show how existing, yet apparently conflicting, aspirations might be harnessed together, and how they might be framed as part of a common goal.

Our contributors also look forward. In this connection, as environmental problems take on an increasingly global character, their focus is upon the prospects for sustainable development at a global level. To talk of environmental problems as 'global' can mean a number of different things. It can refer to problems that are common to all peoples, even though they are affected in different ways and to different degrees – climate change, for example, or the hole in the ozone layer. It can refer to shared problems whose nature is different for different regions – loss of biodiversity for example. Or it can refer to transboundary problems, where events that have a specific location have implications for peoples elsewhere on the globe. The disappearance of the tropical rainforests would be one example, and the 'export' of acid rain another. Here surely lie some of the next century's greatest challenges.

But while the scale of environmental problems reaches ever more widely, the social and institutional arrangements needed to cope with them seem hardly to be keeping pace. There is no doubt that part of the appeal of sustainable development is that it appears to present a practical objective – a practical way of doing something about these problems. But the practicality of this objective depends upon the existence of a whole host of enabling conditions. These include appropriate political and economic systems, at both national and international level; robust social and legal institutions; and the wealth that lies in the habits, practices and skills of individual citizens – in a phrase, 'social capital.' Equally important are the visions and ideals that inform these systems and institutions. Accordingly, the likely social, economic and political realities that will govern any attempt at realising the objective of sustainable development form another central focus of the volume. Our contributors give insight into these complexities. They show how different issues, contrasts and conflicts are thrown into relief when the concept of sustainable development is overlaid onto different backgrounds, or inserted into different contexts. They look beneath the simplifying dichotomies of 'North' and 'South', 'developed' and developing', and find elements that at least give grounds for hope. A recurring theme is the contrast between different approaches to realising the objective. One may be called the prevailing vision, variously referred to by our contributors as 'ecological modernisation', 'global eco-liberalism' or, simply, 'global development.' This assumes the operation of the global market economy and seeks means of accommodating environmental objectives within that framework. It tends to be managerial in style, to favour command and control instruments, and to take an instrumental view of environmental assets. On the other hand, we also glimpse a variety of alternative visions that emanate from and find a response among more marginalised peoples. These tend to involve decentralised, unmanaged approaches that present a challenge to existing institutions of property and power. Perhaps one of the most fertile sources for reflection to emerge from this volume is the issue of how far the objectives of sustainable development can be achieved within the framework of the prevailing vision; and how far real progress depends upon the conversion of our thinking to some more radical vision.

But sober reflection hardly ends there. For in the view of at least some of our contributors, the realisation of sustainable development is not what we should be pursuing in the first place. They argue not only that it is incapable of uniting the hopes of those who fight for justice, those with concerns for the future and those who want to defend nature, but also that it has the potential both to frustrate and to marginalise these very causes.

In taking this view they reflect fairly accurately the note of scepticism and suspicion that has accompanied the concept of sustainable development since it was first formulated. Some environmentalists have suspected all along that what is billed as a constraint on business as usual will prove to be a cover for business as usual. So Vandana Shiva, for one, has commented on the paradox that development and growth, which are creatures of the market economy, are being offered, under the banner of sustainable development, as a cure for the very ecological crisis that they have served to bring about. Moreover, the sustainability agenda has proved a fertile source of mutual suspicion between North and South – the poorer countries suspecting that the constraint on development now judged to be necessary, as a result of patterns of economic activity from which they have received little or no benefit, is being used to justify a constraint on their development. This was already a key issue at the Conference on Environment and Development held in Stockholm in 1972, twenty years before the Earth Summit at Rio de Janeiro in 1992. It continued to underlie the acrimonious exchanges over the Climate Change and Biodiversity Conventions that were hammered out at the Rio conference.

Certainly, conflicts of interest are involved here, but also conflicting values and ideologies. At this point, the siren voices of the pragmatists are increasingly heard, telling us to get real. What matters, they say, is that we develop working solutions on the ground, and lay our disagreements about values to one side. They sometimes add that if we had to settle our ideological disagreements first, then nothing would ever be done. But this approach seems not to do justice to the deep suspicions roused by the sustainability agenda. On the one side are the suspicions that it is a device, whether intentional or not, for blocking 'Southern' development. Resentments are built up by conservation projects, dam-building schemes and the like, that are financed by the wealthy economies. These, as some of our contributors indicate, are seen as expressions of a distinctly 'Northern' agenda, designed to limit the global environmental impact of economic activity of which they are the primary beneficiaries. Nature conservation, in particular, is seen as a value that the developed economies preach but do not practice. But the pragmatists also overlook the fact that a much more potent and insidious force for the corruption and displacement of local, and often 'Southern', values is represented by the values imbibed along with the products, practices and institutions of the market economy. The idea that one can draw a distinction between working solutions and ideology is an illusion experienced mainly by those whose ideology pervades most working solutions undertaken within the framework of the market economy. Ken Saro-wiwa's battle with the Shell oil company, and the French farmers' arson attack on MacDonald's, are sober reminders of the strength of feeling that lies (only just) below the surface.

Meanwhile the capitalist economy trundles on, an immensely conservative force jealously guarded by bodies, such as the World Trade Organisation, who blatantly advance the interests of the most powerful economies. As currently operated, it is simply not geared up to make the kind of difference that is needed – a point eloquently illustrated by President Bush's remark ahead of Rio that the American way of life was not negotiable. However, notwithstanding the obstacles posed by such powerful and entrenched positions, it may well be the case that the most realistic hope for change does indeed lie in the slow and painstaking modification of this juggernaut. But this raises the question: what will motivate such change? When politicians and business leaders dare not say other than that they are putting the interests of their countries and companies first, a modest start may perhaps be made by doing what one can to foster and promote a much enlarged and enriched conception of what those interests are. I appeal here to Desmond McNeill's anticipation of a growing gulf between those whom he calls 'technicists', dedicated to finding technical solutions to environmental problems, and those whom he calls 'humanists', dedicated to finding political solutions. When the technicists, here in the guise of environmental economists, charge that we can only save the environment by costing it properly – a project that stays well within the dominant paradigm – the humanists are entitled to reply that they cannot abide and do not recognise the picture of the human subject that is incorporated in this project. In taking this view they are in a position to make common cause with those in the developing economies whose challenge to the paradigm is not, as Enrique Leff will remind us, based so much upon interests, as upon values and ideology. In doing this the humanists do not merely offer questions and criticism, as technicists frequently allege, but make a real contribution by keeping alive alternative visions of the good life, which arguably are crucial if the capitalist economy is to be steered in a sustainable direction.

From our preceding analysis it is clear that both the foundations of the concept, and the value of sustainable development as a policy objective, are keenly contested. But it is possible to argue that its true value lies elsewhere. This, at least, is the suggestion of Desmond McNeill (Chapter 1), whose contribution begins the volume. McNeill notes that the debate about sustainable development occurs at the interface between theory and practice, where it appears to have been highly effective in loosening entrenched positions and re-shaping debate. It has all the makings, in McNeill's words, of 'an idea that makes a difference.' The fortunes of such ideas can vary. Speaking of the concept of 'pragmatism', for example, the

American philosopher William James claimed that it, like all significant ideas, had passed through three stages: being rejected; being admitted as true but insignificant; and finally, being seen as so important that its opponents claim to have thought of it first. McNeill stops short of predicting how the concept of sustainable development itself will fare, but observes that even ideas that are apparently abandoned can gain a new lease of life when placed in a different context.

Keekok Lee (Chapter 2), on the other hand, presents a case for saying that, in the key area of social justice, the version of sustainable development promulgated by the Brundtland Report is unlikely to make a difference. It is in fact more likely to exacerbate existing inequalities. The nub of her argument is that the Report largely ignores the extent to which affluent societies have already more than met their needs and are hell-bent on the business of satisfying their wants. If views corresponding to those of President Bush are widespread among the G7 countries, this strongly suggests that the famous prescription in the Brundtland Report about leaving enough for everyone to satisfy their needs is likely to be heeded, if at all, only in a minimal sense. Hence the Report sanctions a rather different future for affluent and non-affluent societies.

Andrew Dobson (Chapter 3) is equally sceptical about how far sustainable development as understood by Brundtland will help towards the defence of nature – another key area where it is hoped that it might 'make a difference.' He examines two routes through which sustainable development might be thought to serve the cause of environmental protection. One is through the link with social justice. The idea is that measures to eliminate inequalities will necessarily involve the alleviation of poverty, and this in turn will help to stop environmental destruction. The assumption is that poor people tend to destroy their local environments because they have little choice in the matter. But Dobson's response is that the relations between social justice and the state of the environment are many and various. If nature is to be protected, it had better be done in more direct ways rather than indirectly and instrumentally. The other route is through the link with future generations. Here, the idea is that a robust defence of biodiversity is by far the best way to preserve the options and opportunities for future generations to meet their needs. Dobson is unconvinced. The defence of nature is still instrumental; and nature is bound to lose out when up against the more pressing needs of the present.

In Enrique Leff's contribution (Chapter 4) we meet a liberated, even anarchic version of the concept of sustainable development that appears to have escaped from under Brundtland's skirts. Rooted in the experiences of the indigenous and peasant peoples of Latin America, it expresses a very different understanding of environmental rationality. It looks to improve efficiency not by decoupling industrial activity from its natural resource base – the project of the prevailing paradigm – but by re-integrating productive technology with its ecological and cultural moorings. This is no technical proposal, but a political statement that speaks of rights, self-determination and cultural identity – a reclamation of both cultural and ecological inheritance. Leff's analysis brings out important elements of the sustainability debate that frequently go unrecognised or are rendered invisible by more conventional accounts. These include the distinction between the governments and the peoples of 'Southern' economies, whose interests and instincts may be very different; and a more fundamental distinction still between forms of ownership (or appropriation) expressed by market relations, and forms of ownership (or appropriation) that express cultural identities.

But is the prevailing paradigm such a lost cause? Its natural habitat, after all, is found among the economies of the developed world. Jan Boersema and Joeri Bertels (Chapter 5), in their review of three developed economies – Italy, The Netherlands and the US – are a little more charitable. Bringing a higher level of resolution to bear upon these three economies, they find it possible to detect at least some measure of progress in the direction of sustainability, especially in the case of the Netherlands where a number of regulatory instruments, social and economic, are already in place. Even in these contexts, however, their analysis highlights the acute shortage of suitable indicators for measuring such progress. This is a serious problem indeed, since the use of indicators is crucial to the effectiveness of the prevailing paradigm, and their absence provides governments with every excuse for backsliding.

Michael Redclift's contribution (Chapter 6) is based on the premise that global sustainable development will remain out of reach without some common agreement on and shared commitment to values such as equity. But herein lies a difficulty because, even if many environmental problems are global in their reach, values themselves have a culturally specific location. He illustrates his thesis by posing the question of how far 'Northern' solutions address 'Southern' problems. With what he willingly admits to be the advantage of hindsight, he shows how the policy of economic liberalisation pursued since the Second World War has worked mainly to the detriment of the developing economies: thus, what some will see as the 'equity' of free trade translates into what others experience as the inequitable distribution of power and resources. His analysis crystallises a number of themes raised elsewhere in this volume: it rubs salt into the rift between 'Southern' and 'Northern' approaches to sustainable development and further elaborates the difficulties facing the project of 'ecological modernisation' – itself an expression of culturally specific values.

In apparent contrast, Mark Sagoff (Chapter 7) mounts a forceful attack upon four propositions that many environmentalists will regard as self-evident. These are: (i) that we are running out of raw materials; (ii) that we are running out of food and timber; (iii) that we are running out of energy; and (iv) that the North exploits the South. Using a mix of extensive citation and ingenious argument he suggests that all of these propositions are misconceived. His aim, however, is not to attack the environmentalists' conclusions but to demonstrate that they have chosen the wrong ground upon which to argue their case. The question, he says, is not whether we are going to run out of resources, but 'whether economics is the appropriate context for thinking about environmental policy.' Hence his position is closer to that of other contributors than it at first sight appears.

Mary Mellor (Chapter 8) argues that ecofeminist analyses, while open to criticisms, have many insights to offer into the sustainability debate. Her contribution serves in particular to suggest a broader base for the alternative visions of sustainable development referred to earlier in this introduction. Although she shies away from the idea that there is some essential feature that is common to all women's experience, her analysis shows that Southern women at least have been consistently marginalised by the operation of the global market economy. Since this is a basic constituent of the prevailing paradigm of sustainable development, it is natural that women should stand opposed to that paradigm. Their key role in subsistence-based agriculture, in maintaining social and ecological diversity and in transmitting local ecological knowledge, gives some inkling of what an ecofeminist alternative vision of sustainable living might be like. It would fit well with what Enrique Leff terms 'environmental democracy' – a mode of constructive participation and shared decision-making, based on the values of equity, diversity and sustainability.

Other contributors have said much that puts the values of the prevailing paradigm in their place. Roy Ellen (Chapter 9) does the same for the science upon which it relies. His counterpoint is the phenomenon of local or indigenous knowledge (something that would no doubt play a big part in Leff's 'environmental democracy'). He points out that the comparatively recent tendency to marginalise such knowledge is out of step with a long tradition of interaction between official and unofficial sources of knowledge. He is critical of unduly romantic deference to indigenous cultures, but is more troubled by the practice of trying to extract from them general principles or insights, which misses the essential point: the value of local knowledge lies in its being local. His most pointed observation concerns the status of Western science itself: we should see it, he says, as but another species of indigenous knowledge.

Our contributors canvas a number of different approaches to global sustainable development. What has been missing so far is the direct frontal assault, which many see as a short-cut to sustainability – namely, the method of population control. Avner de-Shalit (Chapter 10) meets the proposal head on, and argues that it is both inefficient and immoral. His case for deeming it inefficient is that there are other factors that have a far greater impact on the state of the environment than human numbers. They include technology, just institutions and education. His case for deeming it immoral is that it amounts to a denial of the right to self-fulfilment. I derive an additional conclusion: that no approach to sustainability is acceptable that does not incorporate the sustainability of certain fundamental values.

Koos Neefjes's contribution (Chapter 11) is based on practical experience gained mostly in the rural South. He argues the importance to the sustainability agenda of promoting various forms of participation. Effective participation allows people to determine their own livelihood strategies – in short to 'define their environments.' In this way, people both carry responsibility for their decisions, and live with the outcomes. The analysis would seem to have implications for decision-makers everywhere, since a great deal of bad decision-making is attributable to the separation of the decision-maker from both the responsibility for, and the consequences of, their decisions. Further objectives of participation are (i) empowerment and (ii) environmental improvement. But both, it seems, are problematic. Empowerment raises problems because it necessarily implies not just the distribution but the redistribution of power. And the link with environmental improvement is uncertain. All the same, what Neefjes describes sounds very like what we might call 'field trials in environmental democracy' (cf. Leff). And although these might not guarantee environmental improvement in an instrumental sense, they do constitute a step towards what he calls civil society, part of the social capital that is crucial to any sustainability programme.

The contributors to this volume track and evaluate a number of different pathways, and different kinds of pathway, to sustainable development. These include procedural, structural and instrumental approaches. In saying this, one risks leaving the impression that global sustainable development is being regarded as an objective in its own right which, strictly speaking, it is not. It is good, then, to be reminded of what we seek to achieve by its means, which is well-expressed in the phrase with which Neefjes ends his piece: 'a healthy environment for everybody, everywhere.'

# Sustainability:

## 'An idea that makes a difference'?

Desmond McNeill draws attention to how the concept of sustainable development has influenced and been influenced by a variety of 'actors' – policy-makers, academics, activists – and also to how it has been shaped by, and has itself re-fashioned, earlier debates about poverty, development and environmental protection. The different 'actors', he argues, have different interests at stake by virtue of their different roles – academics in designing, activists in promoting and policy-makers in implementing the concept. McNeill also shows how we need to be aware of the influence and contribution of different disciplines to the sustainability debate – notably, ecology, anthropology and economics, each of which makes different assumptions about the relation between environment and human subject, and inevitably, therefore, commands different perspectives and proposes a different order of priorities. He notes the uniqueness of economics in offering not only a disciplinary perspective, but also various instruments of policy implementation, and in doing so helps to explain, perhaps, the pervading influence of this discipline in the sustainability debate.

For all his talk of perspectives, McNeill does appear to acknowledge that the concept of sustainable development has at least one essential feature. One of his more striking claims, and one that is borne out in the later contributions, is that there is conflict at its core, a conflict that explains its contested status. It can be manifested (i) as the conflict between the interests of the present and the interests of future generations (see for example Chapter 10), (ii) as the conflict between human well-being and the protection of nature (see for example Dobson's chapter in this volume), (iii) as the conflict between poor and rich, or (iv) as the conflict between a local and a global focus. These conflicts are portrayed as residues of the earlier, and relatively separate, debates about development on the one hand, and environment on the other. In the process of fusion that marks the onset of the debate about sustainable development, McNeill detects the emergence of a new conflict, between those whom he calls 'technicists', including both social and natural scientists, who are looking for technical solutions to environmental problems, and those whom he calls 'humanists', whose approach is altogether more critical and, if it looks anywhere for 'solutions', will presumably look towards the altogether messier realm of politics.

It is worth adding that a difficulty emerging alongside this conflict is how to decide what is to count as a 'solution' to an environmental problem, and how to recognise when a 'solution' has been reached. Thus, in cases of conflict, there are potential losers. But as McNeill hints in his conclusion, the complexity of the conflicts involved makes it hard to see what combinations of policies and actions will forward the sustainability agenda, and what will motivate people to seek them. In taking thought for future generations, we may be helping the rich; whilst some measures taken to protect the non-human environment may damage the poor. As he says, global warming is typical of the problems that a move to sustainable development is designed to tackle, but it is not a priority issue for many of the world's poorest people.

~ O ~

# 1 THE CONCEPT OF SUSTAINABLE DEVELOPMENT

# *Desmond McNeill*

## – INTRODUCTION –

It was the Report of the World Commission on Environment and Development (the Brundtland Report), published in 1987, which put the term 'sustainable development' on the map.[1] This, together with the conference in Rio in 1992, was a massive and, to a large extent successful, agenda-setting exercise. Central to this agenda was the concept of sustainable development. My purpose in this chapter is to offer a critical analysis of the term, showing how it has influenced, and been influenced by, policy-makers, activists and academics; and how the debate on sustainable development has reshaped the largely separate debates – on development and on environment – that preceded it. I shall address the political and ethical aspects of the issue, showing in particular how the perspectives and interests of the poorer countries may be overlooked or misrepresented. Since the different actors have different perspectives and interests, one cannot expect that all will agree even on the meaning of the term 'sustainable development', and it is not my aim to provide the 'ideal' definition; but the concept itself provides an excellent anchor for an analysis of the wider issues.

## – ALTERNATIVE INTERPRETATIONS OF SUSTAINABLE DEVELOPMENT –

Since the publication of the Brundtland Report there have been innumerable debates as to what is meant by sustainable development. I take as my starting point the 'standard' definition in the Brundtland Report: 'Sustainable development is development that meets the needs of the present without compromising the ability of future generations to meet their own needs' (Brundtland 1987, p. 8). Explicit in this definition is a contrast, and indeed a potential conflict, between two interests: those of present and future generations. This is a conflict arising out of a recognition that growth in material well-being has implications for the environment. And this implies the need for a trade-off, a choice arising out of the fact that two goals are at least partly in conflict. Both the sort of definition one prefers and the nature of the trade-off one favours are strongly influenced by one's perspective.

The answer to the question: 'What do you mean by the term sustainable development?' depends on whether one is seeking a definition or a description. A good definition (for scientific purposes) is rigorous, minimal, exclusive. A good description is rich, informative, inclusive. It is important to make a distinction between the two, although in common usage this is often blurred.

In academic debate, the introduction of new terms is quite common – often associated with a new theory, a new species, a new material. In many disciplines (though perhaps less commonly in the natural sciences) a lively debate often rages around the definition of a new term. The term is first coined, then much discussed, and even finally abandoned, perhaps to be picked up again elsewhere.[2]

In such circumstances there are often two interconnected debates being conducted in parallel: one that seems to be about the definition of a term and the other about the issues (theoretical and empirical) to which it relates. But clearly the analytical term and the issues mutually affect each other. It is impossible to have the debate without both a term (such as sustainable development) and at least some degree of consensus as to what it means. It may be necessary to change or qualify the term as a result of debate. But, even so, the term has an important impact on the debate, and it would be wrong either to dismiss debate about definitions as meaningless or to believe that it is possible to arrive at some final, uncontested conclusion.

This debate falls within the realm between academia and practice. Here, at the interface between research and policy, there is a place for what may be called 'ideas that makes a difference.'[3] These are powerful concepts, with a wide appeal. Precisely because they operate in this realm, not only are they contended, but the authority of academia to be the arbiter of the debate is also contended. Indeed, some would argue that academic discussions about the niceties of definition will render the concepts less, rather than more, powerful. But I would argue that such concepts must be clear and rigorous.

In briefly reviewing alternative views on what the term means, I will consider four types of actor: the academic, the activist, the bureaucrat (political), and the bureaucrat (legal).[4] The first two are self-explanatory. The difference between the others is that the third one is a bureaucrat in the position of making policy statements, while the fourth is the bureaucrat in the position of drafting law. I wish to compare how the definition of sustainable development differs for each actor. Do they distinguish clearly between the goals of increased material well-being and environmental sustainability? Do they perceive a trade-off between these two? And what is their attitude to the trade-off? More precisely, it is useful to determine whether the respective actors assume that a conflict is possible or even unavoidable, and whether the actor is engaged or dispassionate in relation to the issue.

### – Academic –

The terms 'sustainability' and 'development' are clearly defined so as to be conceptually distinct. Neither is explicitly valued, either negatively or positively. And whether there is a conflict between the two is an issue which needs to be tested empirically. Thus, for example, development might be defined as a 'process of increasing average material well-being' and sustainable as 'not irreversibly damaging the natural environment.' This position may be characterised as open/uncommitted. (At the extreme it can be taken to justify total inaction, which is why the concept of the precautionary principle has been so important in the debate.)

### – Activist –

Both terms are clearly interpreted, if not explicitly defined, so as to be conceptually distinct; one or both are clearly valued, either negatively or positively. Less emphasis is placed on the importance of empirical testability. The environmental activist is one who favours protection of the environment at the expense of increased material well-being (assumed to be the price one has to pay). An extreme position regards increased material well-being negatively, while a more moderate one regards both positively, but sees environmental concerns as overriding. On the other hand, development activists – those who believe that material well-being (or at least alleviation of poverty) is overriding – would take the opposite viewpoint. These positions may be characterised as closed/committed. Taken to extremes they can be used to propose, and even impose, a wide range of drastic actions which may or may not be justified (or to resist actions which are justified).

– Bureaucrat (political) –

In theory politicians both reflect and influence the views of the people, while bureaucrats implement the policies that politicians choose. Either faces a dilemma which may be well summarised in relation to the UNCED (United Nations Conference on Environment and Development) process. This was initiated by a political decision at the international level; the United Nations had agreed that the environment was an issue of major importance. The process had to be carried through by bureaucrats dealing with politicians, academics and activists. (Obviously many people occupy more than one role – see Glasser et al. 1994.)

In the preparatory meetings leading up to the Rio conference, the academics played a substantial role, writing background papers, describing and analysing the problems. As the process continued, the activists and the politicians took over and the academics found themselves squeezed out. But at the end of the day it was the bureaucrats who had the task of implementation. They had to confront both the empirical questions (what are the facts of the case?) and the policy questions (what should be done about them?).[5]

The bureaucrats had to come up with a form of words which should be as concrete, specific and binding as possible, but also agreed to by as many as possible. This of course involved interesting and complex trade-offs between maximising the number of signatories and being as precise as possible. That process is not my main concern here, but it does of course impinge directly on the subject of this paper, namely the concept of sustainable development. Agreement at Rio was achieved at some cost, in terms of the clarity of this concept, and this process has been extended to numerous subsequent negotiations (see below).

A similar predicament arises in relation to each country's own policy document, and as a result the definition of sustainable development may begin to differ in each country. The extent of commitment to sustainable development as a goal will also vary very greatly. Under pressure from outside, and receiving technical assistance in the drawing-up of policy documents and legislation, some aid-dependent developing countries will present policies that may look impressive on paper but have little meaning in reality.

– Bureaucrat (legal) –

There is an important difference between a policy document and a legally binding agreement, although the distinction is beginning to be blurred with the development of so-called 'soft law.' At Rio, and subsequently, a number of legally binding agreements have been signed. And here the role of the lawyer becomes crucial. If a country is serious about implementation of the agreement, then very precise concepts are needed. It is interesting to note that terms such as 'sustainable' and 'development' then tend to appear only in the preamble to such documents, or simply give way altogether to more concrete and specific terms.[6]

Although this may be a wise response, I shall nevertheless not abandon the term here, but rather investigate further how it might possibly be defined, recognising that perhaps no definition can satisfy all four types of actor. However, an adequate definition should satisfy three requirements:

1. It should be rigorous in the sense that it distinguishes what is true by definition from what is true empirically. (That a bachelor is unmarried is true by definition; that Queen Elizabeth I was unmarried is true empirically.)
2. It should be unbiased, that is it should not have value-laden terms built into it. (Thus a term like 'higher' should be used rather than 'better.')
3. It should avoid self-reference. (Thus, in this case, the definition should include neither the word 'sustainable' nor 'development.')

It is, of course, often difficult fully to satisfy these requirements.[7] (For an early discussion of some of these see, for example, Redclift 1992.) I shall not review these or try to come up with the perfect definition, but simply observe that some fail the test of rigour; some fail the test of bias; some fail the test of self-reference.[8]

However, even satisfying the three suggested requirements may not be sufficient; a fourth must be added, namely, that the definition makes it clear that there is potential conflict of some kind. This is essential to the meaning and significance of the concept; it is what makes it both powerful and contentious. Most definitions do at least do this, but it is important to note that the conflict may be presented in two different, though related ways, either as a conflict between growth in material well-being and the environment, or between the rights of different groups (normally of present and future generations). The former should give rise to hypotheses which are empirically testable. The latter necessarily moves into the ethical/political arena; but academic research should nevertheless be able to make some contribution here too.[9]

## – CONTRASTING PERSPECTIVES OF DIFFERENT DISCIPLINES –

Researchers themselves do not form a homogeneous group. Within academia, too, perspectives on sustainable development differ, although there may be a fair degree of consensus that the concept should be defined according to accepted standards of academic rigour. Both environment and development are very broad terms; and to study the relationship between the two is to study the enormously complex interplay within and between nature and humans.

I shall here focus on three disciplines that are central to the study of sustainable development or, more broadly, of the relationship between development and the environment. These are ecology, economics and anthropology (or sociology). It should be added that within the field of environmental studies, a whole range of other natural sciences – chemistry, physics, geology, and so on – are predominant. And when one moves from analysis to policy, then others, such as law, become more important, while if one is concerned with fundamental issues then philosophy (whether practical ethics or the philosophy of science) is central. Almost all disciplines have something to contribute to the study of either development or environment, and I shall here not seek to comment on their relative merits.[10] The primary reason why I have selected the three disciplines mentioned above is that they mark out the extremes of the space, because they contrast with each other in important ways. Thus:

Economics is concerned with the interactions of individuals as rational, self-interested, autonomous, maximising decision-makers. But it treats nature typically as a material resource/constraint.

Anthropology regards human beings interacting with one another not only as decision-makers but also as meaning-makers, with the emphasis on the collective. It considers nature both as a resource/constraint and as a locus of meaning.

Ecology is concerned with human beings as a species, interacting as biological beings, both with their own and other species and with the inorganic environment; the emphasis is on the whole as a system.

These are different theoretical and methodological perspectives.[11] A separate, though closely related, issue involves distinguishing between three competing or complementary sets of objectives. These are summarised in the so-called ESD triangle (see figure 1.1). This, or some variant of it, is increasingly being used in debates concerning sustainable development.

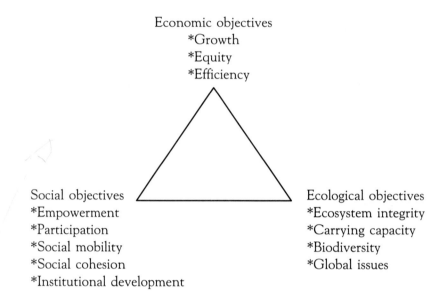

Figure 1.1 Objectives of environmentally sustainable development
(Souce: Serageldin and Steer 1994)

There is no necessary binding connection between the three perspectives and the three sets of objectives, but nor are the links purely coincidental. Thus the methodological approach of each of the three disciplines has certain associated norms which also tend to link with objectives. For example, the economist's model of the maximising individual is easily related to growth as an objective, while social cohesion is much more difficult to take into account.[12]

The debate is further confused by the introduction of terms such as 'a social and economic good' and 'environmental needs.'[13] The confusion in terminology matters as it has significant practical consequences. Such confusion is, of course, not unusual in international policy debate. It arises in part because there is genuine misunderstanding and in part because apparent consensus is sought in obfuscation. But such obfuscation can be dangerous.[14]

Another emerging practice, which I believe confuses rather than clarifies debate, is using the term 'sustainable' to relate to all three sets of objectives.[15] Thus, sustainable development is development (definition unspecified) which is:

- environmentally sustainable
- economically sustainable
- socially/culturally sustainable.

The distinction between 'environmentally sustainable' and 'economically sustainable' is, roughly, the same as that between 'sustainable' and 'development'. There is, of course, a range of solutions as to how this circle can be squared. (See, for example, Pearce et al. 1989, and criticisms by Beckerman 1995.) The meaning of socially or culturally sustainable – as used in publications by United Nations agencies such as UNESCO – is, however, far from clear. The major problem is: what do we mean by 'culture'?[16] And are we concerned with it as a means or an end? Does one argue that sustainable development cannot be achieved unless cultural factors are taken into account? Or is there a third goal? If so, then it is necessary to clarify what it is. Is it to maintain cultural diversity? To make the question more concrete: if the other two goals are economic well-being and environmental well-being, then what could be meant by 'cultural well-being'?[17]

In summary, I believe that it is better to reserve the term 'sustainable' to relate to a concern for the environment, so that the economic and social aspects are two other dimensions which are explicitly identified, instead of being blurred within some broad and unclear concept of sustainability. Ideally, of course, the aim is a unified whole, with all three different perspectives and objectives taken into account, although each of the three should be conceptually separable, and identified by name. In my view, therefore, the term 'sustainable development' is only two-thirds complete, for the social dimension is not explicitly included.

How one combines, or integrates, these different disciplines and objectives is in large part a political question, relating to both the politics of academia and the politics of the real world. Within academic research on sustainable development, I perceive an emerging split not between the three disciplines discussed here, nor even between the natural and social sciences, but rather between what I call the technicist and the humanist approaches. The former category includes most, but not all, natural sciences. The second includes most, but not all, social sciences and humanities. But economics, in particular, is divided. Thus many economists (and perhaps especially those in the mainstream) have a greater methodological affinity with physicists, chemists, geologists, and so on than with anthropologists and historians. The technicists are more policy-oriented while the humanists are more critically-oriented. This may develop into a still more marked split, both in the sphere of policy and within academia. In the sphere of policy, the technicist approach has strong appeal; it appears to provide answers while the humanist approach offers only questions, or even criticism. In the academic field, there is developing, at least in the USA, a growing war between science and what the defenders of science have called 'the academic left': cultural studies, gender studies, and so on (see Gross and Levitt 1994).

The various disciplines also differ with respect to how, if at all, the ethical/political aspect of the sustainable development question is addressed. Ecology, as a discipline, is not concerned with this, although ecologists have, of course, been active in the debate. Mainstream economics also tends to avoid the issue, but within the political economy tradition it has always been of importance. In anthropology, morality or moralities[18] are an important aspect of understanding local society, but researchers have not usually addressed such questions at the global level. I should, however, make reference to what has been called 'political ecology.'[19] Perhaps research in this field will help to counter the centrifugal forces inherent in the technicist/humanist and global/local dichotomies. Alternatively, it may establish one of two clearly opposed poles in an emerging discussion around these issues. To show how this discussion has developed I shall briefly analyse the recent history of the sustainable development debate.

## – A STRUCTURAL ANALYSIS
## OF THE SUSTAINABLE DEVELOPMENT DEBATE –

In most accounts (see for example Hettne 1990; Rist 1997), the development debate, as opposed to more general debates about the causes of poverty and economic growth, is described as dating back to the early post-World War II period, and is closely associated with the process of decolonisation and nation-building, national planning, development aid, and the political debate over the new international economic order. The environment debate dates back many years, but for my purposes it is appropriate to focus on a similar period, taking as a starting point the Stockholm Conference 1972. With the publication of the Brundtland Report in 1987 there occurred, I suggest, a fusion between the two in what may be called 'the sustainable development debate.'[20]

There are interesting lessons to be drawn from comparisons between the debate on the meaning of the term 'development' in the 1960s and 1970s, and the debate about 'sustainable development' in the 1980s and 1990s. Two points in particular merit consideration. The first is the question of whether 'development' is a process or a goal. Both positions are, in my view, quite tenable. But sustainable development, by contrast, must be a goal as it is unambiguously concerned with the normative, what ought to be done, not with describing the actual experience of one or more countries.

Second is the question of whether development means simply increasing real incomes, irrespective of equity considerations, or whether development must also imply something about the distribution of income. This discussion has been pursued both with regard to development as a process ('is increased inequality of incomes a normal or even necessary part of the development process?') and as a goal ('can it be called development if it leaves the majority of people poor?'). This debate has moved on, partly because there is good empirical evidence to suggest that equity and growth are not necessarily in contradiction. But even if one questions this, there can be few who would deny that development as a goal must imply equity as well as growth.[21]

I suggest that sustainable development is a goal (not an empirical process), and that it implies a potential conflict between human material well-being and the environment, a conflict which is captured by the two terms 'development' and 'sustainable', as the former is concerned with human well-being (including equity) while the latter is concerned with the stress that such development places on the environment.

It is possible to analyse both the development debate and the environment debate in terms of what I call 'lines of fission', using dichotomous terms which have been of especial significance in setting the terms of the debate and distinguishing different positions within it. These are summarised below. This is thus a simple structural analysis of the debates, in which it is further implied that the different dichotomies 'map onto' each other, at least to some extent. Thus the first column lists four 'lines of fission' which are of most relevance in defining the development debate; the second column does the same for the environment debate and the third combines these two columns in one, under the heading 'sustainable development debate.' The issue, as discussed below, is how coherent this third column actually is.

| *Development debate* | *Environmental debate* |
|---|---|
| north/south | nature/people |
| right/left | global/local |
| market/state | market/non-market |
| hard/soft | hard/soft |

*Sustainable development debate*
north/south
nature/people
global/local
market/civil society/state
right/left
hard/soft

## – The development debate –

The central concern of this debate was relations between poor and rich, whether presented as First World/Third World, developed/developing, or North/South. This was largely a debate about poverty and power. The relations between North and South might be portrayed as being of mutual interest (as in *North-South* 1980) or exploitative (as claimed by the dependency theory) but there is no doubt that North/South was a significant divide in conceptual and geo-political terms (witness the demands for a new international economic irder). There was a rather clear distinction between radical and conservative, or right and left, analyses of the situation. The major alternatives for development policy were those relying on the market and those based on strong state ownership and control. In terms of academic disciplines, it was predominantly social scientists who were involved, but here there was a divide between development economists and others, which emerged especially towards the end of the period. In this context, development economics was often portrayed as more 'hard', in the sense of rigorous, quantitative analysis, in contrast to other 'soft' social science.

These four lines of fission mapped very closely onto each other, although there were certainly a number of exceptions; for example, by no means all in the South adopted a radical approach, while some development economists undertaking rigorous quantitative analysis were radical.

## – The environment debate –

The lines of fission in this debate were very different. First came the people/nature divide. Clearly all in the debate were concerned with nature, but the contrast identified here is between an anthropocentric and a non-anthropocentric view. Another difference is between those focusing on global and on local levels. (This refers both to concern about priority issues as well as how best to resolve them. The slogan 'think global, act local' was coined in an attempt to connect across this divide.) Some responded to the challenge by favouring market solutions, while others not only emphasised community action but, in some cases, recommended opting out of the money economy. In academic terms, natural scientists were predominant. These came both from the life sciences (with ecology favouring a holistic, in some cases 'soft' approach) and the physical sciences (a more reductionist, 'hard', approach).

Here also I suggest one can legitimately map the four dichotomies on to each other, though perhaps with less accuracy than in the case of the development debate.

– The sustainable development debate –

The combining of the two debates has led to some interesting contradictions and realignments. In terms of politics there is some confusion – what is the relationship between the reds and the greens? They may share a negative view of the market, but their prescriptions are very different. In terms of academic discipline, as I intimated above, the split within this field is not precisely between these two, but rather between what I have called the 'technicist' and the 'humanist' perspectives. There is an affinity between the 'hard' social sciences and the 'hard' natural sciences. Most natural scientists (and especially physical scientists) fall into the 'hard' category, and most social scientists and humanists (especially anthropologists and historians) into the 'soft.'

The question of global/local arenas and the role of the market has been confounded by the whole globalisation debate. Here, there may be allied (but not precisely similar) concerns between those who oppose globalisation because of its exploitative effect and those who are interested in its impact on the environment.

Where there is most confusion, I suggest, is with regard to the North/South and nature/people issues. A conflict is emerging between those in the North who – to put it strongly – prioritise conservation of nature over the alleviation of poverty, and those in the South who invert the order of priority. And the global/local contrast in the environmental debate and the North/South contrast of the development debate are becoming linked. As the radical Third World environmentalist Vandana Shiva has put it 'the global is defined as North, and the local as South':

> The G7 can demand a forest convention that imposes international obligations on the Third World to plant trees. But the Third World cannot demand that the industrialized countries reduce the use of fossil fuels and energy. All demands are externally dictated – one way – from North to South. The 'global' has been so structured, that the North (as the globalized local) has all rights and no responsibility, and the South has no rights, but all responsibility. (Shiva 1993, p. 154)

Thus, the North is seen by many in the South as imposing not only the sustainable development debate, but also its own self-interested conclusions from that debate. And the North claims to represent the global rather than the local. This question 'who speaks for the globe?' raises fundamental ethical and political questions.

## – THE ETHICS AND POLITICS OF SUSTAINABLE DEVELOPMENT –

The central ethical – and thereby also political – issue within the development debate has been the rights of the poor as against the rights of the rich. This has been related to some extent to intra-country conditions, but more especially to inter-country conditions. (This is not to be confused with the empirical question of whether greater equity is positively or negatively correlated with growth.)

The central ethical/political issue within the environment debate has been the rights of humans as against the rights of nature (that is, other living species). But the sustainable development debate has often been cast (by the Brundtland Report and others) in terms of the rights of future generations. I suggest, however, that it necessarily involves all three issues:

1. Rights of the poor in the present generation as against those of the rich.
2. Rights of non-humans as against humans.
3. Rights of future generations as against present generations.

Focusing on issue three alone is not adequate.[22] There is a complex trade-off between all three of these issues which must be addressed. More specifically: should the interests of (rich?) future generations be served at the expense of (poor) present generations? (See the brief discussion by Solow in the UNDP's Human Development Report, 1996.) The precise nature of the trade-off available is an empirical question. With regard to the first issue, there is a great deal of information about degrees of inequality both within and between countries, but there is disagreement both as to whether there is a growth/equity trade-off, and as to how to reduce inequality if this is desired.[23] With regard to the second issue, the situation is more complicated. Can research – for example on pain or consciousness in animals – cast light on this issue? With regard to the third issue, there is clearly a need for more empirical research on the effects on the environment, and hence on future generations, of actions taken now. Certainly they will have an effect (ores mined and consumed now can, though to a limited extent, be reused in the future while energy can never be), but how serious will this be?

The ethical argument for considering the rights of future generations is not generally contested. By contrast, the ethical argument in the case of non-humans is contested, although there seems to be some shift in favour of 'animal rights' in the North in recent years. And few contest the rights of the poor in the present generation. But this is within the realm of theory. In practice, of course, rather little is done within many countries, and very little is done between countries, to counteract the great inequalities of wealth and power. In the real world of politics and personal behaviour, there is a wide gap between ethical ideals and practice. Yet, I suggest, debates couched in ethical terms do have some influence on politics and personal behaviour. And academics contributing to the debate have an influence even when they seek to avoid taking any normative position.[24] The influence of the researcher in the sustainable development debate depends largely on how that debate is framed.

## – CONCLUSION –

The Brundtland Report was a remarkably successful agenda-setting exercise. It focused on a perceived dilemma – between growth and the environment – and encapsulated this very neatly in the term 'sustainable development.' Consensus in the document, and subsequently, was, however, achieved at some expense in both academic and policy terms.

Given the diversity of perspectives and interests, some confusion as to the meaning of the term could not be avoided. But this confusion has to some extent obfuscated the central empirical question of whether, or under what circumstances, there is in fact conflict between increased material well-being and the environment.[25] An equally serious error, I suggest, is the predominant ethical focus on the rights of future generations, for the two other ethical dimensions to the debate cannot be ignored. Both of these limitations in the report can be explained, perhaps excused, on the grounds of pragmatism. Sustainable development is an intensely political issue, and it may be thought that change is more likely to be achieved through consensus than confrontation.[26] But real differences of perspective cannot for ever be ignored, and some of these are clearly beginning to emerge, both with regard to what global policy measures are proposed and with regard to the grounds for proposing them.

The negotiations concerning global warming (notably at the 1997 Kyoto Conference) indicate that there is some slight movement towards an international response in which the burden is predominantly borne by the richer countries. Some will say that it is too little, too late; but it should be recognised that proposals such as the idea of tradable quotas are very radical, and represent a significant shift in political and, arguably, also in ethical terms. Political arguments often require ethical underpinnings, however flimsy these may seem. The future generations argument seems to be effective to an extent that the present poverty argument has not been, at least for the rich countries. But what about big, and increasingly rich countries like India, China and Brazil? What will stir them to action? Global warming has rightly been identified as 'the archetypal global problem'

(Bhaskar and Glyn 1995, p. 5)[27] and the discussions surrounding it will both reflect and determine the broader discussions concerning other aspects of the sustainable development debate. It is archetypical in several respects which relate to what has been discussed in this chapter: the ethical issues that arise concern the rights of present as much as future generations and the empirical evidence for the nature (and even the existence) of a trade-off is disputed. Global warming is certainly not the priority issue for many of the poorest people of the world, but it does in many ways exemplify the challenge – practical, ethical and political – posed by the concept of sustainable development.

## – Notes –

1. I shall not enter the dispute as to when, and by whom, the term was first introduced.
2. Take, for example, the term 'fetishism.' This was coined by de Brosses in 1760 as a category of comparative religion. It became increasingly debased as theories of primitive religion changed and fell into disuse, but psychologists took up the term (in 1887); and so did Karl Marx (in 1848, as festishism, and later as 'commodity festishism'). And it is coming back into fashion in a slightly new guise (Hirsch 1976). A more recent example is the term 'social capital' which some see as a useful theoretical innovation, and others as merely 'old wine in new bottles' (McNeill 1996). As with sustainable development, the link to policy has contributed to both the immense popularity of this phrase and the analytical confusion surrounding it.
3. I would distinguish between 'words that make a difference' (slogans, in the realm of activism), 'ideas that make no difference' (technical jargon, in the realm of academia), and 'ideas that make a difference.'
4. Absent from this list are both the business community and the people themselves. The former is becoming more active in the debate; an important issue will be whether, and on what terms, it comes to act as an organised group. It would be meaningless to try and generalise about what 'the people' mean by sustainable development, but there is some evidence that the concerns raised by the term are being followed up – or even taken over – at the local level.
5. Especially in the case of intensely contested issues, the two tend to be connected – for example, global warming.
6. For an elaboration of the above points, consider Grubb's analysis of the written agreements from Rio. Regarding the forest principles, he writes: 'Agreement was eventually reached by a process of avoiding specific commitments or contentious principles, and incorporating a wide range of generalised observations, recommendations and goals, sometimes in themselves ambiguous or perhaps contradictory. The result is a document with something for everyone, without any clear message or direction' (Grubb 1993, p. 166). On

carbon emissions: 'The detailed wording is convoluted and deliberately ambiguous but clearly implies that industrialised countries should aim, as a first step, to stabilise emissions over the decade' (ibid., p. 14).

We are in the realm of what Kissinger called 'constructive ambiguity.' In addition to ambiguous wording, there are other ways of avoiding commitment. To cite Grubb again: 'An important postscript to the Rio Declaration was the release by the US delegation of "Interpretive Statements for the Record by the United States." These "interpretive statements" were in fact disclaimers on principles 3, 7, 12 and 23 . . .' (ibid., p. 86).

It is also interesting to note mechanisms for excluding the findings of earlier (more expert-dominated) preparatory meetings. Thus the Dublin statement and report of the International Conference on Water and the Environment (1992) was 'a UN-sponsored conference of experts, not governments, with agreement reached by vote rather than consensus; hence formal references to it were rejected in Agenda 21 negotiations' (ibid., p. 131).

7. The result is bad research and bad policy documents. Two examples will suffice. The first involves apparently empirical findings which are actually true by definition. In a study of the informal sector in Sri Lanka, the informal sector was defined as exhibiting several attributes, such as employing mainly family members. A study of informal sector activities was carried out. The results showed that an unusually high proportion of the businesses surveyed did indeed employ family members. The second involves apparent policy choices presented in a way which either allows no room for choice or renders decisions banal. For example, who will oppose 'safe motherhood' or 'good governance' or (the worst and most common case) 'appropriate' levels of investment, tax and so on. It is commendable that some few have dared to protest, by advocating 'unbalanced growth' (Hirschmann 1988) or 'getting the prices wrong' (Amsden 1989).

8. The standard definition quoted above fails this test; but, to be fair, one must point out that it was actually presented as a definition only of 'sustainability.' One must look elsewhere in the Brundtland Report for a definition of what is meant by 'development.'

9. There is likely to be a link between the way the trade-off is expressed (as empirical or moral) and whether the definition is unbiased.

10. One in particular, geography, has, with some justification, claimed that it alone brings together the key disciplines within a single sphere.

11. The question arises: is there a necessary link between discipline and role? Is the ecologist likely to be a bureaucrat or the economist an activist? Although the general answer is no, there is, I suggest, one very important respect in which economists differ from anthropologists and ecologists. Economics offers not only a perspective but also a set of powerful instruments of policy, such as taxes, prices and quotas. What can the ecologist or the anthropologist offer which may compete with these? This is not to claim superiority for economics, but to note its power. In the debate over sustainable development the

economist enjoys, in my view, a special advantage in this respect. And this is by virtue of a number of interacting factors, of which I have just named only one. It is an important question (though well beyond the scope of this chapter) whether economics now faces a fundamental challenge which may have far-reaching effects on this powerful discipline.

12. *Pace* the recent interest in the concept of social capital, and the attempts to measure it and relate it to economic growth performance.

13. Take this example: 'Sustainability 15. There is a need to recognize water as a social and economic good with a vital role in the satisfaction of basic human needs, food security, poverty alleviation and the protection of ecosystems' (UNESCO 1998, p. 4). But it is not clear what is meant by 'a social good.' However, its implication is clear, namely, that water is a basic human need. And in practice the adoption of this expression results in the term 'economic good' necessarily becoming limited to its narrower 'economistic' meaning.

 Another example comes from Lundqvist and Gleick (1997): 'There is a difference between basic human and environmental "needs" for water and the much larger set of "wants" ' (p. viii); between '. . . meeting commitments to nature and [to] the diverse social groups of the present and future generations' (p. 3).

14. There are, I suggest, two related issues at stake here; 'economism' and anthropocentrism. The assertion that 'water is an economic good' has been taken by some as an economistic view, implying, at the extreme, that water has to be paid for at market prices; and the term 'social and economic good', whose meaning is in my view unclear, has been introduced as a compromise to avoid such a position. The term 'environmental needs' (and more extremely, 'environmental wants'), is also, I suggest, ill-defined, though it clearly implies a non-anthropocentric standpoint.

15. In the battle between the competing perspectives, each may seek to encompass the other. Thus, the economist recognises the validity of the other two, but argues that they can easily be incorporated within the overall economic schema; and similarly with the anthropologist and the ecologist.

16. Any researcher concerned with the study of culture is likely to object to the reification of the term 'culture' which runs throughout much of the recent literature (including the UNESCO 1995 report, *Our Creative Diversity*). This appears, however, to be the price one has to pay for moving from the world of academia into the world of policy.

17. The social and cultural dimension of development is extremely important, and substantial efforts are being made to put it high on the international agenda – see the Report of the World Commission on Culture and Development (UNESCO 1995), headed by Xavier Perez de Cuellar. But there is a real danger that confusion of this kind will contribute to its being excluded.

18. See Howell 1997.

19. One recent contribution is 'Enclosing the global commons', in which Lipietz notes: 'We will consider economic tools not only as theoretical means to deal

with our subject but also as objects for our study. In fact, we are witnessing the birth of a social object: the political economy of global environment' (Lipietz 1995, p. 118). Another is the concept of a Third World political ecology, which Bryant and Bailey describe as 'the politics of environmental change in the Third World' (Bryant and Bailey 1997). This is concerned with micro as well as macro level research: for example the detailed work of Fairhead and Leach (1995) on West Africa.

20. In recent years, as noted above, there has been the addition of the socio-cultural dimension, and still more concepts: economically sustainable, socially sustainable, environmentally sustainable.

21. This is still, of course, a very broad statement. Does equity imply equality? Or the meeting of some minimum basic needs? Or what?

22. I should stress that all three issues are discussed in the Brundtland Report. And some of what I have just said is, in effect, stated there. For example: 'Even the narrow notion of physical sustainability implies a concern for social equity between generations, a concern that must logically be extended to equity within each generation . . . The protection of nature is not only a goal of development. It is also a moral obligation toward other living beings and future generations' (Brundtland 1987). But the standard definition of sustainable development, and the thrust of the argument in the Report are, I maintain, focused on only the third issue, namely the rights of future as against present generations.

23. But as C. Jencks succinctly puts it: 'The best way to reduce inequality is still to reduce inequality' (quoted in Le Grand 1982, p. 101).

24. This has been the case, of course, over the controversial question of valuing life as addressed by Working Group 3 of the Intergovernmental Panel on Climate Change.

25. Despite this, there is now considerable evidence against the view – crudely expressed – that 'it is the poor that cause environmental damage.' It would be more accurate to say – if sweeping judgements are to be made – that it is affluence rather than poverty which is the greater threat to the environment. This has led to increased interest in the impact of consumption patterns of the rich and in the concept of sustainable consumption.

26. At Rio, it appears that the issue of consumption in the North was played down in exchange for a similar treatment of the issue of population growth in the South.

27. 'As the developed industrial countries generate about 80 per cent of total global pollution, developing countries often remark that they do not want to sacrifice their development – thus mitigating some environmental damage – in order to manage the problems caused by the industrialised countries. Some of the more radical experts or political figures of the South even accuse the North of environmental imperialism . . .' (Bhaskar and Glyn 1995, p. xii).

## – BIBLIOGRAPHY –

Amsden, A. (1989), *Asia's Next Giant: South Korea and Late Industrialization*, Oxford and New York: Oxford University Press.

Beckerman, W. (1995), *Small is Stupid*, London: Duckworth.

Bhaskar, V., and A. Glyn (1995) eds, *The North, the South and the Environment: Ecological Constraints and the Global Economy*, London: Earthscan Publications.

The Brundtland Report (World Commission on Environment and Development) (1987), *Our Common Future*, Oxford: Oxford University Press.

Bryant, R., and S. Bailey (1997), *Third World Political Ecology*, London: Routledge.

Fairhead, J., and M. Leach (1995), 'Reading history backwards: the interaction of policy and local land use in Guinea's forest-savanna mosaic', *Environment and History* 1, pp. 55–91.

Glasser, H., P. Craig, and W. Kempton (1994), 'Ethics and values in environmental policy: the said and the UNCED', in J. van den Berg and J. van den Straaten (eds), *Towards Sustainable Development: Concepts, Methods and Policy*, Washington DC: Island Press.

Gross, P., and N. Levitt (1994), *Higher Superstition: The Academic Left and its Quarrels with Science*, Baltimore: Johns Hopkins University Press.

Grubb, M. (1993), *The Earth Summit Agreements: A Guide and Assessment*, London: Earthscan Publications.

Hettne, B. (1990), *Development Theory and the Three Worlds*, London: Longman.

Hirsch, F. (1976), *The Social Limits to Growth*, Boston: Harvard University Press.

Hirschmann (1988), *The Strategy of Economic Development*, Boulder: Westview Press.

Howell, S. (1997) ed., *The Ethnography of Moralities*, London: Routledge.

Le Grand, J. (1982), *The Strategy of Equality*, London: Unwin Hyman.

Lipietz. A. (1995), 'Enclosing the global commons: global environmental negotiations in a North-South conflictual approach', in V. Bhaskar and A. Glyn (eds), *The North, the South and the Environment*, London: Earthscan.

Lundqvist. J., and P. Gleick (1997), *Sustaining Our Waters into the Twenty-first Century*, Stockholm: Stockholm Environment Institute.

McNeill, D. (1996), 'Making social capital work', *Forum for Development Studies*, pp. 417–21.

*North-South: A Programme for Survival* (Report of the Independent Commission on International Development Issues under the Chairmanship of Willy Brandt) (1980), London: Pan Books.

Pearce, D., A. Markandya, and E. Barbier (1989), *Blueprint for a Green Economy*, London: Earthscan Publications.

Redclift, M. (1992), 'The meaning of sustainable development', *Geoforum* 23:3, pp. 395–403.

Rist, G. (1997), *The History of Development: From Western Origins to Global Faith*, London: Zed Books.

Serageldin, I., and A. Steer (1994) eds., *Making Development Sustainable: From Concepts to Action*, Washington: World Bank.

Shiva, Vandana (1993), 'The greening of the global reach', in W. Sachs (ed.), *Global Ecology: A New Arena of Political Conflict*, London: Zed Books.

UNDP (1996), *Human Development Report*, Oxford: Oxford University Press.

UNESCO (1995), World Commission on Culture and Development: *Our Creative Diversity*.

UNESCO (1998), Commission on Sustainable Development: *Strategic Approaches to Freshwater Management* (Report of the Secretary-General, Addendum Report of the Expert Group Meeting, Harare, January 1998).

# The wants of the few: the needs of the many

Keekok Lee throws the Brundtland Report into relief by inviting us to consider it alongside another, earlier model of sustainable development which she terms the 'classical model', and associates with the early American conservationist Gifford Pinchot (1865–1946). Her contribution is a useful corrective to the sometimes shallow and ahistorical understanding that is shown of the key ideas that inform the Brundtland Report.

The similarities revealed by her analysis are indeed striking. Lee draws attention to the shared preoccupation with development, quoting Pinchot's remark that 'the first principle of conservation is development', and she shows how the idea of a sustained and sustainable yield is absolutely central to his conservation thinking. She shows, too, how Pinchot shares Brundtland's concern with future generations, taking it as an obvious objective of current policy that generations to come should 'live civilised, happy and useful lives.' Pinchot is equally clear on the point that natural resources should be developed 'for the benefit of the many, and not just for the profit of the few.' In Lee's view, both models are unreservedly human-centred and essentially devoted to 'managing human nature to advance human well-being.' In this sense she regards both as falling squarely within the tradition of utilitarian materialism. In neither model is nature of value in its own right: in Lee's terms, their objective is not ecological sustainability as such, but 'eco-social sustainability' – the conservation of nature insofar as it services human needs.

But here, her critical analysis begins to reveal differences, for she finds that the Brundtland model is not even-handed in its treatment of human well-being, and threatens to accentuate the divide between poorer and richer countries. In terms of the conflicting strands that McNeill has identified, Lee is convinced that the Brundtland agenda weighs in heavily on the side of human well-being as distinct from nature protection, and on the side of the 'haves' as distinct from the 'have-nots.' For Lee, the 'new development path' that Brundtland speaks of involves a commitment to the relief of poverty and the promotion of justice which is no doubt laudable. But it also remains in thrall to the idea that indefinite economic growth is the only means by which these goals can be achieved. This, as she observes, creates a problem. The economic and social organisation of so-called 'developed' economies is very different from that of the 'developing' ones, and commitment to indefinite growth implies a future in which every economy has been transformed from 'developing' to 'developed' status. But if sustainable development is difficult to achieve under existing conditions, and if the idea of ecological limits is taken to heart, its achievement would seem well nigh impossible in a world in which every economy was 'developed'. It is Lee's contention that Brundtland is therefore obliged to recommend a different development path for affluent as opposed to non-affluent economies. Appealing to the distinction between needs and wants, she notes that while Brundtland allows that developing countries may aspire to an improved quality of life, the main objective is framed in terms of the satisfying of needs. The developed economies, on the other hand, whose needs are already tolerably well met, are admonished merely to curb their wants. Accordingly she interprets the burden of the Brundtland recommendations as pointing not to a common, but to a divided future.

Whilst being strongly critical of certain formulations of the sustainable development agenda, however, Lee's conclusions are by no means wholly negative. Perhaps there are absolute ecological limits to growth. Even so, the classical model at least entertains the idea that a dynamic technology might enable all peoples to share a common quality of life, provided only that the social arrangements are in place for effective technology transfer. Hence she judges the classical model to be superior to the Brundtland model. Given their common anthropocentric terms of reference, it at least holds out the hope of a genuinely 'common' future.

~ O ~

# 2 GLOBAL SUSTAINABLE DEVELOPMENT:
# ITS INTELLECTUAL AND HISTORICAL ROOTS

## *Keekok Lee*

### – INTRODUCTION –

The notion of sustainable development is linked in people's mind to the Brundtland Report – referred to from now on as the Report – which has widely publicised and promoted it. It is true that the notion is not entirely new. However, this reflection should in no way lead one to underestimate the significance and impact of the Report itself.

The notion is normally deployed with no reference to its intellectual and historical roots. This chapter makes good that context in order to assess the relevance of the notion of sustainable developmentfor the coming century. Furthermore, the critique will show that two models of sustainable development may be identified, one which takes into account such roots and the other which does not. The first may be called the classical model and is an optimistic global model; the second is the Brundtland model as embodied in the Report, and is a more pessimistic, fractured model with very different prescriptions for the developed and developing economies.

Section 1 of this chapter looks at the core theses commonly understood to constitute the notion of sustainable development as purveyed by the Brundtland model. Sections 2 and 3 delineate the classical model, which will be shown to incorporate a reference to economics through the component called development, as well as a reference to a particular strand in environmental philosophy, often identified today as conservationism, through the adjective which qualifies that development, namely, 'sustainable.' In the light of such provenance, the discussion will go on to make clear that sustainable development is an unashamedly anthropocentric concept primarily in the tradition of utilitarian materialism.[1] That tradition has nothing to say about the future of non-human beings except when they are perceived as being of use, actual or potential, to humans. The discussion will also show, as a touchstone, that while conservationism itself is quintessentially involved with sustainable livelihoods and civilisations, not only of present but also of future peoples, the notion ignores if not rejects outright that (non-human) nature may possess kinds of value independent of the instrumental value it has for humankind. In other words, the concern in the long run is not so much that sustainable development is in principle unattainable, but that its very success could systematically undermine or eradicate nature and its processes as these have operated in the long history of Earth's evolution.

Section 4 points out the similarities between the two models, while section 5 highlights the salient differences and, in the light of that comparison, shows that the Brundtland model may well be internally incoherent. Section 6 argues that it may also be much less relevant to the issues of the twenty-first century than the classical version.

− I −

Sustainable development as generally understood today includes, amongst others, the following themes and presuppositions:

1. That economic growth is both desirable and necessary. 'We see . . . the possibility for a new era of economic growth, one that must be based on policies that sustain and expand the environmental resource base' (Brundtland 1987, p. 1).
2. That the limits to growth are relative, not absolute. They are understood to be imposed by 'the present state of technology and social organizations on environmental resources' (Brundtland 1987, p. 8), although as we shall see later, the Report is ambiguous about this crucial point.
3. That science and technology can be relied on both to render indefinite economic growth possible and to circumvent any short-term scarcities which arise to hinder such growth.
4. That poverty can be relieved and equity promoted through growth. This implies the 'trickle down theory' of economic growth, although the Report does go beyond this explicitly to endorse the need for some active redistribution.

The notion of sustainable development, thus characterised, is deployed by the Report both as diagnosis of, and solution to, the problems facing humankind at the start of this century. If appropriate actions are taken, then a better world will emerge, one rescued from increasing environmental degradation which, in many contexts, affects all, and from poverty, which affects many.

– 2 –

Standard economics divides the world into the developed and the developing. Conceptually, this division implies a certain model of development and a belief in certain processes that transform the developing so that it becomes the developed. What are they? A brief answer shows that the developed world displays these salient features:

1. It is fundamentally urban – most of its population live in towns and are in waged employment, although increasingly in recent years, a good many are unemployed.
2. Inequalities exist but generally there is relative, not absolute, poverty.
3. Literacy is high, with a store of scientific/technological knowledge and personnel together with a back-up of other social institutions and skills to exploit that expertise effectively and economically.
4. Of two of the factors of production, namely capital and labour, it is relatively short of the latter.[2]

In contrast, the developing world display these features:

1. It is predominantly rural and agricultural at the level of subsistence.
2. It has inequalities which may be extreme and poverty which veers to the absolute in many instances.
3. It has high illiteracy on the whole and less scientific/technical and social expertise for efficient economic exploitation.
4. It lacks capital relative to labour.

The success of developed economies lies in their expanding capacity to supply increasingly diverse goods and services to the population at large. That is why such success necessarily involves growth. That growth is to be measured in terms of the GDP per capita: the higher the GDP, the higher the general standard of living. Growth is fuelled through increasing the rate of productivity based on the understanding of efficiency as more output for any given input. This latter objective is achieved through the application of science and technology, resulting in predominantly large-scale capital-intensive industrialisation. The growth rate is ultimately dependent on increasing capital stock and on mobilising savings and investments to augment it. According to this view, of the four major factors behind GDP growth – capital accumulation, technological progress, new resources, population growth[3] – the first is the most important.[4]

Rostow (1960) has delineated five distinct stages in the development path:

1. A traditional society with limited productivity due to lack of developed economic techniques.
2. Emergence of the preconditions for take-off – a 'leading sector' develops with positive effects on the rest of the economy.
3. Take-off – obstacles to growth are finally removed with growth in all sectors, characterised by an increase in the ratio of savings and investment to national income of roughly 5 to 10 per cent, and by the emergence of institutions (political, social and others) to facilitate growth.
4. The drive to maturity – a long period of sustained growth with 10 to 20 per cent of national income invested.
5. The age of high mass-consumption – structural change slows down, economy is geared to producing consumer goods and services.

While the developed world is at 5, the developing world is at the critical stage of 3 and some countries, such as the Pacific Rim 'tiger economies' (until the crisis overtook them from late 1997), might be said either to hover between 3 and 4 or to have reached 4. The model implies that every economy could eventually become developed; and that all economies require growth, because growth, in spite of its drawbacks, is nevertheless indispensable to improving material well-being. This is the model of development as purveyed by standard economic theory at its most optimistic and most inspirational as a global model. However, it is said to have run into difficulties, since it appears no longer to be sustainable even for the already developed economies, never mind the eventual situation when all economies would in theory have become developed. As we shall see, it is this latter realisation which makes the Report take the turn that it does.

– 3 –

The classical global model may also be looked at from a perspective other than the one provided by economics, namely, conservationism, a prominent stance in environmental philosophy. Conservationism includes the following theses:

A. Anthropocentrism, the thesis that only human beings are intrinsically valuable, and instrumentalism, the thesis that (non-human) nature is only of instrumental value to humans. According to this view, nature is a storehouse of potential raw resources for food, clothing, shelter, medicine, and so on. This latter thesis is also referred to as resource conservation.

B. In the modern economy, these resources are turned into commodities whose values are realised in monetary terms, and through transactions of buying and selling them, they enter into the GDP of an economy. In this way, nature contributes to the advancement of human well-being.

C. Conservationsim may also include forms of weak instrumentalism (or resource preservation). Nature is (a) a source of amenity value to humans whether as individual organisms or as part of ecosystems and landscapes. Humans get psychological satisfaction, aesthetic pleasure, or indeed even feel awe which is tantamount to a religious/spiritual experience in the presence of nature. Nature is also (b) a provider of services which constitute public/ collective goods. Biodiversity is such a good as its maintenance is a prerequisite for the survival and well-being of future human generations (and indirectly of non-human species). This is because diverse organisms act as a sink for absorbing waste, and sustain the great biogeochemical and hydrological cycles.

D. It follows that the model is concerned with the survival and well-being of the whole of humankind, and therefore not only of the present but also of future generations.

The most influential original exponent of conservationism[5] in environmental thought is Gifford Pinchot (1865–1946), the first scientific forester (and politician) of the Progressive Era, who had the ear of President Theodore Roosevelt.[6] But before expounding in further detail Pinchot's philosophy of conservationism, a quick comparison between his version of sustainable development and that outlined in Section 1 is called for:

1. Both imply theses A and B above.
2. Both could be said to uphold C(b), although Pinchot would not have put it in precisely those terms, as he was only aware then of the ecological damage caused by certain economic activities on the American environment[7] rather than on the global environment as such.
3. Pinchot, as a private person, was known to be well-disposed to C(a) although he did not think it ought to form part of the official view of conservation he was promoting.[8]
4. However, both Pinchot and upholders of sustainable development in general could agree on a monetised version of C(a). For instance, ecotourism could generate psychological, aesthetic, spiritual and recreational value, and would be a kind of development that could be approved.[9]
5. While sustainable development today holds (D) without qualifications, Pinchot considered a more restrictive application of it: instead of being concerned with the whole of humanity then and in the future, he was concerned primarily with the well-being of the citizens of the USA then and in the future. However, an equivalent of an environmental policy-maker and thinker of the status and influence of Pinchot today would no doubt have cast it in the form which supporters of the notion of sustainable development today uphold.

As we shall soon see, besides these similarities and differences, there are others. But first, let us give a brief account of the salient features which constitute Pinchot's idea of conservation and, therefore, of sustainable development. The following themes may be identified:

1. Development and economic growth.
   The first great fact about conservation is that it stands for development. There has been a fundamental misconception that conservation means nothing but the husbanding of resources for future generations. There could be no more serious mistake. Conservation does mean provision for the future, but it means also and first of all the recognition of the right of the present generation to the fullest necessary use of all the resources with which this country is so abundantly blessed . . . The first principle of conservation is development, the use of the natural resources now existing on this continent for the benefit of the people who live here now. (Pinchot 1910, p. 43)
   In other words, with regard to a non-renewable resource, like coal, Pinchot was in favour of mining and using it as prudently and as efficiently as possible to make the exhaustible, though vast, supply last as long as possible. With regard to a renewable resource, like forests, they ought to be managed to give a sustainable yield. He stood for economic growth, but growth which does not unnecessarily waste resources and/or does not undermine indefinite long-term yield.
2. For him, conservation meant the gospel of efficiency,[10] the elimination of waste and damage, both economic and ecological: 'In the second place,

conservation stands for the prevention of waste. There has come gradually in this country an understanding that waste is not a good thing and that the attack on waste is an industrial necessity' (Pinchot 1910, p. 44). The lumber industry, for instance, had destroyed forests with gay abandon, regarding them as inexhaustible. Lumbermen, until Pinchot's campaign, 'regarded forest devastation as normal and second growth as a delusion of fools, whom they cursed on the rare occasions when they happened to think of them. And as for sustained yield, no such idea had ever entered their heads' (Pinchot 1947, p. 27).

3. Resource conservation for sustained yield[11] required scientific management and planning. Although Pinchot was inclined to say that this meant no more than 'the application of common-sense to the common problems for the common good' (Pinchot 1910, p. 48), involving the simple use of foresight, prudence, thrift and intelligence, nevertheless, in spite of this demotic rhetoric, he really relied on science and technology for achieving the goal of rational, efficient and ecologically sound development. For instance, grazing would have to be regulated in order not to exceed the carrying capacity of the land. Furthermore, he realised that threats to the resource base could not and should not be understood or treated individually, each on its own. Even managing forests involved managing more than trees. The Forest Service had to deal with 'public lands, mining, agriculture, irrigation, stream flow, soil erosion, fish, game, animal industry and a whole host of other matters' (Pinchot 1947, p. 322). He wrote that, one afternoon in 1907 while out riding his horse, he realised in a flash that all these matters constituted a single whole question with many parts. He did not doubt that before him, others had been exercised by particular specific threats to the resource base; he, however, believed he was the first to appreciate their interrelatedness:[12]

So far as I know then or have since been able to find out, it had occurred to nobody, in this country or abroad, that here was one question instead of many, one gigantic single problem that must be solved if the generations, as they came and went, were to live civilized, happy, useful lives in the lands which the Lord their God had given them. (Pinchot 1947, p. 323)

4. The demand for equity.

The natural resources must be developed and preserved for the benefit of the many, and not merely for the profit of a few. We are coming to understand in this country that public action for public benefit has a very much wider field to cover and a much larger part to play than was the case when there were resources for every one, and before certain constitutional provisions had given so tremendously strong a position to vested rights and property in general. (Pinchot 1910, pp. 46–7)

However, Pinchot was not so much against private property and profits *per se*; he emphasised more the rational and efficient use of natural resources, the benefits arising from which, in his view, ought to be shared out more amongst the rest of the citizenry, and not confined largely to the few who owned the resources. Both he and Roosevelt favoured public ownership because they believed that it alone would permit rational development.

He unhesitatingly invoked the utilitarian formula but gave it an ecological slant: 'The conservation idea covers a wider range than the field of natural resources alone. Conservation means the greatest good to the greatest number for the longest time . . . thus recognizing that this nation of ours must be made to endure as the best possible home for all its people' (Pinchot 1910, p. 48).

5. Duty to future generations. 'Conservation is . . . . a question of a vastly higher duty . . . That duty . . . stands for an equal opportunity for every American citizen to get his fair share of benefit from these resources, both now and hereafter' (Pinchot 1910, pp. 78–9).

6. The contribution of women to conservation not merely as activists, such as in their fight for the Minnesota National Forest, but also in their roles as managers of households and educators of the young. Values, like the elimination of waste, are best learnt at mother's knees when they are actually put into practice within the family style of living.

All in all, it is fair to conclude that Pinchot's official philosophy of conservationism reflects the utilitarian materialism which is shared by the standard account of economic development, except for two caveats. First, as a career forester, activist, adviser to the President and politician in his own right, Pinchot's work and thought must be understood in the context of Progressive politics and political theory in the USA. Pinchot was really concerned to ensure American prosperity, then and into the distant future. He wrote: 'Conservation holds that it is about as important to see that the people in general get the benefit of our natural resources as to see that there shall be natural resources left' (Pinchot 1910, pp. 80–1). The US economy of Pinchot's time could be said to be poised between Rostow's stages 4 and 5. His argument for equity is naturally intra-economy, while the classical model, being global, is applicable to all economies. Second, Pinchot has enriched the classical model by adding the gender dimension,[13] through acknowledging the role of women in the conservation cause.

– 4 –

The Brundtland, like the classical, model of sustainable development is unashamedly anthropocentric and to be understood within a scientific/technological framework of managing nature to advance human well-being. Ecological limits may exist, but within these, science and technology are expected to help reduce waste, and to find substitutes for scarcities to ensure continuing economic growth for present as well as future generations of people: 'With careful management, new and emerging technologies offer enormous opportunities for raising productivity and living standards, for improving health, and for conserving the natural resource base' (Brundtland 1987, p. 217).

Like the classical model, the Brundtland model presupposes a philosophy of conservationism which, aside from one or two references (ibid., p. 13, p. 57), has no room for respecting nature for its own sake but only in so far as its flourishing is shown to be necessary to sustain the (material and physical) flourishing of humankind.

According to the anthropocentric perspective, biodiversity, ecosystem health, the integrity of the great hydrological and biogeochemical cycles, and so on are only valuable because they are of either actual or potential benefit to us. If science tells us that the rainforests play a vital part in maintaining the carbon cycle, then this would be a compelling reason not to cut them down in order to promote the more limited and shorter-term benefits derived from the mining or the hamburger industry. But science and technology may also tell another story. For instance, biotechnology today may enable us to genetically engineer trees with a far greater capacity for absorbing and recycling carbon dioxide than those which have naturally evolved in the rainforests. If such research turns out to be successful, the philosophy of conservationism/sustainable development would in principle welcome such an advance – perhaps, the rainforests could be cut down after all (in an orderly fashion) and replaced by their more efficient substitutes, so that the emission of carbon dioxide arising from economic activities would be far less alarming, at least in the longer term.

Biodiversity, too, could be more efficiently catered for in the light of modern scientific and technological developments. Whole plants need not be saved; only their seeds. In the past, seed storage has not been all that efficient, as seeds decay. But cryotoria are now available which store seeds much more efficiently than the old fashioned seed banks. Kew Gardens is planning to store seeds of as many plant species in the world as possible in cryotoria. The habitats of the plants may be destroyed but their seeds live on. With the seeds intact, DNA genetic engineering will enable us to splice the DNA relating to whatever property of the plant is deemed desirable into another, or indeed into bacteria using viruses as a vector, which could replicate that property for us in an infinitely more efficient manner than the original seed/plant can do. In this way, the well-being of humankind could be ensured and sustained into the future. Technology is one of the key factors which makes sustainable development possible at all.

Utilitarian materialism underpinned by science and technology will see humankind right. But nature, whether as whole plants and animals or as seeds and eggs/sperms – indeed even as segments of DNA – is regarded only as providing actual or potential raw resources to enter into the processes of production. On this view, nature may ultimately be regarded and appreciated as sequences of amino acids, rather than as individual plants and animals, as species, as ecosystems in the wild or even as traditional cultivars.

However, the discussion above indicates the need to clarify the concept of ecological sustainability which has of late entered the literature about sustainable development. As the term can be variously understood, for the purpose of this critique it will be understood as follows: ecological sustainability is constituted and maintained by species of plants/animals within their habitats, including the processes of interaction and exchange between the biotic and abiotic components making up the ecosystems, such that these themselves, in the absence of human interference, may be self-maintaining while coping with change. This sense should be distinguished from another which is better termed 'eco-social sustainability',[14] namely, the overlap between what is ecologically sustainable and what the current generation of humans deems desirable for itself and for future generations. In the light of this clarification, it is obvious that the philosophy of conservationism (such as Pinchot's) and sustainable development (behind either the classical or the Brundtland model) is not concerned with ecological sustainability as defined above but only with eco-social sustainability. Eco-social sustainability is predicated upon ecological sustainability but is not identical with it. Sustainable development is eco-socially sustainable development. As such it would involve managing human-made ecosystems and their biogeochemical processes to satisfy human desires on the part of both present and future peoples, but within the constraints laid down by our understanding of ecological sustainability. According to this view, the goal is not so much 'sustained high yield' but 'sustainable yield'[15] which is more efficient (although not in the narrow economistic sense) as a means of securing the survival and material prosperity of humankind, now and in the future.

– 5 –

The above sections have examined some of the grounds shared by the classical and Brundtland models of sustainable development. But wherein lie their salient differences? One crucial difference, from which others flow, has already been mentioned, namely, that the classical model is unitary and global[16] in scope of application, whereas the Brundtland model is fragmentary in character and, therefore, not genuinely global in scope.

The Brundtland model implies that while the now affluent world has reached its developed, mature state following the path of development laid down by standard economic theory, that prescription, contrary to standard economic thought, is not universally applicable. The developing world has to follow another path. The Report implies that it has come to this conclusion by taking seriously certain problems ignored by the standard approach; the key one being that current technology cannot be comfortably accommodated within the framework laid down by ecological limits: 'The concept of sustainable development does imply limits – not absolute limits but limitations imposed by the present state of technology and social organization on environmental resources and by the ability of the biosphere to absorb the effects of human activities' (Brundtland 1987, p. 8).

There are two ways of reading the quotation above: (a) as saying that the limits imposed by the present state of technology on environmental resources are relative, but that the ability of the biosphere to absorb the effects of human activities is absolute,[17] or (b) that either type of limitation is relative. The grammatical construction of the sentence leans towards (b). But if (b) is what the Report means, then it is simply mistaken, as the capacity of the biosphere to absorb waste is not a relative but an absolute or ecological scarcity. Technological progress could conceivably improve thermodynamic efficiency (although thermodynamic efficiency can never be 100 per cent) in the production processes, thereby reducing waste, and in this sense enable economic growth to proceed unimpeded, but this does not mean that the capacity of the biosphere itself as a sink has increased through technological manipulation. Reading (a) coheres better with extant knowledge, and it is this interpretation which lends weight to the view that the Report has singled out something that is normally ignored by standard economic thought.

This new focus, however, has implications for the Report's own prescription to avoid ecological disaster for all and increasing poverty for the many. As the size of nature's sink is absolutely limited, indefinite economic growth for all would overwhelm the biosphere altogether. To date, the mature industrialised economies, covering roughly only a fifth of the world's population, may nevertheless in their production and consumption be held largely responsible for the carbon dioxide emission which contributes to the greenhouse effect and global climatic change. Imagine for a moment what would happen if the developing world were to achieve a similar per capita emission of carbon dioxide within the next two decades or so (and in this process were said to have achieved the status of being developed). The ensuing climatic changes would even be more marked and alarming.

The Report prescribes that:

(a) 'Sustainable global development requires that those who are more affluent adopt lifestyles within the planet's ecological means – in their use of energy, for example . . .' (Brundtland 1987, p. 9) while the more numerous poor reduce the stress on resources through slowing population itself.

(b) To remove gross inequities, belt-tightening on the part of the affluent should be accompanied by economic growth in the poorer economies so that they can meet their essential or basic needs. But what are these essential needs 'to which overriding priority should be given' (ibid., p. 43)? They are for food, clothing, shelter and jobs. However, beyond that, the developing world is merely entitled to 'have legitimate aspirations for an improved quality of life' (ibid., p. 43).[18]

In other words, sustainable development when applied to present generations requires very different things respectively of the affluent and the non-affluent economies. One commonly quoted definition of sustainable development from the Report may therefore be misleading. It reads: 'Sustainable development is development that meets the needs of the present without compromising the ability of future generations to meet their own needs' (ibid., p. 43). Another runs: 'Humanity has the ability to make development sustainable – to ensure that it meets the needs of the present without compromising the ability of future generations to meet their own needs' (ibid., p. 8).

The Report does not explicitly distinguish between the concepts of 'needs' and 'wants.' Although this distinction has been philosophically challenged, the Report implies that it upholds it, that it makes conceptual sense, as evidenced by the earlier quotation (from page 43) showing that it attaches priority to the satisfaction of needs amongst present peoples who are unable to meet them.[19] If the distinction is held to be sound, it follows that by all accounts, the affluent economies have long gone beyond meeting basic needs. Indeed, in Rostow's view, an advanced mature economy is precisely defined in terms of an ability to meet ever-expanding wants. It is tautological to say that such an economy exists to satisfy novel wants.

If the analysis above is plausible, then it follows that the following conclusions may be drawn:

1. The Report is committed to maintaining for the present, at least, the deeply entrenched inequalities which exist between rich and poor countries to which it is itself inordinately sensitive, and in spite of its own clarion call to remove them. But in truth, according to the Report's prescriptions, they would not be removed or diminished but further entrenched. The rich would be permitted to satisfy their ever-changing wants (subject to some efforts to reduce the ecological damage which the pattern of production and consumption causes), while the poor would be permitted to meet their basic needs. As far as present generations are concerned, it looks as if the Report endorses the priority of the wants of the affluent over the basic needs of the non-affluent. This is a

disappointing as well as ironical implication of a study so committed to creating a common human future – see its sub-title.

2. While the countries of the affluent world are allowed to maintain their status as developed mature economies, the rest are allowed, as we have seen, only to aspire to an improved quality of life beyond meeting basic needs. This indeed is a realistic concession, for these hopes had better remain as aspirations, as the chances of them turning into reality are both politically slim and, furthermore, ecologically undesirable. (The Report explictly acknowledges the latter obstacle: 'The simple duplication in the developing world of industrial countries' energy use patterns is neither feasible nor desirable' (Brundtland 1987, p. 59).)

3. Sustainable development includes in its definitional scope not simply the present but also future generations. So perhaps in the long term, there will be a common human future. However, there is no attempt to address the profoundly difficult problems the world would face if it were to adjust to meeting the needs of all, and not merely the wants of some and the basic needs of the many.

In the light of this critique, it would be fair to conclude that the Brundtland model of sustainable development is not unitary but binary in implication; it suffers from serious incoherence in failing to recognise that it operates with two different prescriptions for achieving global sustainable development, a conclusion it appears to have arrived at by recognising that ecological constraints are absolute. The affluent countries are expected to continue on the path of economic growth to deliver an ever-increasing range of goods and services to their citizens (to satisfy their correspondingly expanding wants) while paying due regard to the requirement to reduce waste and environmental damage, in so far as this ecological preoccupation is compatible with the maintenance of their status as advanced mature economies. The non-affluent countries are also expected to commit themselves to economic growth but with this growth geared to meeting basic needs. As failure to meet needs causes environmental degradation in the developing world, once this modest level of growth has been reached, that world could be said to be environmentally virtuous. Strictly speaking, it would then be 'developed' as it has reached its own maturity. Both paths could then justifiably be labelled 'sustainable development' as the Report presupposes that between them the total effects of the activities of all economies in the world would be just below that critical level beyond which biospheric integrity would be undermined.

– 6 –

The classical model is unitary and global in scope because, while tacitly accepting the absolute limits imposed by biospherical integrity, it nevertheless holds that science and technology is not static but dynamic. Such technological optimism permits it to reconcile sustainable yield with growth. On the other hand, the Report appears trapped by the limitations of extant heavily-polluting technologies. However, in the last decade it is increasingly believed that given recent technological developments and innovations, economic growth tempered by the notion of sustainable yield, worldwide, can be accommodated within the absolute limits for the maintenance of biospheric integrity.[20] These dramatic improvements together with others on the horizon promise a much more optimistic scenario than that permitted by the Brundtland model. Under the latter, achieving the status of being a developed economy via economic growth is at best only an 'aspiration', but could never become a reality for the developing nations of the world. However, under the most recent technological dispensation, the new 'realists' are those who believe that a much larger physical resource base, increasingly rendered technologically accessible, will enable even developing nations to reach the status of being developed without subverting biospheric integrity.[21]

The Report is right in singling out the limits of current social organisation as a crucial obstacle to global sustainable development. But it may be mistaken in identifying 'present technological developments' as providing the other great obstacle. While putting its faith in technology, it has at the same time failed to appreciate technology's dynamic nature and, as a result, focused on the ecological limits of economic growth – a focus which has led to very different prescriptions for the developed and developing economies. Developing economies are, naturally, reluctant to embrace a development path which they consider to be inferior to that achieved by the developed economies. But in the light of the critique offered here, all economies could invoke the unitary and global model of eco-socially sustainable development, and, in the coming century, concentrate their efforts on grappling with the politically thorny issue of effecting suitable transfers of technology. At least the classical model has the virtue of promising universal affluence; whatever other drawbacks it may and does have, unlike the Brundtland model, divisiveness is not built into it. As alternatives within an anthropocentric framework, the classical model may well be superior to the Brundtland model provided its assumption about the dynamic nature of technological developments obtains.[22]

## – NOTES –

1. Jeremy Bentham's classical utilitarianism is based on pleasure and pain as the ultimate intrinsically valuable/disvaluable states. It recognises that sentience

extends not only to human beings but also to some of the higher animals. However, this recognition, until revived recently by Peter Singer, has had no bearing on the historical development of utilitarian materialism which has confined itself to humankind as its object of moral concern.

2. Historically, this has been so. For instance, it is said that the Black Death in Europe played a part in the eventual industrialisation of Europe, initially via the agricultural sector. Another example from more recent times is the relative shortage of labour (in spite of slave labour) in the history of the industrialised USA.

3. See Henriot 1983, p. 27 for a cyclical representation.

4. However, this does not mean that technology is not crucial to economic growth. But technological progress can only enter into the economic equation via capital investment in growth-generating technological innovations.

5. Terminology can be very confusing. For the purpose of this discussion, the term 'philosophy of conservationism' is defined as follows: (a) the thesis of resource conservation together with the notions of anthropocentrism and strong instrumentalism which underpin it, and (b) the thesis of resource preservation together with the weak instrumentalism which underpins it.

   Standard economic thought and Pinchot (at least officially, as we shall see later) support a modified version of the philosophy of conservationism through endorsing only thesis (a) and implying a conditional support of thesis (b), that is, only when resource preservation could be seen to contribute to the GDP.

6. On Pinchot as professional forester, conservation activist and presidential adviser, politician, see Pinkett 1970; Hays 1959 and Taylor 1992, ch.1.

7. He was much influenced by George Perkin Marsh's classic, *Man and Nature*, published in 1864, in which Marsh deplored the wasteful aspects of the standard form of development and the conversion of wilderness areas into productive land.

8. He had this to say about some early protesters against the greed of the lumber industry, whom he nicknamed 'denudatics':

   > Their eyes were closed to the economic motive behind true Forestry. They hated to see a tree cut down. So do I, and the chances are that you do too. But you cannot practice Forestry without it. Naturally the lumber juggernaut rolled over them – rolled over them and went on its forest-devastating and home-building way without even paying them the tribute of serious attention. (Pinchot 1947, pp. 28–9)

   As far as he could see, the denudatics 'were marching up a blind alley' (ibid., p. 27). In his view, 'The job was not to stop the ax, but to regulate its use' (ibid., p. 27). (*Breaking New Ground* is Pinchot's 'personal story' about (American) national forestry and conservation movements.)

9. But whether ecotourism – and to what extent in any given context – is ecologically sustainable is another matter. Pinchot's idea of conservation recognises ecological sustainability. In that sense, ecotourism as an economic activity must be predicated upon ecological viability. See section 4 of this

chapter for a clarification of the distinction between 'ecological sustainability' and what is called 'eco-social sustainability.'

10. See Hays 1959.

11. See section 4 for a clarification of the distinction between 'sustained yield' and 'sustainable yield' and for the argument that Pinchot's view (taking into account all the strands of his thought) could be said to accommodate the latter concept, so that it might be truer to say of him that his goal was not so much sustained as sustainable yield.

12. Of course, today, this insight is a commonplace; for instance, the Brundtland Report concurs: '. . . most renewable resources are part of a complex and interlinked ecosystem, and maximum sustainable yield must be defined after taking into account system-wide effects of exploitation' (Brundtland 1987, p. 45).

13. The Brundtland model does not.

14. Maser (1994, pp. 308–10) invokes the term 'ecosystemic sustainability' which this author finds unsatisfactory, though not necessarily disagreeing with him about the meaning of his preferred word.

15. 'Sustained high yield' is ultimately about maximum economic yield (that is, profits) to be got out of any capital invested such as in planting and/or harvesting a forest. Such yield can be sustained for a limited period but not indefinitely. However, 'sustainable yield' recognises that maximum economic yield invariably undermines ecological sustainability and thereby eco-social sustainability.

16. Pinchot's own parochial concerns do not detract from this claim.

17. 'Relative' and 'absolute' in this context have the following sense: a limit is relative if it can be transcended via a (technologically developed) substitute, but absolute when such transcendence is neither available nor possible.

18. The only peoples, belonging by and large to developing economies, who officially are said not to have such aspirations are the indigenous peoples (estimated to be at least 250 millions scattered throughout the world), at least according to the 1997 IUCN report entitled *Indigenous Peoples and Sustainability*.

19. It is probably truer to say that the Report wants to both eat the cake and keep it. On the one hand, it wants to say that needs trump wants, as meeting wants could at some stage hit the ecological limits which growth would run up against. On the other hand, it also seems to want to stay within the neo-classical economic framework which abolishes the distinction between wants and needs, hoping after all, that scarcity would always be relative and never absolute.

20. See Sagoff's contribution in this volume; also, Easterbrook 1996.

21. But this, of course, is subject to the crucial proviso that there is a politically effective way of ensuring technological transfer from the mature affluent to the less or non-affluent parts of the globe. Critics of the contemporary world order are not sanguine that this proviso will ever be met.

22. The emphasis here is on the framework as one within anthropocentrism. Of course, from the standpoint of non-anthropocentrism, both the Brundtland and the classical models are equally fundamentally flawed.

## – BIBLIOGRAPHY –

The Brundtland Report (World Commission on Environment and Development) (1987), *Our Common Future*, Oxford: Oxford University Press.

Easterbrook, Gregg (1996), *A Moment on the Earth: The Coming Age of Environmental Optimism*, Middlesex: Penguin Books.

Hays, Samuel P. (1959), *Conservation and The Gospel of Efficiency: The Progressive Conservation Movement*, Cambridge, MA: Harvard University Press.

Henriot, Peter, J. A. (1983), 'Development alternatives: problems, strategies and values' in Michael P. Todaro (ed.), *The Struggle for Economic Development*, New York and London: Longmans.

IUCN Inter-Commission Task Force on Indigenous Peoples (1997), *Indigenous Peoples and Sustainability*, Utrecht: International Books.

Lee, Keekok (1989), *Social Philosophy and Ecological Scarcity*, London: Routledge.

Marsh, George Perkin [1864] (1965), *Man and Nature*, Cambridge, MA: Harvard University Press.

Maser, Chris (1994), *Sustainable Forestry: Philosophy, Science and Economics*, Florida: St. Lucie Press.

Pinchot, Gifford (1910), *The Fight for Conservation*, Washington: Doubleday, Page and Company, University of Washington Press.

Pinchot, Gifford, (1947), *Breaking New Ground*, New York: Harcourt, Brace and Co.

Pinkett, Harold T. (1970), *Gifford Pinchot: Private and Public Forester*, Urbana and London: University of Illinois Press.

Rostow, W. W. (1960), *The Stages of Economic Growth: A NonCommunist Manifesto*, Cambridge: Cambridge University Press.

Taylor, Bob Pepperman (1992), *Our Limits Transgressed*, Kansas: Kansas University Press.

COMMENTARY ON CHAPTER 3

# Social justice and environmental sustainability: quick marriage, quick divorce?

Andrew Dobson takes his stand on a relatively robust conception of the natural world – as a sphere of events and relationships that is relatively independent of human activity. His central question is how far the Brundtland Report provides a defence of the natural world, understood in this sense. Given that the Report tends to treat the maintenance of biodiversity as proxy for the protection of the natural world, this comes down to asking how far the pursuit of sustainability, as expressed in the Brundtland Report, carries a commitment to the maintenance of biodiversity.

He begins by noting how relatively sparse are the explicit references to biodiversity contained in the Report – a fact which might suggest that the authors of the Report do not give it a very high priority. However, he goes on to note that advocates of sustainable development tend to associate the pursuit of sustainable development both with the promotion of social justice and with the protection of nature. They claim indeed that it brings justice and environmental concerns into harmony. Dobson resists this claim, calling into question one of the key premises on which it rests. For the argument is that justice requires the alleviation of poverty, and that this in turn will help to halt environmental degradation. The argument rests squarely on the premise that poverty is a prime cause of environmental degradation. Dobson points out that the relation between poverty and environmental degradation is in fact poorly understood, and such evidence as there is suggests that the relation obtains only in particular sets of circumstances (see also Neefjes's contribution in this volume). Empirical studies are likely to reveal important differences between developed and developing countries depending on the type of degradation that is involved. Dobson pointedly observes that the connection between poverty and environmental degradation in developed countries arises not because the poor create such environments, but because those are the environments into which they are forced. His conclusion thus far is that nature will receive but fitful protection from policies designed to sustain development or to sustain justice, since the connection is at best a purely contingent one.

However, a further potential link to environmental protection is provided by the Brundtland Report's concern for future generations, and Bryan Norton, for one, has argued that the interests of the human species and the interests of nature will converge 'in the long run.' Humans with a proper regard for the future will refrain from replacing nature with human-made substitutes, from assuming redundancy in the system, and from taking unnecessary risks. Once again, though, Dobson is sceptical. The needs of the present as regards both development and justice are bound to take precedence over the needs of the future; and as a result, inhibitions over substitution, redundancy and risk will be undermined, at nature's expense. In his view, it seems, the marriage of social justice and environmental sustainability looks set for a quick divorce.

~ O ~

# 3 SUSTAINABLE DEVELOPMENT AND THE DEFENCE OF THE NATURAL WORLD

## Andrew Dobson

My plan in this chapter is to explore the meaning and intention of sustainable development, as set out in the Brundtland Report, and to examine the idea in the context of the objective of the defence of the non-human natural world. In this regard, the Report's authors set out their stall early on: 'A first priority is to establish the problem of disappearing species and threatened ecosystems on political agendas as a major economic and resource issue' (Brundtland 1987, p. 13), and much of what follows is given over to examining this objective and its implications for environmental protection and the defence of nature.

Much of the debate will be about the meaning of sustainable development itself, which I shall argue has rather little to do with the defence of nature as a primary objective. The 'defence of nature' is of course itself an indeterminate idea: there are many who say that nature does not exist, and others who say that even if it does, there is no way of working out whether it is being successfully defended or not because all suggested indicators are flawed. These are important points, and if they are completely right then the intentions of this chapter are undermined right at the outset. I do not have the space here to debate the issues raised by these objections, but I do need to say – far too baldly – that they are not so firmly grounded as to make talk of the defence of nature otiose. I believe that nature, as something in a relationship of relative independence from the actions (mental and physical) of human beings, does exist,[1] and that there are ways of assessing whether it is being successfully defended or not.

The maintenance of biodiversity, for example, is often regarded as one of the objectives of environmentalists, and there are certainly ways in which its increase or decline can be measured. Here I shall be taking the maintenance of biodiversity as a proxy for 'the defence of nature.' I understand the problems with this – not least, that the value of non-human nature cannot be comprehensively expressed in terms of biodiversity. It is not necessarily the case, for example, that building a pond in an otherwise dry garden, thereby introducing aquatic plant and animal species to the local environment, amounts to a 'defence of nature.' Building the pond will alter the configuration of the garden as it previously stood – a configuration of nature (worked by humans, of course) which may have had value in itself. In other words the history of natural objects, as well as their diversity, is an important source of natural value (Goodin 1992), and this is not adequately captured by using biodiversity as a proxy for the defence of nature. However, I have chosen to concentrate in this chapter on the Brundtland Report itself, and biodiversity is certainly the Report's proxy for estimating the state of the non-human natural world. Rather than import critical tools from outside the Report, then, I think it best to perform an immanent critique of it – testing it by its own lights, as it were. This will not invalidate other critical tools that might be brought to bear, of course, but if sustainable development can be shown to have fallen short of the mark in terms of its own measurements of what a defence of nature might consist in, then things will look especially bleak.

There are a number of ways in which the question of 'falling short of the mark' might be addressed. One would be statistical. That is to say that we could look at the Brundtland Report's targets for the maintenance of biodiversity and see whether they had been met. One problem with this approach is that there are no targets set by the Report – target-setting was not part of the Report's remit. The most we can say is that since the Report was published, biodiversity has been in aggregate decline. But this is already saying quite a lot, since if part of the project of sustainable development is the maintenance of biodiversity, and if, even in the absence of specific targets, we can say that, overall, biodiversity has been in decline, then we seem entitled to conclude that sustainable development is failing in this particular objective.

Another way of discussing the issue of 'falling short of the mark' would be to interrogate the Report as to its actual intentions as far as the maintenance of biodiversity is concerned. That is, we could perform an immanent critique on the Report by examining the discursive commitment it makes to biodiversity, so as to try to arrive at some sort of conclusion regarding the relative importance attached to biodiversity by sustainable development, as expressed in The Brundtland Report. This is the course of action I propose to follow here, not only because a barrage of statistics would speak past the Report rather than to it, but because of my belief that part of the explanation for sustainable development's failure to halt the decline of biodiversity lies, precisely, in its reluctance to prioritise it. This reluctance can, I think, best be displayed through analysing the Report's discourse as far as biodiversity is concerned.

There is no point denying that the defence of nature is a feature of the project of sustainable development: those who think that not enough has been done by the architects of sustainable development to defend the natural world cannot say that such architects have done nothing to defend it. The Report recognises at several places that biodiversity is in decline, and it bemoans this fact. Part of the point of what follows, though, is to show that references to biodiversity in the Report are few and far between and that the bulk of the World Commission on Environment and Development's work was taken up with other issues relating to population, poverty, food security, sustainable industries, and the like. A rough-and-ready count shows that about one-fifteenth of the main body of the Report is taken up with biodiversity issues – that is some 6 to 7 per cent – with the rest devoted to sustainable development as such. One should treat figures like this with a degree of caution, of course, but they do give an indication of the influence the issue of biodiversity had on the preparation and writing up of the Report. At the outset, then, and without saying anything specific about just what this 6 to 7 per cent contains, we can suggest that biodiversity was some way down the list of the Commission's priorities.

It is of course contentious to distinguish between 'biodiversity issues' and 'sustainable development' as I have just done, but this is precisely the wider point of what follows. The standard view (or at least the view of sustainable development enthusiasts) is that sustainable development and biodiversity are two sides of the same coin, or that sustainable development is a precondition for the protection of biodiversity and vice versa. From a political progressive's point of view, this would be marvellous if it were true. Sustainable development has come to be associated with issues of social justice, and particularly with issues of justice between the so-called 'developed' and 'developing' worlds. It has, therefore, resonances with 'old left' objectives revolving around the relief or elimination of poverty and the deepening of national and international social justice. The defence of biodiversity, on the other hand, can be read as a shorthand (as I am doing here) for the defence of the non-human natural world, and this in turn is what has animated one of the most influential of the new social movements of recent years – the environmental movement. So if it were true that sustainable development, as a political project, were to be about both social justice and environmental protection, then two broad streams on the progressive wing of political life would have common cause. And this is, of course, precisely one of sustainable development's main claims – that it does bring justice and environmental issues into harmony, and that therefore it has the political capacity to unite potentially disparate progressive factions.

My own belief is that the temptation to subscribe to this view needs to be resisted. In the first place, the evidence for one of sustainable development's principal arguments – that poverty is a prime cause of environmental degradation – is not overwhelmingly compelling, even where it exists. It is remarkable how little empirical evidence there is to corroborate this central claim in sustainable development literature, and in the absence of clinching empirical evidence, we are left with broad supposition. The supposition tends to be that poverty is a prime cause of environmental degradation, but even if it is accepted that it is, we might equally well suppose, first, that it will not always be so, and second, that often there will be causes other than that of poverty.

Put differently, the first point should be that the sustainable development claim that poverty causes environmental degradation is only true for certain times and places and under certain conditions. The Commission says, for example, that, 'poverty itself pollutes the environment . . . those who are poor and hungry will often destroy their immediate environment in order to survive' (Brundtland 1987, p. 28). It would be foolish to deny that this is often true, but it does not describe every poverty-environment relationship. It is not a good description, for example, of the relationship between poverty and the environment in representative parts of the 'developed' world. It cannot be said in any meaningful way of the poor of a major British city like Birmingham that they 'destroy their immediate environment in order to survive.' Nor, to draw a closer parallel, can it be said of the rural poor in Britain that they typically destroy their immediate environment in order to survive. The causal relationship between poverty and environmental degradation posited in sustainable development literature seems better suited to the lived experience of the Southern poor rather than the Northern poor. This is entirely appropriate in the context of a political project which is designed for developing countries, but this in itself should make us wary of transposing the arguments to contexts in which they are less likely to work.

In truth, no-one can be sure exactly what the causal relationship between poverty and environmental degradation is until it has been examined in all its dimensions. We need a raft of studies which can claim to be truly representative of the range of possible situations within which it might be claimed that poverty 'produces' environmental degradation. This would involve differentiating between types of environmental degradation, because it is likely that poverty will contribute more to certain types of environmental degradation than to others. Such a study would make it clear that many environmental problems are caused by wealthy styles of life rather than poor ones, and this would be a useful political corrective to the handy view (for wealthy Westerners/Northerners) that most of the world's environmental ills are due to the activities of poor people. It will also point up the important truth that poor people sometimes live the most environmentally sustainable lives of all, out of sheer necessity. In brief, both poverty and wealth need to be in the frame when discussion of environmental degradation takes place.

Such a study should also involve, as I suggested in the previous paragraph, examining closely the conditions under which poverty leads to environmental degradation, since the relationship is unlikely to hold at all times and in all places. What is true of the environmental impact of the activities of poor people in marginal lands is not necessarily true of poor people in inner cities. Sustainable development literature is markedly lacking in empirical studies organised analytically around these sorts of questions, yet such studies are surely a precondition for speaking with any authority on one of sustainable development's central claims: that poverty causes environmental degradation.

As I have suggested, part of the significance of this is that while we might accept that the defence of nature goes hand-in-hand with poverty alleviation in developing countries, the same cannot necessarily be said of 'developed' countries. This is particularly pertinent in the context of debates about the 'environmental justice' movement in the United States of America. This movement is the developed world analogue of the sustainable development movement in the 'developing' world, and it is based on the widespread truth that poor people live in poor environments. Ever since Love Canal was found, in 1978, to be poisoned, after a new housing estate had been built into which predominantly poor people had moved, the connection between poor people and poor environments has been explored and established. In many parts of the developed world the poor inhabit poor environments, just as they do in many parts of the developing world.

In truth, though, the relationship between poverty and environmental degradation differs in the discourses of environmental justice and sustainable development. As we have established, sustainable development has it that poverty produces environmental degradation, but the gist of environmental justice is that poor people are sold degraded environments. Unsurprisingly, sustainable development is about development, and environmental justice is about justice, but perhaps more suprisingly, neither is really about the protection of nature as such. Sustainable development is about the sustaining of development, and its commitment to environmental protection is dependent upon such protection being functional for development. Just as sustainability has its discourse, centred around the question 'what is to be sustained?', so justice has its discourse, and one of its central questions is, 'what is to be distributed?' For the environmental justice movement, the environment is viewed under the sign of social justice discourse, as no more and no less than something to be distributed (along with all the other goods and bads that society distributes). The environmental justice movement tends to focus on the distribution of environmental 'bads' (toxic waste dumps, landfill sites and so on) rather than environmental 'goods', and its principal observation is that the distribution of environmental bads is skewed towards poor people. This is undoubtedly true, and is a useful corrective to the widespread 'apocalypse' strain of environmentalism which argues that environmental calamities are, and will be, visited upon everyone equally. But the question for us is: how strong is the connection between environmental protection and environmental justice?

On one reading, the environmental justice movement is even further removed from environmental protection than the sustainable development movement. Sustainable developers at least have environmental protection on their radar, even if only in functional and instrumental guise, but the environmental justice movement is explicitly concerned with how good and bad environments are most fairly to be divided up, rather than how they might be best protected. It is possible to think of the environmental justice movement having achieved its principal objective of the fairer distribution of environmental goods and bads without focusing on the protection of the non-human natural world at all. Of course, environmental justice need not stop at the fairer distribution of goods and bads; it is not a large step from there to the proposition that the incidence of environmental bads should be reduced rather than just shared out more equally, and in this case the causes of environmental protection and environmental justice would come closer together. But if this step is not taken – and the evidence suggests that it is only patchily taken, if at all – then it is important to distinguish between 'environmental justice' and 'justice to the environment', and to see that they are not the same thing. What is more, the former does not necessarily entail the latter, and this confirms the remark made earlier in the context of sustainable development: that justice-based approaches to the environment which do not have interspecific justice within their respective remits will not necessarily result in its protection.

All this relates to the second of the two points made above, that while poverty may be one cause of environmental degradation under determinate circumstances, there may be other causes too. This means that if the defence of nature is an objective, then it will not always be achieved by hitching the project to the star of poverty alleviation, and it may therefore require strategies aimed directly at its defence, rather than indirectly as a hoped-for result of reducing poverty. Sustainable development has a markedly instrumental view of environmental protection, which is to say that environmental protection is regarded as a necessary condition for development. As with all instrumentally-based arguments, the instrument is only regarded as valuable so long as it works, and where it does not work, or is unnecessary, its value declines.

None of this is to say that the objectives of sustainable development are unimportant. Far from it. The justice-based initiatives and intentions of sustainable development need the widest possible implementation, and where this results in environmental protection too, this is to be welcomed by environmental campaigners. My purpose here is simply to point out that the cause of the defence of nature is not always and everywhere best pursued through the political, economic and ethical mechanisms tied up with the project of sustainable development.

Another way into this is to consider the range of questions to which any discourse of sustainability must have an answer, and to analyse the range of answers. Such an analysis helps to differentiate between the various sustainability discourses by grouping the answers in families. Each family of answers to the common questions around which the sustainability discourse is organised represents a 'conception' of sustainability. I have carried out a detailed analysis of this sort elsewhere (Dobson 1996), and this is not the place to go over that ground again.

The two important points to remember here, though, are, first, that sustainability discourses are multiple, and second, that perhaps the most important question to which these discourses have to give an answer is: 'sustainability of what?' Recognising that there is a multiplicity of sustainability discourses is the first step to seeing that sustainable development is only one of them, and acknowledging that there is one particularly foundational question to which they all must give an answer is the route to differentiating them in interesting ways. This is because each conception of sustainability gives a different answer to that foundational question: just what is to be sustained into the future? Some of these answers accord with the objectives of environmentalists, and some do not (necessarily). It is this fact that helps us to see why the objectives of sustainable development should be – and are – regarded with some suspicion by environmentalists.

Environmentalists, or at least environmentalists of the sort I am concerned with here, have as their objective the sustaining of natural value – the value that inheres in naturally-occurring objects – into the future. To the obvious rejoinder that there is no such thing as natural value, I can only say here that I think there is, although just what it is, is contested (just as there is such a thing as 'sustainable development', although its meaning is contested). In this chapter, as already indicated, I am taking 'biodiversity' as a proxy for natural value, so we can reinterpret the environmentalist answer to the 'what is to be sustained?' question to be: biodiversity.

What is striking about this is the difference between the environmentalist answer to the principal organising question of sustainability discourse, and the sustainable development answer. Unsurprisingly, the sustainable development answer to the question of what is to be sustained into the future is 'development.' Now there is no obvious connection – certainly no necessary connection – between the environmentalist and sustainable development answers. There is no necessary connection, that is, between 'biodiversity' and 'development', and it is the normative distance between the two that generates the doubts (legitimate doubts, I believe) of environmentalists in respect of the intentions of sustainable development.

Of course, to stress that there is no necessary connection between 'development' and 'biodiversity' is to leave the door open to arguments of contingent connection, and it is right to do so. Moreover, there are both broad and narrow contingent connections. At the broader end of the spectrum, what sustainable developers are arguing for is the sustaining of the conditions for development, and sustainable development theorists and activists have taken an enormous stride in recognising that there are environmental as well as other sorts of preconditions for successful development over time. At the narrow end, it will obviously be the case that industries that depend on biodiversity (such as, perhaps, the pharmaceutical industry) will see the sustaining of development and of biodiversity as mutually enhancing. But as far as a broader defence of nature is concerned, these contingent connections have their limitations, for it is clear that by these lights any aspect of the non-human natural world that is not regarded as preconditional for sustained and sustainable development will receive little, if any, protection.

A cursory glance at the language used in the Brundtland Report confirms this instrumental engagement with the non-human natural world. A representative extract runs as follows:

> The loss of forests and other wild lands extinguishes species of plants and animals and drastically reduces the genetic diversity of the world's ecosystems. This process robs present and future generations of genetic material with which to improve crop varieties, to make them less vulnerable to weather stress, pest attacks, and disease. The loss of species and subspecies, many as yet unstudied by science, deprives us of important potential sources of medicines and industrial chemicals. (Brundtland 1987, p. 35)

In each of these cases, the value of the non-human natural world is tied to the uses to which it might be put for industrial, medicinal and agricultural purposes. This instrumental attachment to biodiversity will of course result in a considerable degree of protection, and sustainable development's achievement in this regard should not be underestimated. It might also be argued that these instrumental reasons are sufficient to generate the very wide-ranging protection that environmentalists want, so long as they are deployed in the context of the very considerable uncertainty that surrounds the potential uses of biodiversity. Given, in other words, that we do not know what might be useful and what might not be, precaution suggests that broad policies for protection are the most appropriate. What more could environmentalists intent on the protection of nature want?

Something of what they might want is suggested by the sentence that follows the ones quoted above, in which the loss of species is bemoaned because: 'It removes forever creatures of beauty and parts of our cultural heritage; it diminishes the biosphere' (Brundtland 1987, p. 35). Even these reasons for protection of the biosphere are mostly human-interested, in that 'beauty' is in the eye of the (human) beholder' and humans are the only 'culture-producing' creatures, so far as we know. I pointed out above that the vast bulk of the Brundtland Report is taken up with 'industrial, medicinal and agricultural' reasons for the protection of biodiversity, and in the light of the comments in this paragraph we might add 'aesthetic' and 'cultural' reasons to the list. Once again, the list is self-evidently human-interested, so in fact the only part of the paragraph on which we have been commenting which amounts to a defence of biodiversity for its own sake is the last four words: 'it diminishes the biosphere.' This is a reason for protection which attaches to biodiversity in itself, rather than instrumentally. The very limited support for biodiversity protection for its own sake exhibited in this paragraph is representative of the Report's attention to the intrinsic value of the non-human natural world as a whole.

On the face of it, then, environmentalists and sustainable developers give very different answers to the same organising question – what is to be sustained? – and it is this that lies at the root of their disagreements. Again, there seems little possibility of bringing the two camps together except in cases of reciprocal contingency. But sustainable development has one more very important card up its sleeve – the futurity that is built into the Brundtland definition: 'development that meets the needs of the present without compromising the ability of future generations to meet their own needs' (Brundtland 1987, p. 43). It is possible to argue, in a way most comprehensively explored by Bryan Norton, that taking future human interests adequately into account entails defending the non-human natural world in practically the same way, and up to practically the same point, as the most enthusiastic intrinsic valuer could want. Norton puts it like this:

> [I]ntroducing the idea that other species have intrinsic value, that humans should be 'fair' to all other species, provides no operationally recognizable constraints on human behavior that are not already implicit in the generalized, cross-temporal obligations to protect a healthy, complex, and autonomously functioning system for the benefit of future generations of human beings. Deep ecologists, who cluster around the principle that nature has independent value, should therefore not differ from longsighted anthropocentrists in their policy goals for the protection of biological diversity. (Norton 1991, p. 227)

Put differently, Norton's general point is that, '[e]nvironmentalists believe that policies serving the interests of the human species as a whole, and in the long run, will serve also the "interests" of nature, and vice versa' (ibid., p. 240). This is a very suggestive idea, and it certainly presents a considerable challenge to those who argue that sustainable development does not do enough for nature. Sustainable developers will say that given the degree of our uncertainty as to just what the 'needs' of future genera- tions (referring to the Brundtland definition) will be, it would be wrong avoidably to deprive them of the opportunities which the present range of biodiversity (our proxy here for 'nature') affords us. A robust defence of biodiversity seems therefore to be built into sustainable development's concern for the needs and interests of future generations.

Two things need to be said about this, though. In the first place, 'future generationism' still only provides an instrumental defence of the non- human natural world. When all is said and done, only those features of that world which present-generation policy-makers think will be of value to future-generations will have any chance of protection. Norton himself says that the actual degree of protection will depend on three variables: the degree of substitutability that is believed to exist between 'natural capital' and human-made substitutes; the extent to which ecosystems are believed to be 'redundant', that is, in terms of their importance to the production and reproduction of human life; and, finally, the degree of risk aversion that is accepted as appropriate – see Norton 1989, p. 156). Actually existing views on these variables are not very promising as far as environmentalists are concerned: the search for substitutes for naturally-occurring objects and processes is not only regarded as permissible, but is often a driving force behind scientific and industrial innovation; the very language of 'redundancy' as far as ecosystems is concerned betrays an almost pathological instrumentalism; and while a precautionary approach to risk would be very welcome in environmental policy-making, there is presently little sign of it being built into the policy-making process in the required systematic way. Despite all this, though, environmentalists do need to recognise that future-generationism affords greater opportunities for the defence of nature than they might suspect, and they might regard it as their political obligation to screw down the lid on Norton's three variables as tight as possible, rather than throwing away the opportunities presented by his enlightened, future-generationist, anthropocentrism.

The second thing that needs to be said about future-generationism, though, is that while sustainable development – at least in its Brundtland guise – pays lip service to it, most of the day-to-day attention is paid to the conditions for sustaining development in the present generation. This is entirely understandable, given the desperate straits in which most of that generation live. Returning to the theme of justice, it is intra-generational rather than inter-generational justice that moves sustainable developers on the ground, and this has a considerable impact on Norton's three variables, discussed above. Sustainable development's discounting of the future (in both the formal economic sense and the more metaphorical sense) has the effect of turning questions of substitutability, ecosystem redundancy, and risk, into luxuries rather than necessities. These questions are much more central to inter-generational than to intra-generational justice, since the former has to do with the distribution of environmental goods across time, and is therefore intimately related to the discourse of sustainability itself. Intra-generational justice, with its time-slice view of distribution, need not concern itself with sustainability over time at all, and this, at present, is where sustainable development stands: concerned most consistently with justice in the present generation and therefore only contingently interested in the defence of the non-human natural world.

## – CONCLUSION –

All this suggests that the Brundtland Report's commitment to the defence of the non-human natural world – for its own sake – is extremely patchy. The Report, and sustainable development more generally, have been credited with harnessing two important political agendas in a mutually enhancing fashion: the agendas of justice and of environmental protection. The discussion in this chapter, though, suggests that social justice and environmental protection are not part of a seamless web. The empirical evidence to back up claims of compatibility is sparse, and analysis of the terms 'justice' and 'sustainability' indicates that while they may sometimes have common cause they certainly will not always do so. For these reasons, the marriage of social justice and environmental sustainability looks insecure as the new millenium beckons, and this shows that those for whom the defence of the non-human natural world is a prime consideration need to pick and choose their political allies with care.

## – NOTE –

1. For various possible defences, see, for instance: Rolston 1997; Soper 1995; Lee 1999.

## – BIBLIOGRAPHY –

The Brundtland Report (World Commission on Environment and Development) (1987), *Our Common Future*, Oxford: Oxford University Press.
Dobson, Andrew (1996), 'Environmental sustainabilities: an analysis and a typology', *Environmental Politics* 5:3, pp. 401–28.
Dobson, Andrew, (1998), *Justice and the Environment: Conceptions of Environmental Sustainability and Dimensions of Social Justice*, Oxford: Oxford University Press.
Goodin, Robert (1992), *Green Political Theory*, Cambridge: Polity Press.
Lee, Keekok (1999), *The Natural and the Artefactual: The Implications of Deep Science and Deep Technology for Environmental Philosophy*, Lanham, MD: Lexington Books (Rowman & Littlefield).
Norton, B. (1989), 'Intergenerational equity and environmental decisions: a model using Rawls's veil of ignorance', *Ecological Economics* 1, pp. 137–59.
Norton, B. (1991), *Toward Unity Among Environmentalists*, New York and Oxford: Oxford University Press.
Rolston III, Holmes (1997), 'Nature for real: is nature a social construct?', in T. D. J. Chappell (ed.), *The Philosophy of the Environment*, Edinburgh: Edinburgh University Press.
Soper, Kate (1995), *What is Nature?*, Oxford UK & Cambridge, MA: Blackwell.

# The social re-appropriation of nature

In Enrique Leff's contribution we learn how the indigenous and peasant peoples of Latin America are mobilising to challenge the prevailing model of sustainable development. He sees this challenge as arising less from a conflict of interests than from a conflict of values.

For Leff, the prevailing model of sustainable development is an expression of 'global eco-liberalism', wherein environmental policies are subservient to economic objectives, and actually depend upon the success of the economic policies for their implementation. The environmental policies themselves are often limited and impoverished in their vision. They typically result in the setting-up of protected enclaves, but have little impact on mainsteam economic activity, which continues unabated. The prevailing model is global in its outlook and managerial in its approach. It deploys economic instruments to protect nature, and believes that assigning property rights and putting a price on the environment is the only way to achieve this end. On the ideological front, it likes to speak of the environment as the common heritage of mankind, and will take steps to instil a love of nature and to moderate the habits of the affluent. It looks to technological innovation to improve efficiency and uncouple industrial activity from its natural resource base.

Leff cautions against resorting to easily to the North/South dichotomy, pointing out the distinction between 'Southern' governments and their advisers on the one hand, who buy into the global economy and protest against obstacles to their country's growth; and the 'rural South' on the other hand – the peasants and the indigenous peoples who tend to opt out of the global economy. It is among the latter that he finds the countervailing view of sustainable development. According to this view, sustainable development stands for the liberation of both the ecological and the cultural potentials of the region. It expresses a new conception of environmental rationality, by which I take Leff to mean the pursuit of policies that follow the 'logic' of local cultural diversity and ecological potential. It is not a movement for environmental justice as this is commonly understood, nor does it involve claims to compensation for environmental damage. Rather, it voices a new sense of cultural identity, and demands self-determination and the re-appropriation of its own ecological potential. It looks to a new form of technological productivity that integrates ecology and culture. In these cultural stirrings Leff describes the makings of a 'new social order' which he terms 'environmental democracy' – a mode of constructive participation and shared decision-making, based on the values of equity, diversity and sustainability.

~ O ~

# 4 SUSTAINABLE DEVELOPMENT IN DEVELOPING COUNTRIES: CULTURAL DIVERSITY AND ENVIRONMENTAL RATIONALITY

## *Enrique Leff*

### – INTRODUCTION –

The discourse on sustainable development is not homogeneous. It cuts across diverse cultural perceptions and divergent economic and social interests. In this essay, I intend to challenge the dominant global discourse on sustainability from the standpoint of developing countries and, particularly, from the perspective of emergent theoretical, cultural and political movements in Latin America.

It is not my aim here to set out the particular ways in which Latin American countries are implementing a global strategy for sustainable development. Instead, I shall develop the argument that, beyond the conflictive interests surrounding the policies of sustainability, a new paradigm for sustainable development can be constructed from the perspective of the poor tropical countries; and that this is being mobilised by emergent social movements. A new concept of environmental rationality is built, underlying the ecological potentials and cultural values that give support to this emergent paradigm for sustainable production. This rationality is not merely a theoretical construction but, as I shall argue, is being mobilised by new social actors in their struggles to re-appropriate nature.

Thus, the environmental question is being radicalised. It turns from environmental (administration, which aims to protect nature by internalising the ecological costs of growth, by 'dematerialising'[1] production and reducing throughput by means of technological innovations), to a social re-appropriation of nature, where new ethical values and political goals (recognition of environmental potentials, poverty alleviation, democracy and autonomy) intermingle in the emergent arena of political ecology. This new paradigm is being constructed by social movements through which indigenous and peasant peoples are struggling to regain control over their natural resources by legitimising their cultural rights. The politicisation of the environmental question is reflected in the discourse of indigenous peoples and in the course of a democratic transition which re-signifies the concept and practice of sustainable development.

## – FROM GLOBAL AGENDA TO DIFFERENTIATED VISIONS OF SUSTAINABLE DEVELOPMENT –

From the late sixties, catastrophic views about ecological collapse (Ehrlich 1968; Meadows et al. 1972) challenged but failed to stop the inertial tendency for economic growth. Sustainability then emerged as the foremost goal to save the Earth and life on it. However, economic globalisation has become a homogenising force which moulds the notion of sustainable development. The special World Commission on Environment and Development, whose remit it was to inquire into the causes of environmental degradation and to re-orient thinking and action in more clear and efficient ways, ended up promoting a common approach to sustainability (the Brundtland Report). With the purpose of building international consensus, meetings were held in the different world regions and public hearings opened a space for multiple voices to be heard. However, the Brundtland Report did not integrate the divergent, sometimes even antagonistic, interests and contradictory visions of sustainability (see Redclift 1992). After the Rio Summit in 1992, and with Agenda 21 as a global programme for action, an international effort started, with a triumphal economistic vision of sustainability dominating policies in economic and trade agreements.

Sustainability as a major attainable objective involves a complex discourse embedded in diverse and divergent theoretical visions and strategic actions. Sustainable development emerges from a common purpose, that of re-valuing nature as an ethical principle and as a general condition for global sustainability of population and production. However, this general purpose is mobilised by contrasting and sometimes antagonistic visions, practices and politics for sustainability. These differences cannot be traced in the usual North/South divide. In fact, conservationism, biocentric and non-anthropocentric ecologism as well as technocratic and economic environmentalisms are not found exclusively in the more developed countries, as they are disseminated to governments and NGOs in the underdeveloped regions.

Ideologues and politicians in the North, as well as the ecologically concerned citizens in those countries, are dominated by a false conception of post-scarcity and post-materialist society, imagining an ideal society liberated from material needs and open to moral values in keeping with an ethic and love for a 'civilised' nature. Furthermore, they are seduced by the belief that technology will solve environmental problems by dematerialising production and recycling waste, thus re-opening the possibility of a clean, unpolluted, ecological nature and unlimited economic growth. In addition, with the emergence of a new discourse on sustainable development, optimism has been re-installed in the minds and hearts of former pessimistic scientists. If technology and instrumental rationality have been considered by critical rationalists to be the driving causes of ecological destruction (Marcuse 1964), salvation is now expected from new environmental values to moderate consumption habits in affluent societies, and from technological innovation to dematerialise production and improve its efficiency (Commoner 1990; Meadows et al. 1992; Ehrlich and Ehrlich 1991; Hinterberger and Seifert 1997).

However, a basic question remains: how to reverse, stop or balance the ineluctable environmental degradation that results from energy use in every productive process? The discourse of sustainable development has shifted away from the claim that economic processes should be embedded in the larger geochemical-ecological system that establishes the conditions and potentials for the economic extraction and transformation of natural resources. From the standpoint of the second law of thermodynamics, Georgescu-Roegen (1971) constructed a radical critique of economics which was followed by proposals for a steady-state economics (Daly 1991). However, the neo-liberal discourse on sustainable development has turned causes and effects upside down. Assigning property rights and market prices to the commons is the dominant neo-liberal strategy to control environmental degradation and to recover ecological equilibrium. Environmental economics claims that affluence will be the driving force to generate ecological values and a new ethic for nature, and that economic growth will provide the budgets for environmental protection.

Ecological economists find in ecology and thermodynamics physical conditions that constrain economic growth and world food production for a still growing population, overlooking the fact that the ecological productivity of the planet offers a new base and new potentials for a sustainable economics embedded in nature and in culture (Leff 1995; Leff and Carabias 1993). As population growth and current practices of resource use exceed the planet's carrying capacity, they see the actual trends in the human appropriation of net primary productivity as another sign of ecological collapse, rather than a new potential for sustainable development (Vitousek et al. 1986).[2]

However, ecological productivity should be viewed as a potential for sustainable production based on the transformation of ecological systems to enhance their eco-technological productivity. Entropy in the metabolism and food chains of living organisms cannot be avoided; nor can technology stop and reverse energy degradation in the process of production. But we can envision a sustainable economy as the balance between the negentropic production of biomass on the one hand and the entropic degradation of matter and energy in the productive process on the other. Thus, we can envision new scenarios where economic and population growth can be stabilised, by constructing a sustainable but dynamic and productive complex system (Leff 1986; 1996a; 1997).[3]

Scientists from Latin America responded to 'limits of growth' global models by demonstrating that beyond technological and ideological solutions, social change, democracy and economic distribution are the basic conditions for a more rational and sustainable use of the natural resource endowment of the region (Herrera et al. 1976). Gallopin (1995) has provided convincing arguments for a view of sustainable development based on the endowment of natural resources and the ecological potential of Latin American countries.

In Latin America, as in other underdeveloped areas, most governments have engaged in sustainable development policies driven by the ideals of economic progress endorsed by global neo-liberalism. Overall, environmental policies have adopted and followed the objectives of economic policies. Environmental protection is generally marginalised as second priority, awaiting economic success to provide the budgets necessary for environmental programmes. The aim of internalising environmental externalities has encouraged the development of environmental legislation and the application of new economic instruments. However, in many countries, the explicit aim of re-orienting economic development towards sustainability has yielded restricted conservationist policies, establishing natural parks and biosphere reserves, while the main sectors of the economy continue 'business as usual' in an ecological void, sometimes accompanied by advanced environmental legislation, but with insufficient institutional capacities for enforcing it.

Beyond this general statement, if we analyse the policies, processes and actions pursued by Latin American and other countries belonging to the

South[4], significant differences between them are noticeable. Consider a country like Costa Rica, seduced and subdued by the benefits of joint implementation agreements, trying to benefit from comparative advantages in its endowment of natural resources, valuing its biodiverse forests as carbon sinks and sites for ecotourism, and trading its absorption capacity for greenhouse gases and its contribution to global sustainability as an environmental asset; or countries where decision-makers are willing to sign bilateral agreements to trade their biodiversity, ignoring the global agreements and protocols drawn up by the Convention of Biological Diversity. However, indigenous and peasant groups in Latin America and countries belonging to the South have alternative visions of sustainability; they are mobilising to resist economic globalisation, to regain property over their lands and ethnical territories and to re-affirm common rights to their patrimony of natural resources.

Ever since the Stockholm Conference on Human Environment, governments in the countries of the South have reacted against any hint of stopping economic growth, fearing that this would undermine much needed development aimed at alleviating poverty and providing jobs. However, this outlook has not necessarily been followed by academicians or by the people. In rural parts of the South, sustainability is not viewed as integration with the global economy, but rather as a strategy to deconstruct and delink from world market constraints and to build up a new rationality based upon the cultural diversity of the peoples and the ecological potentials of the environments where their cultures have evolved (Escobar 1995; Leff 1995).

We find examples of these social processes in the Zapatista movement in Chiapas, Mexico, where the *Ejercito Zapatista de Liberacion Nacional* made its political appearance on the same day that NAFTA was signed. The struggle for democracy, political autonomy, self-determination, ethnic identity and cultural diversity is the struggle not only of the indigenous peoples of Chiapas and indigenous peoples of Mexico in general (Díaz Polanco 1991; Gómez 1997), but also of the organisations of indigenous peoples in the Amazon basin (Torres 1997) and, in general, in the Latin American and Caribbean region (Grünberg 1995). Thus, according to indigenous peoples, political ecology is being defined as political culture and politics of place (Escobar 1997b). These emergent indigenous peoples' movements point to the re-invention of nature and the re-signification of cultural identities, as exemplified by many ethnological studies of indigenous peoples such as the Achuar (Descola 1996), or the black communities of the Atlantic coast in Colombia in their struggle to re-appropriate their biodiversity (Escobar 1997a). These social movements are mediating between cultural identities and environmental rights and, re-defining territorial spaces where new 'extractive reserves' are being established through strategies for sustainable appropriation of nature, as shown by the *seringueiros* in Brazil (Gonçalvez 1997).

Two different views have emerged from strategies for sustainability, informed by antagonistic social interests. The first seeks to solve the problem of environmental degradation through capitalisation of nature, international consensus, command and control policy instruments and free-market mechanisms. The second, opposing this economistic approach, sees environmental rationality as being constructed in grass roots organisations, at local community and municipal level. This ecological path, taken by peasant and indigenous communities for the socialisation of nature and self-management of their environmental potentials for sustainable development, constitutes the new environmentalism of the South. It is giving impulse to new social actors in the rural areas of such economies, who are struggling to regain control over their heritage of natural and cultural resources.

## – Cultural diversity, political autonomy and environmental rationality: emergent social movements in rural areas of the South –

Once viewed from the standpoint of cultural diversity and conflictive interests, sustainable development cannot be reduced to an homogeneous concept or practice. Environmental problems are perceived from different theoretical visions, social interests and political strategies. Ecologism encompasses different meanings, from deep ecology, biocentrism and conservationism to social ecology and political ecology (Naess and Rothenberg 1989; Devall and Sessions 1985; Bookchin 1989; Guha and Martínez 1997). Ecologism as an ideology portrays an understanding of the world built on ecological relations; it views population dynamics and human behavior as determined by the 'carrying capacity' of their environment, reducing the symbolic order that organises culture and power relations to the complex interdependencies of nature (Leff 1998b).

However, beyond the dominant conservationist vision and technological solutions to resource exhaustion and environmental pollution, a new concept of environment is emerging. Environment is being conceived as a complex productive system that integrates the ecological potential of nature, technological productivity and cultural diversity (Leff 1995; 1998a). Thus, a new paradigm of production can be constructed, based on the sustainable eco-technological productivity of different regions, where nature is recognised, signified and transformed through diverse cultural values. This new paradigm for sustainable production goes beyond the ecological approaches to determine ecological footprints (Rees 1992) – extra-boundary extensions of the resource consumption of cities to their surrounding environments – and bioregionalism, an ecological ordering of the territory for a more decentralised and sustainable development.

In rural areas of the South, new social actors are emerging in response to extreme poverty, dispossession of their traditional land, destruction of their natural means of production, social marginalisation and political exclusion, questioning dominant economic power relations and their effects in terms of ecological destruction and socio-environmental degradation. In many cases, these social actors mobilise against neo-liberal policies and state centralisation and authoritarianism. They demand direct participation in decision-making regarding public policies, and claim new rights of access to, and control over, the common environmental resources of their locale.

These movements are organised under the protection of a new ecological and democratic culture. They demand new forms of representation and criteria of environmental justice to solve conflicting interests over the ownership of land and nature, the appropriation of environmental re-sources and wealth distribution. Environmental issues incorporate new meanings and perspectives, introducing a further dimension of complexity to the traditional social struggles over land and resources of rural commu-nities, with forest-dwellers emphasising the need to construct new schemes to re-appropriate nature as a productive potential, and to develop their patrimony of natural and cultural resources through sustainable use practices.

Thus, the claims of peasants and indigenous peoples are being enlarged from demands for cultural rights regarding language, traditions and terri-tories to include the re-appropriation of the productive potential of the ecosystems within which they live to satisfy their needs and develop their cultures. Their claims are then redefining human, cultural and property rights related to the possession and sustainable use of nature's wealth and ecological recources.

These emergent sustainable development movements integrate 'environ-mental rights' with new demands for democracy and autonomy, that is, for a more direct appropriation of nature based on consensual decisions of popular organisations and communities themselves. These demands oppose centralised decision-making and hierarchical structures, opening up a more decentralised and democratic process. Sustainable development led by such principles in grass-roots social organisations is mobilised by cultural values which depart from a unidimensional conception of progress in terms of technological productivity. These grass-roots organisations also reject the current mechanisms of political representation; their cultural values also inform negotiation of their interests, such as credits and productive inputs, with mediating agencies. These new social actors are claiming their right to self-organise their productive processes and their living conditions.

This emergent environmental democracy strives to halt the current homogenisation and fragmentation forced by economic globalisation, searching socio-environmental integration based on new social solidarities, ethnic identities, cultural diversities and the multiplication of different styles of sustainable development (based on principles of environmental rationality).

Environmental justice movements are not simply demanding more equity – understood as a better and more just distribution of environmental costs or compensation for environmental damage – nor more participation in the prevalent economic and political system, with its global or national homogeneous rules to be complied with by conflicting groups in society. Instead, they struggle to construct a new social system, a new rationality and a new ethic to develop sustainable productive projects and to give meaning to their lives. They thereby depart from the concepts of conservationist ecologism and individual choice. These movements cannot be understood as deviant social behavior which simply rejects existing society, its economic system and its political order; or as cultural self-exclusion. They are guided by new reasons and desires to question the established order. These new movements defy the hegemony of actual economic and political forces, of legitimised decision-making and governing processes. They are struggles for democracy and production mobilised by new principles of rationality (Leff 1996b).

These social groups are re-valuing and modernising their traditional productive practices and gearing them towards sustainability. Thus, strong movements for agro-ecology are spreading out in rural areas of the South. They are establishing new identities, solidarities and alliances; opening up history to the construction of a new productive rationality through a cultural and political re-appropriation of nature. The strategies of this environmental democracy go beyond the need to solve conflictive interests over ecological distribution (of ecological costs and environmental impacts) through peaceful negotiations; they promote direct democracy, establishing common rights for community management of natural resources, subject to different ecological and cultural conditions. Thus democracy is re-signified in terms of social rules that define access, property and actual possession of environmental resources, integrating social equity and cultural diversity with ecological sustainability.

Environmental democracy integrates the values of social equity in the objectives of sustainable production and turns power relations into the politics of diversity, difference and otherness, as a means of solving socio-environmental conflicts. Today, many legitimate democratic regimes have been established in which conditions of poverty and environmental degradation keep growing.[5] Ideological and power domination have been imposed upon traditional forms of social cohesion and cultural identities, generating passive attitudes towards inequity; they function as a mechanism to control or dissolve social conflict and political unrest. However, these mechanisms of social control are being challenged by emergent ecological and democratic values which are legitimising the reconfiguration of ethnic identities and cultural diversity, as well as peoples' and communities' rights to autonomy and self-reliance. Thus, social equity, cultural diversity and environmental democracy define new political values and a new social rationality for sustainability.

Environmental democracy stands for the creative participation of communities in the construction of the new environmental rationality for sustainable production. It advocates the integration of theory and practice in agro-ecology and agro-forestry (Altieri 1987), as well as in the productive strategies of peasants and indigenous peoples founded in the ecological potential of each region and in the cultural values of every community.[6]

Thus, environmental rationality translates the values of ecologism into decentralised production, and the concept of the global market into pluri-ethnic nations (González and Roitman 1996), promoting the emergence of sustainable local and regional economies to solve the basic needs of each community. The construction of a national economy integrated by different productive environmental units is thus defined in terms of diverse ethno-eco-development styles (Sachs 1982). This strategy does not intend to restrict itself to self-sufficient micro-economies guided by parochial utopianism, or an ethic and aesthetic of nature, or nostalgia for an idyllic past. Democracy in production means re-appropriating life, nature and production. This new productive rationality entails a complex process of productive transformations, technological innovations, state reforms and juridical changes to establish a new political culture based on principles of equity, diversity and sustainability. Here, equity recognises the value of difference; equity is defined through a diversity of means and goals and of conceptions about the quality of life. It implies the need to solve conflictive interests over the appropriation of nature, but to do so respecting differentiated cultural codes and values.

The demands for democracy worldwide, together with the emergent rights of indigenous peoples and principles for sustainable development, gained legitimacy in 1992 with the coincidence of the Rio Earth Summit and 500 years of ecological imperialism following the European conquest of today's regions belonging to the South (Crosby 1986). This has led to a cross-fertilisation of the environmental and indigenous peoples' movements, which has encouraged the indigenous peoples to claim the ecological debt to their territories and cultures as well as their legitimate historical right to regain control and re-appropriate their control over natural resources.

Thus the indigenous peoples' demands have hybridised with those expressed in environmental and democratic discourses leading, in the last few years, to the eruption of numerous social movements guided by ecological demands (Moguel 1992). These struggles for the reconstruction of the productive process are intermingled with claims for land ownership, for revaluing traditional practices and cultural identities, for re-appropriating knowledge, science and technology and for integrating a new productive paradigm which articulates ecological, technological and cultural processes in sustainable eco-technological productivity, thereby strengthening the capacities of communities to manage their own social and productive life.

Such struggles, which have penetrated both the discourse and the practices of emergent social actors in rural areas of the South, have generated demands that go beyond established social rules and juridical laws. Their critical and innovating character is not yet contained by the codes of positive law and environmental legislation. As juridical rules always follow and reflect the established social order and its dominant interests, they, therefore, cannot currently accommodate the complex demands, desires and rights claimed by this new broad-ranging environmentalism clamouring to construct a new social order.

Through these struggles, indigenous peoples intend to legitimise their rights to appropriate and manage their cultural legacy and their patrimony of natural resources. They also intend to delink from and deconstruct the global homogenising economic model and juridical order which construe rights and demands of communities as mere adjustment to a conception of 'the common good', decided and established by centralised state and global market interests, which determine the conditions of production, the laws for resolving conflicts and the means to distribute natural wealth and income from the merchandising of nature.

In challenging the established economic and political systems, indigenous peoples are redefining their ethnical identities and establishing autonomous organisations and municipalities. New indigenous and peasant movements have emerged in Mexico; for example the Purépecha Nation, the National Movement of Autonomous Pluri-ethnic Regions, the *Consejo Guerrerense 500 Años* and (more recently) the National Indigenous Plural Assembly for

Autonomy and the Union for the Defense of Indigenous Peoples' Rights, Culture and Autonomy, together with numerous agrarian and communalist movements in Chiapas, Oaxaca and other regions in Mexico. These include organisations of producers whose expressed aim is to develop according to their own cultural identities, traditional uses, customs and practices. Their vision of autonomous sustainable development leads them, in practice, to link the principle of cultural diversity with an emerging conception of environmental rationality.

## – CONCLUSION –

Environmental indigenous movements are changing the juridical order for peaceful settlement of conflicts over uneven ecological distribution by posing a radical challenge to the dominant economic rationality. In their demands, they go beyond the legalised spaces previously gained by the struggle for human rights now sanctioned by law. Their claims for new rights are asserted in their struggles for resistance, their power strategies for the defence of their control over natural resources, thereby playing an essential role in mobilising profound social changes. The emergent environmental agents in rural areas of the South are attempting to lay the basis for a new social order and a new productive rationality.

## – NOTES –

1. This word is ambiguous. In this context, it is simply used to mean the decrease of raw material/energy as input in the production of goods and services (instead of x units of steel to produce a car, technological innovation permits $x - n$ units), rather than the total dispensation of material/energy in the processes of production. The latter amounts to thermodynamical nonsense.
2. Thus, 'potential NNP [Net Primary Production] comprises the ultimate constraint on human population growth . . . In future decades, the impoverishment of biotic systems may play an increasingly important role in determining the limits of food production' (Ehrlich and Ehrlich 1991, p. 202). Commoner might be the one exception. He views photosynthesis as a limit, but also as a potential for sustainable development:

    The 'limits to growth' approach is based on a serious misconception about the global ecosystem. It depends upon the idea that the Earth is like a spaceship, a closed system isolated from all outside sources of support and necessarily sustained only by its own limited resources. But the ecosphere . . . is totally dependent on the huge influx of energy from an outside source – the sun . . . Solar energy, captured by photosynthesis, sustains every form of life and drives the ecological cycles in which they participate . . . Hence, the ultimate limit of economic growth is imposed by the rate at which renewable, solar energy can be captured and used . . . We are at present nowhere near the limit that the availability of solar energy will eventually impose on production and economic growth . . . The issue we face, then, is not how to facilitate environmental quality by limiting economic development and population growth, but how to create a system of production that can grow and develop in harmony with the environment. (Commoner 1990, pp. 146–48)

3. For a scientific assessment of the potential of photosynthesis in primary productivity of natural ecosystems, see Leigh 1975; Lieth 1978; Rodin et al. 1975.

4. 'The South' in this context does not have geographical connotations. It stands for what used to be called 'The Third World.' But given today's politics, the latter appears to be an inappropriate term to use.

5. In democratic India, the caste system is, nevertheless, alive and well, imposing restraints on the utilisation of natural resources (Gadgil 1985). On the other hand, class differences break norms of ecological equilibrium by merchandising humans and nature under capitalism.

6. The objectives of self-sufficiency and ecological equilibrium are incorporated into peasants' ecological strategies through processes of 'community democracy which are expressed in two ways: 1) through the equal distribution of resources among community members in all domestic and family units, and 2) through collective and consensual decision-making in the ejido assemblies' (Toledo 1994).

## – BIBLIOGRAPHY –

Altieri, M. (1987), *Agroecology: The Scientific Basis for Alternative Agriculture*, Boulder: Westview Press.

Bookchin, M. (1989), *Remaking Society*, Boston: South End Press.

The Brundtland Report (World Commission on Environment and Development) (1987), *Our Common Future*, Oxford: Oxford University Press.

Commoner, B. (1990), *Making Peace with the Planet*, London: Gollancz.

Crosby, A. (1986), *Ecological Imperialism*, New York: Cambridge University Press.

Daly, H. E. (1991), *Steady-State Economics*, Washington, DC: Island Press.

Descola, P. (1996), *La Selva Culta: Simbolismo y Praxis en la Ecología de los Achuar*, Quito: Ediciones Abya-Yala.

Devall, B., and G. Sessions (1985), *Deep Ecology*, Salt Lake City: Gibbs Smith Publishers.

Díaz Polanco, H. (1991), *Autonomía Regional: La Autodeterminación de los Pueblos Indios*, Mexico: Siglo XXI-UNAM.

Ehrlich, P. (1968), *The Population Bomb*, New York: Ballantine Press.

Ehrlich, P., and A. Ehrlich (1991), *Healing the Planet: Strategies for Resolving the Environmental Crisis*, New York: Addison-Wesley Publishing Company.

Escobar, A. (1995), *Encountering Development: The Making and Unmaking of the Third World*, Princeton: Princeton University Press.

Escobar, A. (1997a), 'Cultural politics and biological diversity: state, capital and social movements in the Pacific Coast of Colombia', in O. Stern and R. Fox (eds), *Culture and Social Protest: Between Resistance and Revolution*, New Brunswick: Rutgers University Press.

Escobar, A. (October 1997b), 'The place of nature and the nature of place', given at *II Congreso Internacional de Etnobotánica*. Mérida, Mexico.

Gadgil, M. (1985), 'Social restraints on resource utilization: the Indian experience', in McNeely & Pitt (eds), *Culture and Conservation*, Great London: Croom Helm.

Gallopin, G. C. (1995), *El Futuro Ecologico de un Continente: Una Vision Prospectiva de America Latina*, Mexico City: Fondo de Cultura Economical/United Nations University.

Georgescu-Roegen, N. (1971), *The Entropy Law and the Economic Process*, Cambridge: Harvard University Press.

Gómez, M. (1997) coord., *Derecho Indígena*, Mexico City: INI-AMNU.

Gonçalvez, C. W. P. (November 1997), 'Movimento social como mediador entre a cultura e o direito: o caso do movimento dos Seringueiros da Amazônia Brasileira e sua proposta de reserva extrativista', *IV Foro del Ajusco*, UNEP/Colegio de México.

González C. P., and M. Roitman (1996) coords, *Democracia y Estado MultiJtnico en América Latina*, Mexico City: La Jornada Ediciones/CIICH-UNAM.

Grünberg, G. (1995) coord., *Articulación de la Diversidad: Pluralidad Etnica, Autonomías y Democratización en América Latina*, Quito: Ediciones Abya-Yala.

Guha, R., and J. Marténez Alier (1997), *Varieties of Environmentalism*, London: Earthscan.

Herrera, A. O. (1976), *Catastrophe or New Society: A Latin American Model*, Ottawa: IDRC.

Hinterberger, F., and E. Seifert (1997), 'Reducing material throughput: a contribution to the measurement of dematerialization and human sustainable development', in A. Tylecote and J. van der Straaten (eds), *Environment, Technology and Economic Growth: The Challenge to Sustainable Development*, Cheltenham, UK: Edward Edgar Publishing.

Leff, Enrique (1986), 'Ecotechnological productivity: a conceptual basis for the integrated management of natural resources', *Social Science Information* 25:3, pp. 681–702.

Leff, E. (1995), *Green Production: Towards an Environmental Rationality*, New York: Guilford Publications. (See also the Spanish revised and extended edition, *Ecología y Capital: Racionalidad Ambiental, Democracia Participativa y Desarrollo Sustentable*, Mexico City: Siglo XXI/UNAM.)

Leff, E. (1996a), 'From ecological economics to productive ecology: perspectives on sustainable development from the South', in R. Costanza (eds), *Getting Down to Earth: Practical Applications of Ecological Economics*, Washington DC: Island Press.

Leff, E. (1996b), 'Los nuevos actores sociales y los procesos políticos en el campo', in

H. Carton de Grammont & H. Tejera (eds), *La Sociedad Rural Frente al Nuevo Milenio*, vol 4, Mexico: UNAM/INAH/UAM/Plaza y Valdez Editores.

Leff, E. (1997), 'Ecotechnological productivity: the emergence of a concept and its implications for sustainable development', *Proceedings of the European Association for Bioeconomic Studies* (Second International Conference on *Implications and Applications of Bioeconomics*), Milano: Edizioni Nagard.

Leff, E. (1998a), *Saber Ambiental: Sustentabilidad, Racionalidad, Complejidad, Poder*, Mexico City: Siglo XXI Editores-UNAM-PNUMA.

Leff, E. (1998b), 'Murray Bookchin and the end of dialectical naturalism', *Capitalism, Nature, Socialism*, 9:4.

Leff, E., and J. Carabias (1993) eds, *Cultura y Manejo Sustentable de los Recursos Naturales*, Mexico City: CIICH-UNAM, Miguel Angel Porrúa.

Leigh, H. (1975), 'Primary productivity in ecosystems: comparative analysis of global patterns', in W. H. van Dobben and R. H. Lowe-McConnell (eds), *Unifying Concepts in Ecology*, The Hague: W. Jung B. V. Publishers (Centre for Agricultural Publishing and Documentation).

Lieth, H. F. H. (1978), *Patterns of Primary Production in the Biosphere*, Stroudsbourg, PA: Dowden, Hutchinson and Ross.

Marcuse, H. (1964), *The One-Dimensional Man: Studies in the Ideology of Advanced Industrialized Society*, Boston: Beacon Press.

Meadows, D. H. (1972), *The Limits to Growth*, New York: Universe Books.

Meadows, D. H. (1992), *Beyond the Limits*, Vermont: Chelsea Green Publishing Company.

Moguel, J. (1992), *Autonomía y Nuevos Sujetos Sociales en el Desarrollo Rural*, Mexico City: Siglo XXI Editores.

Naess, A., and D. Rothenberg (1989), *Ecology, Community and Lifestyle*, Cambridge: Cambridge University Press.

Redclift, M. (1992), *Sustainable Development: Exploring the Contradictions*, London and New York: Routledge.

Rees, W. (1992), 'Ecological footprints and appropriated carrying capacity: what urban economics leaves out', *Environment and Urbanization* 4:2, pp. 121-30.

Rodin, L. E., N. I. Bazilevich and N. N. Rozov (1975), 'Primary productivity of the world's main ecosystems', in W. H. van Dobben and R. H. Lowe-McConnell (eds), *Unifying Concepts in Ecology*, The Hague: W. Jung B. V. Publishers.

Sachs, I. (1982), *Ecodesarrollo: Desarrollo sin Destrucción*, Mexico: El Colegio de MJxico.

Toledo, V. M. (1994), 'La via ecolgico-campesina de desarrollo: una alternativa para la selva de Chiapas', *La Jornada del Campo*, Año 2, No. 23, 25 de enero.

Torres, R. (1997), *Entre lo Propio y lo Ajeno. Derechos de los Pueblos Indígenas y Propiedad Intelectual*, Quito: COICA.

Vitousek, P., Paul R. Ehrlich, Anne H. Ehrlich, and Pamela A. Matson (1986), 'Human appropriation of the products of photosynthesis', *Bioscience* 36:6, pp. 368-73.

COMMENTARY ON CHAPTER 5

# Sustainable development: can we all be winners?

In the eyes of Jan Boersema and Joeri Bertels, sustainable development stands for a relationship between human society and the natural world that can be sustained and at the same time provides for human development. It is (or appears to be) 'a concept that recognises only winners.' They point out that merely to diagnose current patterns of economic activity as unsustainable provides no guidance at all as to what kinds of activity are sustainable. We lack indicators, both of the limits within which the required relationship can be sustained, and of human development.

In formulating such indicators, consistent spatial and temporal parameters are crucial, they argue. Even within the category of 'developed economy', their analysis shows how differently the sustainable development agenda plays out in the different social and institutional contexts of Italy, The Netherlands and the US respectively. In Italy, progress towards sustainable development is fitful: driven by external treaty obligations and internal environmental crises, it is hampered by a variety of institutional obstacles such as complex legal machinery and lack of monitoring arrangements. Being a more densely populated country, The Netherlands is some way ahead of most countries in implementing policies aimed at environmental protection; indicators and monitoring procedures are in place at least for levels of pollution and waste disposal; and there is already some experience of economic instruments such as the 'polluter pays' principle and cradle-to-grave responsibilites on the part of maufacturers; the trend has been towards greater integration. In the US, the President's Commission on Sustainable Development interprets the concept in very broad terms, as indicated by the title of its first report, which speaks of 'Prosperity, Opportunity and a Healthy Environment.'

Boersema and Bertels are particularly exercised by the problem of how progress towards sustainable development is to be measured. They point out that apparent improvements may be illusory: gains in the efficient use of resources may be offset by increases in their use, and unsustainable practices may merely be transferred elsewhere. One aspect of the difficulty is how to build an overall integrated perspective that embraces social, economic and environmental factors. In this connection they point to the Human Development Index as holding out some promise, since it relates levels of well-being to environmental conditions. Their own constructive suggestion is that indicators relating specifically to environmental conditions might most usefully be focused on the more efficient use of energy and space, and the maintenance of biodiversity.

The analysis offered here seems to corroborate that of other contributors in identifying as generic concerns: (i) how to uncouple economic growth from environmental impact, and (ii) how to ensure that the voices of the weak are heard – specifically the poor, future generations, and non-humans. On both fronts one is left to wonder how far the developed economies really mean business.

~ O ~

# 5 Sustainable Development in the Developed Countries: Will Theory and Practice Meet?

## Jan J. Boersema and Joeri Bertels

### – Introduction –

It is generally accepted that the concept of sustainable development (SD) was internationally coined and achieved the status of a shibboleth following the 1987 publication of the UN-sponsored Brundtland Report. This is notwithstanding the fact that the term 'sustainability' has a long tradition and was widely used by environmentalists in the eighties, while even the term 'sustainable development' can already be found before 1987.[1] From the very beginning it was quite clear that in using the concept of SD, one is faced with an inherent tension. Combining these two words 'sustainable' and 'development' implies having aspirations to achieve a balanced relationship between human society and the natural environment, one that can be sustained, and at the same time implies striving for a certain kind of development. According to the Brundtland Report, development is to be taken as economic growth and there is as yet no evidence that such growth can be realised without leading to additional environmental pressure. A concept giving expression to these human endeavours and at the same time suggesting that these two apparently contradictory aims might be compatible is obviously highly attractive and explains, by and large, the enormous popularity of the Brundtland Report and the willingness with which it was taken on board by a great many governments. Who could be opposed to a concept that recognises only winners? All over the world, and particularly in certain developed countries, formal adoption of SD has led to a great deal of scientific and political effort to analyse the idea and to put the concept into practice.

This chapter deals mainly with the concept of SD in the developed world over the past decade. The content of the concept will be discussed, the practical progress made as well as the difficulties encountered in the implementation of the concept will be examined and, finally, the prospects it holds out will be explored. For the purpose of this chapter, the term 'developed countries' is taken to be synonymous with the countries of the Organisation for Economic Cooperation and Development (OECD).[2] The developed world being far too large to describe as an entity, (data from) three OECD countries will be singled out to illustrate the line of reasoning pursued and to underpin the points made.

## – SUSTAINABILITY AND DEVELOPMENT –

Acceptance of sustainable development as an overall guiding framework led to an explosion of studies and publications in which the concept was critically analysed and fleshed out in increasing detail. Once the aforementioned tension between sustainability and development is taken seriously, the key question becomes how prosperity can be increased while at the same time reducing environmental pressure. Three essential clusters of related questions have emerged.

In characterising our interaction with the environment, the first question is: what exactly does 'sustainable' or 'sustainability' involve? Merely establishing that our present environmental conduct is 'unsustainable' does nothing to elucidate the positive essence of the concept. Where do they lie, those limits we have apparently exceeded? Can they be unambiguously defined? If not, to what extent are they value-based, and to what extent do they imply subjective choices? How much hard scientific evidence do we have at our disposal, and when must we be content to base ourselves on estimates or on opinions about acceptable risks? Who sets the limits, and on what grounds? Closely linked to this is the question of whether or not we have devised overall good indicators that enable us to measure accurately the very diverse impacts on the environment. Many useful indicators have been developed over the years, but nearly all of them are confined to specific domains.[3] There is an urgent need to develop reliable methods for integration and a general desire for integrated indicators. Today, appropriate indicators to measure overall environmental pressure are still lacking.[4] Emissions from energy use seem a good candidate for such an overall indicator, but we will come back to that later.

A second cluster of questions revolves round the notions of development, economic growth, prosperity and welfare. This implies a need to measure and develop indicators for the latter two terms. Welfare is a broader concept than prosperity, which in turn encompasses more than economic growth. While there has long been a standard international yardstick for economic growth – Gross Domestic Product or GDP – such generally accepted indicators have always been lacking for prosperity and welfare. Consequently, there has been too much emphasis on GDP as the sole measure of a country's development. Environmental economists have long agreed on the shortcomings of GDP and there is broad consensus that GDP should be 'greened' by incorporating external effects. However, it is unclear to what extent this aim can be duly achieved and how far this process will bring us towards sustainability. Within the economic domain, one of the most promising as well as far-reaching proposals is the Index of Sustainable Economic Welfare (Daly and Cobb Jr. 1994; Daly 1996). Critics of such efforts take the stand that we should employ several indicators instead of attempting to integrate them. To arrive at common ground there is still much work to be done.

The last cluster of questions has to do with the temporal and spatial scale at which sustainability is to be achieved and analysed. Time is a crucial parameter to take into account – environmentalists and investors use different time horizons. Consistency in scale is also very important because of the danger of roll-off (shifting negative effects outside the system under consideration). In the long term, it is not really sustainable to achieve sustainability at the expense of others elsewhere, future generations or non-human organisms. Consequently, there is a growing tendency to link environmental sustainability to social sustainability.[5] As system boundaries are hard to define, let alone to draw, this is a serious difficulty to overcome.

In everyday policy-making, we are faced with a considerable gap between the more integrated and theoretical manner in which sustainability is analysed and the more pragmatic and fragmented manner in which politicians in fact do, and perhas must, put the concept into practice. In the next section we shall illustrate this point, providing a concise overview of the efforts made in three quite different OECD countries.[6]

# – Three cases: Italy,
## The Netherlands and United States of America –

### – Italy –

Policy framework
Although environmental protection and conservation measures have a long history in Italy, it was not until 1986 that concrete federal environmental policy goals were introduced in this country. Italy's environmental efforts have been driven mainly by external influences, such as requirements resulting from international treaties, directives of the EU or agreements made within the UN. In addition, Italian policy has developed partly in response to domestic environmental crises, such as the notorious Seveso accident in 1976 (exposing people and animals to high doses of dioxins) and the pollution of the Adriatic Sea.

The official Italian policy regarding sustainable development is laid down in the National Plan for Sustainable Development, which was approved in 1993. Practical implementation of this plan is coordinated by the Committee for the Implementation of Agenda 21, but few measures have actually been taken to date. In 1994 a new body was created in response to the outcome of a national referendum. This National Environmental Protection Agency (ANPA) was intended to fill organisational gaps and fulfil missions that were not yet being tackled. The ANPA took over jurisdiction on environmental health issues from local institutions. Several other responsibilities were transferred from local to regional environmental councils. Whether the ANPA will be a genuine success is presently unclear.

Indicators
There is little evidence that the Italian government is using indicators for sustainable development. In the Italian response to the RIO+5 inquiry of the UN Commission on Sustainable Development in 1997, answers to most of the questions are lacking (UNCSD 1997a).

Measures taken
Voluntary agreements with industry were introduced in Italy as early as the 1970s. In recent years government and industry signed contract programmes designed to align industrial environmental initiatives with government priorities. Control and monitoring of the agreements are poor, however.

Despite the weakness in environmental policy implementation, the

Italian government has adopted an active approach to the prosecution of violations of environmental regulations. However, prosecution is less effective than it might be, owing to the complexity and incompatibility of laws and regulations (OECD 1994).

In conclusion, it can be said that in Italy sustainable development is still an abstract principle that is being inadequately applied in policy development and implementation at the national and regional levels, as is indeed recognised by the Italian government (UNCSD 1997). The tempo at which centrally planned measures are actually put into practice is fairly slow. At times, the bureaucratic apparatus proves to be misinformed, and communication and coordination between and within administrative bodies is poor.

## – The Netherlands –

Policy framework
The Netherlands is a highly urbanised and intensively cultivated country. Its culture has been shaped by well-integrated planning and public participation. Because of its high population density, intensive use of land for agriculture and horticulture, a large bulk-goods industry and heavy traffic, the country imposes a heavy burden on the environment compared to other developed countries. Consequently, The Netherlands introduced specific policies on the environment at a relatively early date. The country was already applying environmental policy planning procedures involving both governmental and non-governmental actors even before the Brundtland Report. Perhaps for this reason, the Netherlands does not have a formal national council for sustainable development. Nevertheless, current Dutch environmental policy is strongly influenced by the Brundtland Report.

As in most other countries, Dutch environmental policy was initially aimed mainly at local or regional disturbances having an impact on human health. At the national level it was part of the competence of the Ministry of Public Health. Until the late seventies, policy was enacted separately for waste, water, soil and air. In the early eighties it became clear that these medium-term-based policies had to be integrated if environmental problems were to be more effectively tackled. In 1982 national environmental policy was delegated to the Ministry of Housing, Spatial Planning and the Environment (VROM).[7] The medium-based approach came to be complemented by a strategy focusing on substances, target groups, regions of special concern and the so-called 'environmental themes.'

In 1989, The Netherlands' first National Environmental Policy Plan (NEPP) was published, prepared with the active involvement of national, provincial and local governments as well as target groups, and jointly signed by four ministers. The plan set out a comprehensive strategy for sustainable development which explores the economics and social concerns of maintaining a healthy environment. Current environmental policy is still based on this plan and the subsequent government documents NEPP+ (1990), NEPP2 (1993), and NEPP3 (1997).

The principal goal of current Dutch environmental policy is to secure sustainable development, both within The Netherlands and throughout the world. The Dutch definition of SD is essentially the same as that put forward in the Brundtland Report: 'satisfying the needs of the present generation without compromising the ability of future generations to meet their own needs' (NEPP 1989). However, the Dutch have elaborated on this definition by stating that environmental problems are not to be transferred to the next generation and must therefore be solved within one generation, taken to be 25 years. At the practical level, however, the plan focuses primarily on a substantial reduction of emissions.

Increasingly, the environment has become a touchstone for assessing the general record of the various target groups (industry, refineries, the energy sector, the retail trade, transport and traffic, and consumers).

Indicators
Sustainability is measured mainly in terms of levels of pollution (in a broad sense) and waste production. The government has set targets such as reduction percentages, ordered by theme: climate change, acidification, eutrophication, dispersion of toxic waste and hazardous substances, waste disposal, disturbance, groundwater depletion and squandering of resources. Indicators are monitored by a national agency, RIVM (the Dutch Institute of Public Health and the Environment).

In practice, then, the Dutch conception of sustainable development focuses primarily on environmental protection. However, there is certainly a tendency to broaden the scope. A white paper on environment and economy (1996) adopts the idea of 'delinkage' (striving at the same time for lasting economic growth and diminishing environmental pressure). A full integration with socio-cultural development has not taken place. Public debate on this issue is beginning to emerge.

Measures taken
The Dutch government has developed and successfully used a variety of policy instruments, including financial incentives, regulations and negotiated agreements (covenants). The last type of instrument may be con-

sidered typical of Dutch culture, aiming at consensus, and has attracted international attention.

Considerable reduction percentages have been achieved for emissions of many substances, although for some, targets are still beyond reach. Emissions of $CO_2$, in particular, have continued to rise. With the aid of economic instruments such as levies and incorporation of the polluter-pays principle, water pollution has been successfully reduced. Implementation of the concept of 'cradle-to-grave' producer responsibilities has provided a major incentive for recycling initiatives. The impact of the recently introduced energy tax has yet to be evaluated.

In response to mandatory measures and in attempting to evade them, many voluntary programmes have been adopted by the private sector (that is, actors are allowed to meet requirements in a manner best suited to their individual constraints and capacities). Generally speaking, these have yielded good results.

– The United States –

Policy framework

The United States has a long history of conservation and resource management: conservation efforts date back to 1872, when Yellowstone Park was established. Nevertheless, the United States federal government has never adopted an overall, comprehensive environmental strategy. The US responded at a relatively early stage to the growing pressures on the environment, but on an issue-by-issue basis rather than within a comprehensive framework.

In the 1980s a number of books, reports and studies were published by both non-profit environmental and conservation organisations and federal agencies stressing the importance of SD and the necessity of changes in the structure of the federal government. Nevertheless, it was not until after the UN Conference on Environment and Development (UNCED) that any policy reforms were implemented. In 1993 President Clinton established the President's Council on Sustainable Development (PCSD) whose objective is to forge a consensus among the various stakeholders (government, business and industry, private citizens, non-profit organisations, labour, and so on) and create a viable sustainable development strategy which articulates the interests and concerns of all groups. In 1996 the PCSD produced its first report, *Sustainable America*. The report includes an adoption of the Brundtland definition of SD, ten policy goals as well as several indicators of SD, and recommendations for necessary changes at all levels of government, in business and community institutions, and at the individual level. It was adopted unanimously by all parties participating in the commission. The PCSD is presently in the process of endeavouring to have its recommendations implemented, at both federal and state levels.

Indicators

The PCSD has given the concept of SD a broad meaning. In addition to environmental aspects, social development and civic engagement are emphasised. The PCSD formulates policy goals relating to ten areas: Health and the Environment, Economic Prosperity, Equity, Conservation of Nature, Stewardship, Sustainable Communities, Civic Engagement, Population, International Responsibility and Education. For each policy goal, several 'indicators of progress' are proposed and policy actions recommended. However, the goals and indicators are all described in qualitative terms only. No quantitative targets or time frames are set or proposed.

Measures taken

During the 1970s and 1980s federal rules, specific to various issues and implemented at the state level, were very effective in reducing emission of traditional air pollutants. There was strict law enforcement and a high degree of compliance. In some cases the USA (as a whole or as individual states) has set world standards (such as the regulations for vehicle emissions set by the state of California).

However, there is continuing pressure on the country's environment, in particular regarding urban air quality, river and lake water quality, the number of endangered species and the declining area of wetlands. Resource-intensive lifestyles, low-density housing, extensive use of automobiles and high waste production are the main causes of this pressure.

## – MEASURING PROGRESS –

Has progress been made in the realm of environmental performance over the last few decades and, if so, can this progress be attributed to policies aimed at sustainability? Are developments sustainable?

Overall, OECD countries have made significant progress on the abatement of environmental pressures. National and international policy agreements have led to considerable reductions in the emissions of toxic or hazardous substances, achieved by means of end-of-the-pipe measures, efficiency improvements and cleaner technologies. Some of the original objectives of environmental policy in these countries, linked primarily with human health, are no longer relevant in the environmental context. For example, almost the entire population of the developed countries has access to a clean supply of domestic drinking water and to wastewater treatment facilities. Just one example of successful reduction is the production of ozone-depleting chlorofluorocarbons (CFCs). As a result of the 1985 Vienna Convention on Protection of the Ozone Layer and subsequent agreements, CFCs have gradually been replaced by other, less harmful substances, at least for most purposes.[8] Global production of CFCs, which presently account for roughly two-thirds of the total ozone-depleting potential (ODP), was reduced by about 77% between 1986 and 1995. Aggregate OECD production of CFCs declined by 90% over this period, with production in Italy, The Netherlands and the US being reduced by 83%, 71% and 89% respectively.[9]

Many other examples of emission reductions could be mentioned here. The last few decades have seen substantial improvements in resource consumption per unit of production or service, the so-called eco-efficiency. Given these improvements, the overall impression is one of a society moving in the right – sustainable – direction. However, there are two unpleasant facts that must not be overlooked. In the first place, although products may be becoming 'cleaner', we see an ever-growing number of those products. And secondly, it is unclear to what extent reductions have been achieved at the expense of an (un-perceived) roll-off onto other environmental media or resources, to other (less developed) countries, or into the future.

This brings us back to the pivotal question: how is progress towards sustainability to be measured? Since the publication of the Brundtland Report there have been many attempts to develop indicators for sustainable development, by individual OECD countries as well as by the World Bank, the UN Commission on Sustainable Development (UNCSD) and a number of NGOs. As yet, there is no international consensus on suitable indicators, but the OECD is striving for publication of a common set of sustainable development indicators by the end of 1999 (OECD 1998a).

As explained above, the concept of SD links economic, environmental and social aspects. An important question is how far these essential dimensions can be integrated. It seems logical to develop indicators for each dimension, with further integration being envisaged in a subsequent phase. Indicators should be drawn up from (or representing) more detailed and specific indicators at a lower level. Each indicator should allow for inter-country as well as temporal comparison.

In fact, for all three dimensions of SD, such efforts have been or are being undertaken. As to the environmental dimension, the most authoritative current set of environmental indicators is the OECD core set (relating, *inter alia*, to climate change, air and water quality, waste production and biodiversity).[10]

As to the social dimension of SD, major progress has been made in recent years on developing indicators. One example is the recently introduced concept of the Human Development Index (HDI). The HDI measures the average achievements in a given country for three dimensions of human development: longevity (life expectancy), knowledge (educational attainment) and living standard (real GDP per capita, in Purchasing Power Parities or PPPs).[11] However, it does not yet encompass disparities and gaps among regions, or between urban and rural areas, ethnic groups or the sexes.

As to the economic dimension, indicators such as GDP, currency inflation, national debt and so on have been in use worldwide for decades. Here, the problem is how to integrate these economic indicators with those of the other dimensions of SD. The discussion about greening GDP and the Index of Sustainable Economic Welfare have been mentioned already. Work on indicators highlighting the economy/environment interface is already well-advanced; eco-efficiency, resource productivity and societal costs of environmental damage are relevant concepts in this respect.

It may prove more difficult to integrate the social dimension of sustainable development with the economic and environmental dimensions. The health effects of environmental pollution and economic circumstances are among the aspects to be included in an integrating indicator or index. Although the HDI includes some economic aspects, it does not yet consider such criteria as political freedom, guaranteed human rights and self-respect: nor is it linked with environmental pressure.[12] An interesting new measure that does link environmental pressure with health (but not with other aspects of the social dimension of SD) is Disability-Adjusted Life Expectancy (DALE), a measure of years lived adjusted for each year lived in incomplete health due to environmental pressures and other health-related factors (assessing complete health as 100 per cent).[13]

We shall now focus solely on the environmental dimension of sustainability. Many ways to measure environmental pressure and status have been developed over the past few decades. In view of a comprehensive assessment of progress on SD, the aforementioned OECD Core Set of environmental indicators (OECD 1993) must be considered a first step. In order to assess progress towards a sustainable environment, indicators must be compared or linked. What is needed in the end is (preferably) one integrated indicator, reflecting developments in all relevant environmental aspects.

Such an 'overall' environmental indicator is still to be developed. But let us give a suggestion for a next step. SD may be covered by three essential indicators, relating to energy, biodiversity and space. These three resources are crucial in ensuring the supply of the world's other reserves and resources. The idea behind this aggregation is that, in principle, sufficient levels of these three resources would be adequate to supply and recycle all other resources and deal with pollution and other environmental problems. In addition to its intrinsic value, biodiversity offers many goods and services necessary for our survival. In order to reach sustainability, substances and materials which biodiversity cannot supply must and can be recycled – with adequate technology and probably a lot of (sustainable) energy. But both for the production of sustainable energy and for a sustainable biodiversity, space is a prerequisite (de Boer 1995). In this sense, one could argue that of the three, space seems to be the most fundamental; however, this is not to deny that there are other 'final' resources, apart from space, such as time and technology.

– Energy –

Performance vis-à-vis energy use can best be expressed in terms of $CO_2$ emission levels. All over the world, $CO_2$ emissions are highly correlated with overall resource use. If these emissions were successfully reduced while maintaining growing GDP, this would be a strong indication that society was heading towards sustainability. Given current technological potential, such delinking of economic growth and $CO_2$ emissions is inconceivable without a drastic reform of the economy, including a switch to sustainable sources of energy.

Now let us take a brief look at these indicators in the three countries examined. Throughout the OECD, emissions of $CO_2$ and other greenhouse gases continue to rise. Since 1980, however, $CO_2$ emissions due to energy use have grown more slowly in the OECD area than worldwide; this is due to a combination of changes in economic structure and energy supply mix, energy savings and, in a few countries, depressed economic activity. OECD countries currently account for 53 per cent of global $CO_2$ emissions, compared with 59 per cent in 1980.[14]

Figure 5.1 shows an almost continuous growth of GDP for Italy, The Netherlands and the US, with minor recessions or reduced growth around 1982 and in the early 90s. $CO_2$ emission still seems to be firmly coupled to economic growth (although it is not a 1:1 relationship) – but with only temporarily reduced emission figures corresponding to decreases in GDP.

– Biodiversity –

Measuring biological diversity (or biodiversity) is a difficult task. Following the Convention on Biological Diversity launched in 1992 at the UNCED conference held in Rio de Janeiro, distinctions between ecosystem diversity,

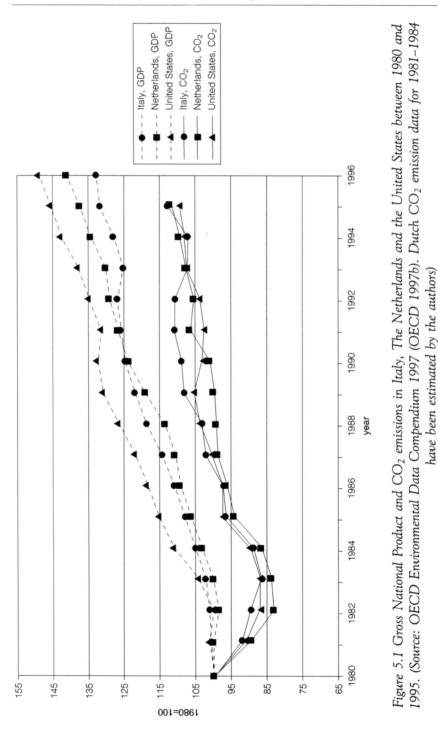

Figure 5.1 Gross National Product and $CO_2$ emissions in Italy, The Netherlands and the United States between 1980 and 1995. (Source: OECD Environmental Data Compendium 1997 (OECD 1997b). Dutch $CO_2$ emission data for 1981–1984 have been estimated by the authors)

species diversity and genetic diversity are made. Measuring genetic diversity on a large scale is unfeasible, however. One yardstick for comparing species diversity would be the number of threatened or declining species within a country or region. However, use of even such a relatively simple parameter is awkward, since in many countries knowledge of the present status of many species is rather limited and knowledge of the past status even more so.

The current status of species varies significantly among individual OECD countries: from 8 to 70 per cent of mammal species are threatened, and from 4 to 100 per cent of amphibian species. For many groups and species, little is known about their status in the past. It is therefore impossible to present reliable trends. Without points of reference, data about the present situation cannot properly be evaluated. The same holds for knowledge about the number of endemic species amongst those which are threatened. One should also bear in mind that the presence of species is not only related to environmental conditions, but also to biogeographical factors, such as the surface area. For this reason, the number of species is much higher in the USA than in The Netherlands or Italy.

Despite the limited availability of data, OECD figures (OECD 1997b) make clear that biodiversity is under severe pressure in the three countries, especially in the densely populated Netherlands, where not only amphibians and reptiles are seriously threatened, but also fish and more than one-third of the vascular plant species.

An additional parameter that might be used as an indicator of species (and ecosystem) diversity is (the trend in) the relative size of national parks and other protected areas, since an adequate habitat area is a prerequisite for sustainable biological diversity. Then again, our knowledge of the spatial 'requirements' of a species is rather limited and there are many other relevant factors when it comes to sustaining biodiversity. For a comprehensive assessment, these indicators should be supplemented by additional information about the sustainable use of biodiversity as a resource.

– Space –

A suitable key indicator for the use of space is also lacking. As physical space is finite, expansion of the area used for one function (housing, for example) will be at the expense of the area in use for other functions, such as agriculture. Spatial conflicts are increasing in The Netherlands (housing versus infrastructure and nature), but also in other densely populated regions such as South-East Asia (agriculture versus nature).

For a few activities, reclaiming land from the sea may be an option, although this may also have adverse effects on nature. To a certain extent, non-conflicting forms of land use may be combined or 'integrated.' For example, car parking, goods storage and several forms of transport can often be put in the underground parts of buildings. But for many other activities, such multifunctional land use is not feasible.

Alternatively, the 'spatial efficiency' (the functional 'output' per unit of space) of some functions might be increased (Nijpels and Boersema 1998). We ought to strive for better functional performance on the same or a smaller surface area – without roll-off to other functions or areas. This requires new quantitative measures.

## – DISCUSSION –

In most developed countries there has been substantial progress in the abatement of many environmental pressures since 1980. Through a combination of funds, technology and management, the developed countries have managed to 'solve' a number of environmental problems, or at least keep them within acceptable bounds. In many cases, however, improvements in environmental efficiency are being offset by population growth, and decreased emissions or resource use per unit product are being offset by increased per capita consumption. Examples include the steady growth of use and ownership of motor vehicles, waste production and water supply.

A useful framework for the identification and description of the main causes of environmental impact is the Ehrlich-Holdren equation, $I = PAT$ (I being the total impact on the environment; P the total population; A the affluence, that is the total amount of products and services consumed per person; and T technology, measured by the total environmental impact per product or unit of service).

Looking at the three developed countries examined more closely in this chapter, it can be concluded that sustainable development policy has not yet become widely established. For example, although many environmental laws have been enacted in Italy in recent years, this country does not yet have any guiding principles to provide a coherent framework for sustainable development policy. It is merely following international rules and agreements, and implementation of environmental laws is still weak. Still, overall Italian performance with regard to SD does not appear to be any worse than that of many other OECD countries (OECD 1998). On the other hand, one should take into account that initially, the per capita pressure on the environment was relatively low in Italy. One possible explanation may lie in the great differences existing within the country (its south being poor and using relatively less energy and resources compared with its wealthier north). Italy's overall performance has shown much less progress than that of the USA or The Netherlands. This is also reflected in the HDI, where Italy ranks well below the other two.

The Dutch developed specific environmental policies at a relatively early date. Through well-designed and integrated environmental policies and the use of quantitative measures, they have been fairly successful in reducing a number of pressures. On the other hand, the social dimension of sustainable development has not been a focus of debate in The Netherlands.

The enormous per capita resource use of the USA, resulting from high living standards, combined with the country's size and complex federal structure, appears to be a complicating factor in reducing environmental impact and achieving sustainable levels of production and consumption. The USA have now developed a comprehensive plan suggesting several useful indicators for assessing progress towards a sustainable situation and prescribing many necessary actions; concrete targets that may serve as yardsticks are lacking, however.

In many cases, declining pollution trends started before 1980, in other words, well before the concept of SD became fashionable. No clear breaks can be distinguished in trends after 1987; there is, therefore, no proof that the concept has substantially altered existing trends. Minor changes in growth or decreases in a particular indicator (such as $CO_2$ emissions) appear to be the result of standing policies and economic developments rather than SD policy measures. However, it may also be too early to draw such a conclusion, for in many countries, such as the USA, SD policy plans are just starting to be implemented, while in others, such as Italy, implementation may improve.

It is certainly clear that the concept of SD has stimulated the international acceptance of broad environmental policy goals. It has broadened the debate on environmental issues and probably speeded up the process of further reducing environmental pressures.

Generally speaking, three main phases in the development of environmental policies can be distinguished:

1. The acknowledgement of adverse effects of human activities on human well-being, crops, wildlife and cultural heritage. In this phase, policies are aimed largely at emission reduction, mainly through end-of-the-pipe measures such as dilution and filtering. Typically, in this phase, laws on clean air and surface water are introduced and large point sources dealt with. 'Green' policies are mainly aimed at conservation.

2. The phase of integrated policy regarding the physical environment ('grey' policy: efficiency improvements, environmentally friendly production or 'clean' technology, restrictions and bans on the use of environmentally harmful substances and materials, and source-oriented measures). Green policies are characterised by nature-development programmes.

3. The sustainability phase. Sustainability is explicitly perceived as dealing with socio-economic developments, equity and the quality of life. This phase is characterised by economic reform, a re-orientation towards the physical environment, and 'dematerialisation.' In this phase, grey and green policy become truly integrated, with environmental aspects also being integrated in all other relevant policy domains.

In this schema, Italy could be positioned early in the second phase, while the USA and The Netherlands are somewhat further ahead, although still in the same phase. Considering its lower per capita pressures, and its decreasing population, Italy could potentially swiftly enter the third phase, if institutional and political barriers could be overcome. The USA, on the other hand, with its high per capita pressures and continuing population growth, will probably stay in the second phase for a much longer time. The Netherlands is in the front when it comes to implementation of the sustainability concept, although the social dimension is still lacking. It is in a position, relatively quickly, to enter the final phase as Dutch society is well-organised with a population set to start decreasing within two decades, its per capita pressures in many cases being not much higher than those in Italy. However, making progress in the third phase might be far more difficult than in the previous two.

– CONCLUSION –

The concept of SD has been widely accepted by developing countries and developed countries alike. Although there are many different interpretations, there is broad agreement that SD comprises economic, environmental and social development. Although the process of implementation of the concept in national policy is still going on, there has also been growing international attention and funding for SD. This is an important first step.

The three developed countries examined here have also drawn up policy plans outlining the route toward sustainability. However, delinking environmental and economic performance and integrating social development aspects into sustainability policies is proving to be a difficult task. In addition, implementation of SD policy plans turns out to be a slow process, due to institutional barriers or lack of political will, as is most clearly illustrated by the case of Italy. Typically, SD policy develops in phases, starting with human-health-related environmental policy and conservation, through integrated policy towards the final phase of sustainability. In the first phase, there have been major gains in environmental quality in the developed countries. But these gains do not involve all aspects, and have also partly been realised at the expense of a roll-off to other environmental or non-environmental areas. These countries are now in the second phase, that of integrated policies. So far, political adoption of the sustainability concept has not led to a clear improvement in environmental performance over existing trends. Sustainability is still a phase that lies far ahead in the future.

Further steps are necessary to achieve true delinkage of economic growth and environmental pressures. A prerequisite is that we can measure progress. As yet, we do not have adequate indicators for SD. As a first step, key indicators for the three dimensions of SD need to be determined. For the environmental dimension, it seems logical to focus on the key resources, namely, energy, biodiversity and space. A next step is to further integrate these indicators so as to reflect interactions between economic development, social development and environmental pressure.

Active government involvement is required to set goals and targets, while leaving target groups freedom of action within sustainable limits. A strong government is also needed to speak out for the weaker groups: those who live in the less developed economies of the world, future (human) generations, and non-human organisms and populations (in particular the unknown, unfamiliar and less attractive species). Strict measures are needed to protect, conserve and use ecosystems, species and genetic diversity in a sustainable manner.

Furthermore, we must enhance the quality of life while decreasing the throughput of materials. In order to tackle the increasing competition for space in several regions, a spatial quality enhancement is also needed.

All factors influencing the environmental impact must be considered coherently. The first is stabilisation of population, which in most developed countries will be realised within a few decades. As already observed, we must adopt a different view to welfare and prosperity: less material-based and delinked from environmental pressure. This will mean a phase-out of fossil fuels with their prices reflecting environmental costs, and environmentally appropriate technological innovations.

## – Notes –

1. See IUCN 1980; Clark and Munn 1986.
2. According to the World Resources Institute, the World Bank and the UN, developed 'regions' include North America, Japan, Europe (including the European successor states of the former Soviet Union), Australia and New Zealand. A large group of countries within these regions have joined the OECD. The OECD presently has twenty-nine member states.

3. See Adriaanse 1993; OECD 1998b.
4. For recent suggestions on this point, see Wackernagel and Rees 1995; Von Weizsäcker et al. 1997. For a discussion of the pros and cons, see Daly and Cobb Jr. 1994; Kuik and Verbruggen 1991; Pearce et al. 1993; Weterings 1996.
5. See Smith et al. 1994.
6. These have been selected rather arbitrarily, using criteria such as size, environmental pressure, population density and type of democracy.
7. Policy regarding nature management is the domain of the Ministry of Agriculture, Nature Management and Fisheries.
8. After the 1985 Vienna Convention, agreements to reduce and eventually eliminate the emissions of human-made ozone-depleting substances were laid down in the *Montreal Protocol on Substances that Deplete the Ozone Layer* (1987), the *London Amendment to the Montreal Protocol* (1990), the *Copenhagen Amendment to the Montreal Protocol* (1992) and the *Montreal Amendment to the Montreal Protocol* (1997).
9. The Dutch figure appears to be in non-compliance with the 75 per cent cut (compared to 1986) agreed in the Montreal Protocol for 1994. However, an increase of production of up to 10 per cent of baseline levels (15 per cent after total phase-out) is permitted under the Protocol for purposes of satisfying the basic domestic needs of developing countries. This is the explanation of Dutch non-compliance in 1995, as indicated by the Ozone Secretariat. (See Oberthür 1997.)
10. OECD 1993; see also OECD 1998b.
11. PPPs are the rates of currency conversion which eliminate the differences in price levels between countries, so as to enable international comparisons between real GDP and real GDP per capita.
12. See UNDP 1998.
13. Barendregt et al. 1995; see also Murray and Lopez 1996.
14. The present per capita $CO_2$ emission is slightly below the 1980 levels for the OECD and for the world as a whole. The same holds for the USA, although the emission level is still more than twice the OECD mean. Per capita trends are slightly upwards in The Netherlands and Italy (OECD 1997b).

## – BIBLIOGRAPHY –

Adriaanse, A. (1993), *Environmental Policy Performance Indicators: A Study on the Development of Indicators for Environmental Policy in The Netherlands*, The Hague: SDU.

Barendregt, J. J., L. Bonneux and P. J. van der Maas (1995), 'Health expectancy: from population health indicator to a tool for policy making.' Paper presented at REVES 8, 5–7 October 1995.

Boer, Margaretha de (1995), *The Environment, Space and Living Quality: Time for Sustainability*, The Hague: Ministry of Housing, Spatial Planning and the Environment.

The Brundtland Report (World Commission on Environment and Development) (1987), *Our Common Future*, Oxford: Oxford University Press.

Clark, W. C., and R. E. Munn (1986) eds, *Sustainable Development of the Biosphere*, Cambridge: Cambridge University Press.

Daly, H. E. (1996), *Beyond Growth*, Boston: Beacon Press.

Daly, H. E., and J. B. Cobb Jr. (1994), *For the Common Good: Redirecting the Economy Toward Community, the Environment and a Sustainable Future* (2nd ed.), Boston: Beacon Press.

IUCN (1980), *World Conservation Strategy: Living Resource Conservation for Sustainable Development*, Gland, Switzerland: International Union for the Conservation of Nature.

Kuik, O., and H. Verbruggen (1991) eds, *In Search of Indicators of Sustainable Development*, Dordrecht, Boston and London: Kluwer Academic Publishers.

Murray, C. J. L. and A. D. Lopez (1996) eds, *The Global Burden of Disease: A Comprehensive Assessment of Mortality and Disability from Diseases, Injuries and Risk Factors in 1990 and Projected to 2020*, Cambridge: Harvard School of Public Health.

NEPP (1989), *Netherlands' National Environmental Policy Plan: To Choose or Lose*, The Hague: Dutch Ministry of Housing, Physical Planning and the Environment/SDU.

Nijpels, E. H., and J. J. Boersema (1998), 'Land use and the concept of environmental space', in E. M. Barron and I. Nielsen (eds), *Agriculture and Sustainable Land Use in Europe*, The Hague, London and Boston: Kluwer Law International.

Oberthür, Sebastian (1997), *Production and Consumption of Ozone-Depleting Substances 1986–1995: The Data Reporting System under the Montreal Protocol*, Bonn: Deutsche Gesellschaft für Technische Zusammenarbeit.

OECD (1993), *Core Set of Indicators For Environmental Performance Reviews*, Paris: Organisation for Economic Cooperation and Development.

OECD (1994), *Environmental Performance Reviews: Italy*, Paris: Organisation for Economic Co-operation and Development.

OECD (1995), *Environmental Performance Reviews: Netherlands*, Paris: Organisation for Economic Cooperation and Development.

OECD (1996), *Environmental Performance Reviews: United States*, Paris: Organisation for Economic Cooperation and Development.

OECD (1997a), *Environmental Performance Reviews: An Introduction*, Paris: Organisation for Economic Co-operation and Development.

OECD (1997b), *Environmental Data*, Paris: Organisation for Economic Cooperation and Development.

OECD (1998a), 'Sustainable development (a discussion paper on work to be undertaken over the period 1998-2001)', Paris: Organisation for Economic Co-operation and Development.

OECD (1998b), *Towards Sustainable Development: Environmental Indicators*, Paris: Organisation for Economic Cooperation and Development.

PCSD (1996), *Sustainable America: A New Consensus for Prosperity, Opportunity and a*

*Healthy Environment for the Future*, Washington DC: The President's Council on Sustainable Development.

Pearce, D. (1993), *Blueprint 3: Measuring Sustainable Development*, London: Earthscan Publications Ltd.

Rees, W. E., and M. Wackernagel (1994), 'Ecological footprints and appropriate carrying capacity: measuring the natural capital requirements of the human economy', in A. Jansson, M. Hammer ect. (eds), *Investing in Natural Capital: The Ecological Economics Approach to Sustainability*, Washington DC: Island Press.

Smith, P. H., S. E. Okoye, J. de Wilde, and P. Deshingkar (1994), *The World at the Crossroads: Towards a Sustainable, Equitable and Liveable World*, London: Earthscan.

UN (1997), *World Urbanization Prospects: The 1996 Revision, Annex Tables*, New York: UN Population Division.

UNCED (1992), *Convention on Biological Diversity* (UN Conference on Environment and Development, Rio de Janeiro, June 1992).

UNCSD (1997a), *Implementation of Agenda 21, Country Profile: Italy*, New York: UN Department for Policy Coordination and Sustainable Development.

UNCSD (1997b), *Implementation of Agenda 21, Country Profile: Netherlands*, New York: UN Department for Policy Coordination and Sustainable Development.

UNCSD (1997c), *Implementation of Agenda 21, Country Profile: United States of America*, New York: UN Department for Policy Coordination and Sustainable Development.

UNDP (1998), *Human Development Report 1998*, London: Oxford University Press.

US Bureau of the Census (1998), *International Data Base* (July 15 Update), Washington: US Bureau of the Census.

Von Weizsäcker, E. U., A. B. Lovins and L. H. Lovins (1997), *Factor Four: Doubling Wealth, Halving Resource Use*, London: Earthscan.

Wackernagel, M., and W. E. Rees (1996), *Our Ecological Footprint: Reducing Human Impact on the Earth*, Philadelphia: New Society Publishers.

Weterings, R. (1996), 'Sustainable development: a challenge to technology policies', in H. Wiggering and A. Sandhövel (eds), *European Environmental Advisory Councils: Agenda 21 – Implementation Issues in the European Union*, London: Kluwer Law International.

World Bank (1997), *World Development Indicators*, Washington DC: The World Bank.

Worster, D. (1988), ed., *The Ends of Earth: Perspectives on Modern Environmental History*, Cambridge: Cambridge University Press.

WRI (1996), *World Resources Report 1996–97*, New York: Oxford University Press.

# Northern solutions provide no Southern comfort

Michael Redclift makes the point that a global approach to environmental problems requires global agreement and global compliance, and these in turn require some shared commitment to values such as equity. But whereas environmental problems may exist on a global scale, global values are difficult to locate. The environment might seem to provide a common point of reference, and therefore potential ground for agreement on values, but as Redclift observes, environmental values are often invoked in support of more human-centred, and therefore more divisive projects, which concern power over the distribution of resources as much as access to the resources themselves.

We noted earlier (in the commentary on Chapter 1 by Desmond McNeill) the difficulty of deciding what counts as a solution to an environmental problem and how to recognise such a solution. Redclift shows clearly how different the problem itself looks from developed and developing points of view respectively. Developed economies see the problem as one to be tackled by using cleaner technologies so as to minimise the impact of economic growth upon the environment. This is the project known as 'ecological modernisation', whose central proposition is that economic growth can be adapted to meet environmental goals. (This is similar, I think, to Enrique Leff's 'global eco-liberalism.') In developing economies, on the other hand, a cleaner global environment is a much lower priority, as compared, say, with the problem of securing a supply of drinking water (cf. Keekok Lee, who makes a similar contrast between securing the necessities of life and improving its quality.)

Redclift identifies a number of problems with the project of ecological modernisation. It fails to recognise the need for specialised production and the existence of differentiated labour markets. It does not address the predicament of stagnant economies, nor a future in which growth is worldwide. It makes environmental goals subservient to economic ones, and is unable to deal with certain kinds of environmental risk – those events that are highly unlikely to occur, but would be highly damaging if they did. Redclift has a grim tale to tell of the 'long shadow' cast by economic liberalisation since the war, mostly to the detriment of the developing economies which are drawn into trading their natural resources for consumer goods which benefit the few, and at ever-worsening exchange rates. Yet even after Rio, the same style of environmental management persists, reliant on the setting of targets, financial inducements and voluntary compliance.

In more optimistic vein Redclift notes the increasing importance of the role played by international NGOs, especially in developing economies where they may assist in implementing government policies. He closes with a strong hint as to the importance of cultural and political factors in working towards more adequate solutions: coming to terms with the equity question will, he suggests, go hand in hand with our coming to grasp what it is to be global environmental citizens.

~ O ~

# 6 GLOBAL EQUITY:
## THE ENVIRONMENT AND DEVELOPMENT

## Michael Redclift

### – INTRODUCTION –

In a book about global sustainable development, global equity must raise some important questions. Even if we concede that the environment is best regarded within a global framework, is this the appropriate way to look at values such as equity? As values are always located culturally, somewhere, where are 'global values' located? 'Global' usually implies an absence of location, a geopolitical space that encompasses everything; the home in which we live and the way in which we live within it.

There have been a number of useful suggestions recently, however, which might help us to ground the global. Tim Ingold, for example, has pointed to the way in which globalisation is used conceptually. Are we 'inside' or 'outside' the global? he asks (Ingold 1993). It is clear that globalisation is, in some sense, a cultural process implying, as this does, that concern with the distributional effects of the development process is also prone to cultural distortions, and that we are part of it.

A few years ago I was watching the television news in a small guest-house, built of cane, on the Colombian Pacific coast. This village, in the Choco, had been exposed to horrific sea conditions, high waves, winds and thunderstorms. The year before I arrived almost a third of the village had been either flooded or swept away. We were watching the news in the only house to have television, and about a dozen people were crammed into the room. One of the news items was about a strike of refuse collectors in Vienna, and the parlous condition of many of the city's streets littered with domestic rubbish. The peasant farmers and fishing people of the Choco were stunned – 'what a terrible thing to happen', they choroused, 'imagine having mounds of rubbish lying outside your house! Dreadful things happen these days, all over the world!' In their village, of course, the rubbish was dumped, or washed directly into the ocean. There was not much domestic waste anyway, and there were no municipal services to collect it.

We might begin by recognising that 'global' does not equate with 'international.' Some global changes in the media, in consumer behaviour, in interest rates, transcend national boundaries but are not located territorially. To this list we might add some very important global issues such as those introduced by information systems and genetically engineered organisms. We are told that most of the genetic material for the world's grapefruit is located in laboratories in Florida, the globe compressed into a few hundred square metres. When we refer to global change we are referring to universalising processes, but not necessarily territorial ones.

It is also clear that some physical processes of a global nature are, literally, extra-territorial, global climate change being perhaps the best example. Human societies, particularly the most 'advanced' of them, have become particularly adept at shifting their waste from one medium to another, usually from the land to the sea, and from the sea to the air, the atmosphere. Everytime we do this it is accompanied by a raft of regulations, which seek to limit the inevitable damage this causes. As Robert Ayres (1994) has pointed out, if this did not happen, we would not believe such a cumbersome and dangerous process could be invented by the human mind.

The point about extra-terrestrial changes is that since they are everybody's concern they are also nobody's concern. In this they seem to point to the need for global environmental management, by means of international agreements and targets for individual countries. However, we are learning, post-Earth Summit (held in Rio in 1992) that it is extremely difficult to get agreement about global management, and to fund the bodies which will police it. Implementation lies ahead in a rather obscure future, muddied by conflicts between countries over trade, investment, indebtedness and radically different political goals. If global environmental agreements are difficult, global compliance will be even more difficult.

We need to return to these questions later. For the moment it is enough to register that global environmental values imply some degree of agreement about what I would call 'underlying social commitments', or everyday practices, in the sense used by Bourdieu (1977) and Redclift (1996). They are about the implications of our patterns of 'getting and spending.' Without some degree of agreement, and eventually, convergence over these commitments, it will be difficult to build consensus nationally, let alone globally. And without consensus-building, as most international reports have argued (from the Brundtland Report to Agenda 21), there is unlikely to be lasting agreement on the environment. However, instead of convergence in our underlying social commitments, and in our pattern of consumption, the globe is increasingly divided about them. Much has been made of the 'end of history.' However, the triumph of global capitalism also marks challenges for sustainable development. The emphasis on market convergence should not be allowed to obscure the importance of other economic dimensions – such as scarcity and need – in addressing problems of sustainability.

The final point to be made about environmental values is that, unless you attribute to nature primary importance, as 'deep ecologists' do, they refer to human values about the environment. This sometimes needs emphasising because, in the absence of a 'biospheric imperative', a clear sense of the signals of vulnerability given by nature (Dasmann 1975), groups of human beings tend to invoke the 'environment' in support of their own project. Environmental interests reflect and are constructed by human groups. Such groups regularly have recourse to nature, and to naturalisation, when political obstacles frustrate their own political, social and economic objectives.

Environmental values may refer to the way we organise 'social time-space' rather than the environment and resources we exploit. They are part of the 'authoritative resources' (including life chances) with which we distribute rights over the environment rather than 'allocative resources', in Giddens's terminology. Giddens distinguishes between 'allocative resources', (raw materials, technology, the physical environment) and the constellations of power, the distributive mechanisms, used to exploit them (Giddens 1984, pp. 258–62).

During the last couple of decades major changes have taken place in the discussion of the global environment. If we think of the environment essentially as a resource system, as we have tended to do historically, then environmental values are about the distribution and use of resources. However, some people, including the Norwegian anthropologist Fredrik Barth (1996), have argued that global responsibilities require a wider definition to include sinks as well as sources. Barth reminds us that we still do not have a theory of sinks to match our many and various theories of resources, and the urgency of some global issues (including climate change and biodiversity losses) suggests this is an omission social scientists should not tolerate for much longer (Redclift 1996). The need to formulate such a mission for the social sciences is one that I suspect many social scientists would be wary of, but those of us who endorse a realist position, without in any sense ignoring the importance of culture, need to ensure that the contribution of the social sciences is not lost by default. The implication, which is not lost on most ordinary people, is that we need to engage with environmental problems in the real world which exist outside us, but not completely independently of us. To understand these problems we need to understand why they assume the status of 'problem', as well as what we need to do about them.

## – The global environment as a 'problem' –

The global environment is regarded as a problem by most countries, but the nature of the problem differs significantly throughout the globe. In the developed countries the problem is seen as how to achieve sustainable growth, that is, how do we get the benefits of a cleaner environment without sacrificing continued economic growth and increasing consumption? This takes the North towards anticipating solutions that are immediately seen as global in scale: addressing climate change and biodiversity losses, for example. But it also leads to attempts to internalise environmental externalities, retaining the central idea of free trade and industrial competitiveness. The key concept, at least in pale Green circles, is that of ecological modernisation. This is the process through which societies try to internalise environmental externalities. The question then becomes, how do we engineer cleaner technologies and production systems?

In the developing countries the global environmental problem is usually looked at differently. In the larger economies of Asia, such as China, India and Indonesia, economic growth is also a priority, as it has been throughout the 1980s in the so-called Newly Industrialising Countries (the Asian 'Tigers'). However, economic growth is also a means to address poverty, and a cleaner global environment (atmosphere, oceans and forests) is a much lower priority than the immediate environmental problems associated with poverty, like securing clean drinking water, sustainable farming systems and adequate shelter. Ecological modernisation can be expected to remain a marginal concern in most of these countries. The situation will continue at least until the failure to meet higher environmental product standards prevents developing countries from reaping the benefits from trade. As we shall see, efforts in some quarters to introduce environmental protection by refashioning global trade agreements meet resistance from the advocates of trade liberalisation in the North, and the opponents of checks on poverty eradication in the South.

The Earth Summit in 1992 demonstrated how a global agenda could be grafted on to the existing global economic system, in many cases using the same institutions, such as those of the United Nations and the World Bank, to implement the new environmental agenda. The only acceptable definition of the global environmental 'problem' was one that each state could (theoretically) endorse. It was one based on voluntary compliance, targets, marginally enhanced budgets for existing international institutions, and principles of environmental management derived from the historically unique, and localised, experiences of the developed countries.

We need to ask, seven years after Rio, whether there is significant evidence of global convergence over the environment, of an accelerating pace in reaching workable international agreements. Are there ways in which existing differences could provide the starting point for global solutions, perhaps through joint agreements, or environmental taxes? In the 1990s, most of the OECD (Organisation for Economic Cooperation and Development) countries have been preoccupied with their own economic recovery. Ecological modernisation is seen as one way of achieving economic recovery, and without sacrificing higher standards in the immediate environment. But we also need to ask what in the North would help the poorer countries of the South and their environments? If the answer to these questions is an emphatic 'no', then perhaps the problem of the global environment, as understood in the North, is completely misconceived. Let us examine the proposition in more detail.

## – THE NORTHERN SOLUTION: ECOLOGICAL MODERNISATION –

Ecological modernisation has been reviewed in a variety of publications (Simonis 1989; Spaargaren and Mol 1991; Weale 1992; Janicke 1992; Hajer 1994; and Gouldson's forthcoming work on ecological modernisation). The central proposition behind ecological modernisation is that economic growth can be adapted to meet environmental goals.

As Gouldson has expressed it: '(It) assumes that there can be a synergy between environmental protection and economic development, where in the past there has been conflict' (forthcoming). The prime mover is government, which helps to provide a broader context than is usually provided by environmental policy alone. In specific terms this means the creation of new products and services that demonstrate improved environmental and economic performance. Essentially, ecological modernisation proposes to internalise externalities, designing cleaner, more sustainable goods, which meet clear environmental standards.

In seeking greater integration of environmental policy goals with those of other sectors, ecological modernisation seeks to accommodate late industrial society. It seeks to redefine international competitiveness in such a way that early technological innovators reap market advantages. It does not represent a threat to capitalist development, however, and those who argue for ecological modernisation do not challenge the logic of international capital. As Gouldson puts it: 'ecological modernisation can be viewed as very selective in just where it apportions blame for environmental degradation' (forthcoming). It is assumed that advanced industrial societies can shift their technologies and patterns of production while leaving the structures of private capital accumulation fundamentally intact.

There are a number of problems with this approach on the global scale. First, it is insufficiently grounded in international political economy, where recent debates have focused on flexible specialisation in production, the primacy of information and associated technology and internationally differentiated labour markets. Ecological modernisation suggests that economic restructuring can be modified to incorporate environmental ends, providing a convergence between productive capital and the environmental goals of society. These Green goals serve to act upon the real world of contemporary capitalism, enabling new environmental values to penetrate the very heart of the industrial process. The result is that companies and governments will be more competitive in the longer term within the global system. The economic restructuring of global capital is a reality, but in some of the most dynamic economies environmental externalities remain just that, external. In the 'Tiger' economies of East Asia, for example, air pollution in cities is growing faster than the rate of economic growth. As yet, however, there is little evidence that economic competitiveness has been refashioned to reflect more sustainable objectives – see the UN survey (*Environmental Management in Transnational Corporations*), published in 1993, of 794 TNCs with sales over US $1billion.

As with other concepts, including sustainable development, different writers have found different things in ecological modernisation. Gouldson (forthcoming) argues that the concept represents a challenge to the nation-state and to national regulation. Fleming (1994) questions whether ecological modernisation is an effective way of addressing the problem of economic growth, in economies where growth is beginning to flounder. He draws attention to the contradictions between the European Union's goal of increased employment and that of labour-saving ecological modernisation.

The problems are more severe if we look outside western Europe. The White Paper from the European Commission published in 1993, *Growth, Competitiveness and Employment*, states that extrapolating current consumption and production patterns within the European Union to the entire world would require a ten-fold increase in resources. Europe's environmental protection industries, the nub of ecological modernisation, are currently incapable of shouldering the burden of growth within Europe. It remains to be seen whether social coupling, the organisation of the workplace around best environmental practice, can work in Germany, Scandinavia or The Netherlands, where it is advocated most strongly. To 'globalise' from European experience would not merely require major shifts in global economies, but would also exacerbate divisions and distributional problems. Where does competitive advantage take you, if everybody gains from it?

There are other problems, too. At the moment ecological modernisation is largely confined to end-of-pipe technologies, where environmental regulation is usually operative. It is significant, then, that whose who favour environmental regulation usually see ecological modernisation as a facet of business development, rather than a means of raising environmental standards. It is argued that business will take ecological modernisation seriously once it benefits financially from doing so.

The real challenge, however, as Daly and Goodland (1992) noted some time ago is to reduce energy throughput in the economy, rather than in the production of a limited range of 'greener' goods and services. What is required is not the creation of 'greener' management accounting and environmental regulation, but a shift towards the wider recognition that sustainability might drive the economy. Until the globe's sink capacities have been assessed and production modified to reflect these capacities, we will not have turned the corner to greater sustainability.

Finally, as Spaargaren and Mol (1991), among others, have shown, ecological modernisation does not extend environmental protection to many global environmental problems and risks. Such risks tend to be what Ulrich Beck (1992) has called risks of 'high consequence' but 'low probability', such as those of nuclear accidents or chemical warfare. Ecological modernisation, by contrast, seeks to allay uncertainties in policy formulation. Risk is materialised, in production, as part of a longer-term strategy of economic harmonisation. The universality of high consequence risks may make management responses, such as those of ecological modernisation, an irrelevance. Further, even if one dissents from Beck's view that the 'positive logic' of wealth distribution has been overshadowed by the 'negative logic' of risk distribution, it remains clear that only preventative action on the global scale will enable us to deal with global risks of this kind. This has served to redefine distributive problems; but they have not disappeared. Economic harmonisation around products and markets exposes the poor to exploitation as a cheap resource. The poorer one is, the less effective is preventative action.

In practice, as we shall see, effective international action to address environmental problems is not amenable to technical solutions alone. It requires agreement about both means and ends, in which the internalisation of environmental costs (through ecological modernisation) can represent a market advantage from which the rich reap most of the benefits. Economic convergence towards 'greener' production, measured by indicators of sustainability, can be seen as a substitute for restructured economies and restructured international institutions which were designed, in the wake of the Second World War, to address world peace by reducing economic vulnerability and world poverty (MacGillivray and Zadek 1995).

## – THE SOUTHERN AGENDA:
### DEVELOPMENT AND POVERTY REDUCTION –

According to the United Nations:

> If current patterns [of development] continue unchanged, the world distribution of income between countries [will] worsen, that is, the gap between the richest and the poorest countries [will continue] to widen. Some social indicators show a slowdown in progress in many developing countries, and even some absolute declines. The risk of serious deterioration of the physical environment will increase unless patterns of production and consumption are radically altered. (United Nations 1990, p. 2)

Let us look briefly at the genesis of an alternative to economic liberalisation. With hindsight, the development decades of the 1950s and 1960s and the eventual prospect of unallayed economic growth and prosperity appear exceptional and politically contingent. The conditions for optimism for most of the South no longer applied. Cheap energy prices had enabled economic growth to obtain a boost, without environmental costs being counted. This legacy of mining natural resources and simultaneously subsidising energy pricing persists today, and underpinned some economies, for example, those of the former Soviet Bloc. At the same time the competition fostered by the Cold War protagonists created artificial (that is, non-productive) economic investment in defence and military security. Ultimately, of course, this expansion in rearmament served to undermine the economies of the developing countries by contributing to higher international interest rates. United States defence procurements (the Strategic Defence Initiative) not only served notice on the Soviet military economy, but also exacerbated the international debt crisis.

Another element in the post-war development decades was the process of decolonisation, which appeared for some time to offer alternative economic models, even a 'third road', but which has largely been abandoned in the 1980s and 1990s. The economic success stories of recent years have served to point up the underlying problems in the larger economies of Asia, Latin America and Africa, from which the assault on poverty must begin. For most countries in the South, the economic imperatives of the free market sit uncomfortably with the political agenda of development and poverty.

What happened to global macro-economic planning as a way of addressing the poverty agenda? The United Nations system has been peculiarly ineffective in addressing development and poverty issues. The reasons have been persuasively argued by somebody with a lifetime's dedication to their resolution, Hans Singer (1994). He points out that the Bretton Woods institutions (the International Monetary Fund and the World Bank) are still legally part of the UN system although they do not consider themselves in this light. The United Nations was created in a separate process from the two global financial institutions, almost a year later, and in a different place (New York rather than Washington).

The effect of decolonisation has been to shift the voting power of UN institutions away from the industrial countries and towards post-colonial states in Africa and Asia. The Bretton Woods institutions, by contrast, became the chosen mechanism for the developed world in fashioning economic recovery and liberalising world markets. The original division of labour between financing development projects (World Bank) and global macro-economic management and aid (the other UN bodies) has disappeared, almost without trace. The World Bank has enlarged its role from project finance to programme lending and, in the 1970s and 1980s, structural adjustment lending. Since 1982 the Bank has advocated global debt collection, in the demise of global economic harmonisation.

The shift from global institutions away from the role of harbinger of a better economic future towards that of international debt collector was taken via a series of modest steps, which are worth recalling. The Bretton Woods institutions advised borrowers to increase their exports, largely to the North. All borrowers attempted to follow this injunction. The prices received by primary exporters began to fall, against relatively inelastic demand from the industrialised world. As a result the total receipts from exports from the South fell, leading to higher production to compensate for the shortfall in receipts. This, in turn, produced further falls in prices and receipts.

This Alice-in-Wonderland scenario is no mere fantasy; it is precisely what happened after the imposition of structural adjustment policies in Africa in the 1980s. Some of the same processes are at work in India in the 1990s. Economic reforms, far from facilitating long-term sustainability, have served to worsen environmental problems in many areas of the globe where sustainable livelihoods were always precariously balanced. What was required was strengthened environmental security and the protection of communal resources. Instead, natural capital was privatised and public infrastructure starved of cash.

This enterprising new 'development role' has left the World Bank, which was largely unaccountable politically, short of the economic success stories it most covets. At the same time, and on its own admission, the quality of much of the Bank's project lending has declined. The 'development' function has passed to an assortment of international NGOs and a few enlightened bilateral agencies preoccupied with poverty issues. Economic liberalism has cast a long shadow. As Hans Singer has expressed it: 'as for the "facts of life" argument (that the developing countries must face the facts of life on international markets), the counter-argument is that the Bretton Woods institutions were not created to impress the facts of life on deficit countries, but to *change the facts of life*' (Singer 1994, p. 13; my emphasis.

These arguments about the way in which global economic management has been pursued, through monetarist rather than Keynesian policies, also have application to trade liberalisation. For the last ten years the deregulation of trade has accelerated, under the mandate of the General Agreement on Tariffs and Trade (GATT). The remit of the GATT is to extend the 'welfare gains from trade', through emphasising comparative advantage, rather than total welfare gains. In poor countries welfare gains might be expected from increasing the domestic production of non-traded goods and the maintenance of the 'natural capital' (environment) on which flows of income depend. Such naive expectations have been dashed. As Herman Daly and Robert Goodland put it: 'Would it not make sense for Third World countries to focus more on transforming their *own* resources into products for their *own* peoples, rather than exporting them to the North, in exchange for consumer goods for Southern elites?' (1992, p. 15; my emphasis).

The use of 'free trade' to cement global economic integration removes the principle of sustainability from local communities across the globe. It does so by stimulating the trade in natural resources and their products without strengthening local communities or encouraging responsible environmental management. Resources are depleted to provide foreign exchange and sustainable livelihoods are eroded. In the North, capital mobility and free trade serve to force down wage levels and create unemployment, without raising wages or creating employment in the South, where the reproduction of the labour force is frequently at the margin of market systems. Environmental asset stripping is the inevitable consequence of unbridled market gain.

Finally, it is clear that prices under 'free trade' do not reflect social and environmental costs. Trade is only 'free' in the sense that it is not encumbered by having to meet its own social and economic reproduction costs, including the costs of seeking to return natural resources to their previous state. As Daly and Goodland argue: 'Until the price of traded goods reflects their full environmental and social costs in each trading country, unregulated trade will undermine efficient national policies of internalizing external costs' (ibid., p. 7).

Put in a different way, free trade enables best practice in German industry to be set against that in Taiwanese or Malaysian industry, without tracing the ecological footprints beyond the borders of Germany. The externalities generated in Taiwan, in both the labour force and the environment, are not part of the equation. In poorer countries, impatient to develop their links with global markets, such externalities have a habit of disappearing. They are frequently invisible and manifest in the health and living conditions of women and children, located at some distance from the main roads. The internalisation of environmental costs needs to proceed through both global agreements and local participation. In the absence of global agreements to protect social conditions and the environment, free trade agreements exacerbate both. They marginalise productive systems whose logic lies outside, or in association with, the market. At best they constitute a vehicle for organising the corporate response to global economic pressures.

Where does this leave the Southern agenda, of poverty and the environment? Daly and Goodland argue that 'since resources are finite, then more Northern growth inevitably means less room for Southern growth' (ibid., p. 23). Certainly, Northern consumption gains in the future should come from improvements in utilising energy more efficiently rather than increased throughput in the economy. The prospect of 'freer' trade does nothing to advance this prospect; indeed it may actually contribute to the problem. Ecological modernisation, as advocated in the North, is at best only a partial solution to the problem and no substitute for policies which assume global responsibility for poverty, especially in the South.

## – THE GLOBAL ENVIRONMENT AND NON-GOVERNMENTAL ORGANISATIONS (NGOs) –

This chapter has focused on the economic processes through which international business has, under ecological modernisation, sought to incorporate environmental costs, utilising technological change and market incentives. It has also considered the effects of economic liberalisation on the environment and the fallacy of viewing 'free trade' as anything but unfair. Again, we note that values intrude into international trade, whether explicit or otherwise. We have also given some consideration to the international institutions, particularly those established under Bretton Woods, whose remit has been to promote 'development', frequently at some considerable cost to the global environment.

It is also important to consider the role of the international institutions of civil society, the Non-Governmental Organisations, which frequently play a large part in seeking to protect the environment of developing countries from the depredations of transnational economic activity. International NGOs represent a distinct contribution to environmental policy-making in two respects: they are both non-governmental and non-profit-making. In the developed world we tend to view NGOs as part of the fabric of our society; they acquire legitimacy from the wide support of ordinary members of the public. Indeed, the environmental movement in most industrially-developed countries is largely an expression of the activities of NGOs.

The situation in the South is somewhat different. As Potter (1996) demonstrates, NGOs in the South are often as large as those in the North; some, such as the Bangladesh Rural Advancement Committee (BRAC), with a paid staff of over two thousand, are larger than most northern NGOs. What characterises their activity, however, is that they are usually engaged in networking with other organisations, frequently forming coalitions and alliances. Some large NGOs such as Greenpeace have become, in effect, networks of their own, with national offices in over thirty countries and almost five million supporters worldwide.

As the international environmental agenda has grown, so the role of some NGOs has enlarged. International conventions and protocols provide opportunities for NGOs to effect leverage on behalf of an environmental issue or a group of interested people. When the parties to international agreements meet, the NGOs shadow them, so to speak, seeking to gain access both to governments and to the forum in which they operate. Governments, in their turn, frequently have recourse to NGOs to help implement their policies. This is particularly true in many developing countries, where governments have fewer resources with which to mount environmental campaigns and may have less public legitimacy than the NGOs with which they work. Finally, governments rarely have the kind of continual presence that NGOs have, with their local supporters and roots in local communities and, therefore, the capacity to help implement environmental measures.

International environmental NGOs confront severe pressures, especially when faced by a policy community made up of governments and international institutions. First, policy communities engaged in environmental management frequently have to work closely with business interests; indeed, many of their activities can only be undertaken with the tacit support of international business. Second, although NGOs may be vitally important to the effective implementation of environmental policy, they cannot be too closely identified with governments without losing the very basis in public support that they need for their own survival. The 'poacher' can become a 'gamekeeper' but only at the cost of courting opposition from the local community from which the poacher comes. In this sense, too, NGOs that pride themselves on their independence from government interference often rely heavily on the notion that governments take them seriously – another paradox that can hinder their development.

Perhaps the most fundamental aspect of the NGOs' role, at the international level, is the way that their mission mirrors the interests (and prejudices) of the public in both developed and developing countries. In the North, the perception of many lay people, if not the more active campaigners, is that poor people themselves are partly to blame for the precarious state of the environment in the South. The popular solution to environmental problems is deemed to be population control. At the same time the message of most campaigners on development and the environment is that it is over-consumption in the North which undermines global sustainability. International NGOs, particularly, face a dilemma, in that the issues on which they need to rally public support are frequently ones where their own analysis diverges dramatically from that of the mass of the public. They therefore seek to persuade and educate people, including their own followers, while trying to keep the pressure up on governments, especially those of Northern countries. For these reasons, among others, it is extremely difficult to assess the influence of international NGOs on the majority of public issues involving the South.

## – THE FUTURE OF GLOBAL INEQUALITIES OVER THE ENVIRONMENT –

Global inequalities will need to be subjected to more interrogation during the next century. On the one hand, the global economic system requires more uniformity in economic goals and more competition to achieve them. The possibilities offered by a 'third way' between capitalism and communism have largely evaporated after the demise of the Soviet Union. Protecting the environment, for developing countries, comes with an increasing price tag attached to it. On the other hand, many of the global environmental problems that confront us today, in both developed and developing countries, were not anticipated, even a couple of decades ago. Environmental problems seem to exhibit a tendency to surprise; we are rarely able to predict with any degree of accuracy the next challenge to sustainability. A new geopolitics is also arising, in which the sources of our consumption (our 'getting and spending') assume enormous strategic importance on the world stage. The Gulf War in the early 1990s was probably a watershed in this respect. Finally, poverty will continue to underpin the most pressing environmental problems in the South.

Poor water quality may still contribute to the death of $13\frac{1}{2}$ million children under five. Having failed to rise to the challenge of post-war Keynesian management, all the indications are that global environmental management will be a very steep learning curve. There will be increasing calls for post-hoc international regulation but with much more difficulty in carrying precautionary agreements. In addition, ideological differences will recur, over rival accounts of what constitutes 'progress.' Secularisation or religious fundamentalism (the West or Islam)? Materialism or spiritual regeneration? What kind of society do we seek to sustain?

– CONCLUSION –

How do we address the issues of global environmental equity at the dawn of the next century? It will require attention to the following: inter-generational justice; recognition of the rights of non-human species; the elevation of use values over commodity values; the acknowledgement of diversity in biosystems and in human cultures.

Global environmental equity will be indissolubly linked to wider questions of citizenship. Rather than thinking in terms of citizenship and the environment as two separate categories, we may find that global environmental change alters the notion of citizenship itself. Global environmental citizenship would be conferred, and understood in much the same way as national citizenship is today. It would provide material evidence of the primacy of global equity over narrower self-interested values. That would be a real achievement in the much-vaunted twenty-first century.

## – BIBLIOGRAPHY –

Ayres, R. (1994), 'Industrial metabolism: theory and policy', in Robert Ayres and Udo Simonis (eds), *Industrial Metabolism: Restructuring for Sustainable Development*, Tokyo: United Nations University Press.

Barth, F. (1996), 'Global cultural diversity in a "full world economy" ', in L. Arizpe (ed.), *The Cultural Dimensions of Global Change: An Anthropological Approach*, Paris: UNESCO.

Beck, U. (1992), *Risk Society: Towards a New Modernity*, London: Sage.

Bourdieu, P. (1977), *Outline of a Theory of Practice*, Cambridge: Cambridge University Press.

Daly, H. E., and R. Goodland (1992), 'Ten reasons why Northern income growth is not the solution to Southern poverty', *International Journal of Sustainable Development* 1:2.

Dasmann, R. F. (1975), *The Conservation Alternative*, Chichester: John Wiley.

European Commission (1993), *Growth, Competitiveness and Employment: The Challenges and Ways Forward into the 21st Century*, Luxembourg: Office of Publications, White Paper.

Fleming, D. (1994), 'Towards the low-output economy: the future that the Delors White Paper tries not to face', *European Environment*, July 1994.

Giddens, A. (1984), *The Constitution of Society*, Cambridge: Polity Press.

Gouldson, A. (forthcoming), 'Ecological modernisation and the European Union', *Geoforum*.

Hajer, T. (1994), 'Ecological modernisation and social change', in S. Lash, B. Szerszynski and B. Wynne (eds), *Risk, Environment and Modernity: Towards a New Ecology*, London: Sage.

Ingold, T. (1993), 'The local and the global', in Kay Milton (ed.), *Environmentalism: The View from Anthropology*, London: Routledge.

Janicke, M. (1992), *State Failure: The Impotence of Politics in Industrial Society*, Cambridge: Polity Press.

MacGillivray, R., and S. Zadek (1995), *Sustainability Indicators*, London: New Economic Foundation.

Potter, David (1996), 'Non-governmental organisations and environmental policies', in A. Blowers and P. Glasbergen (eds), *Environmental Policy in an International Context: Prospects for Environmental Change*, London: Arnold and the Open University.

Redclift, M. R. (1996), *Wasted: Counting the Costs of Global Consumption*, London: Earthscan.

Simonis, U. (1989), 'Ecological modernisation of industrial society: three strategic elements', *International Social Science Journal* 121.

Singer, H. (1994), 'The Bretton Woods institutions and the UN', *Bulletin of the Development Studies Association*, UK.

Spaargaren, G., and A. Mol (1991), *Sociology, Environment and Modernity: Ecological Modernisation as a Theory of Social Change*, Wageningen: Landbouw University.

United Nations (1990), *Global Outlook 2000*, New York: United Nations Publications.

United Nations (1993), *Environmental Management in Transnational Corporations: Report of the Benchmark Corporate Environmental Survey*, New York: United Nations Publications.

Weale, A. (1992), *The New Politics of Pollution*, Manchester: Manchester University Press.

# Why over-consumption is bad for you

Mark Sagoff offers a robust challenge to some common analyses of our environmental predicament, including several that are represented in this volume. He asks whether it is true to say, as many representatives of developing economies say, that the industrialised nations 'consume too much' – whether indeed this (rather than, say, overpopulation) is the problem facing the world's environment.

In the body of his essay, Sagoff assembles an impressive array of reasons for denying this claim. In terms also used elsewhere, he mounts a stout defence of the project of 'ecological modernisation' or 'global liberalism' that Lee, Leff, Redclift and others have roundly attacked. The idea that nature sets ecological limits to economic growth, and that therefore increased consumption inevitably leads to the depletion of resources and the collapse of ecosystems is, he claims 'mistaken both in principle and in fact.' He points out that previous predictions of resource scarcity have been proved false, due in part to improved methods of extraction, partly to replacement and substitution, and partly to new technologies that make more efficient use of new and lighter materials. Citing developments in aquaculture and silviculture, improved water-delivery systems and the development of water-efficient and salt-resistant crops, he argues that the only limits to growth are the limits of our knowledge, and that the elimination of hunger is constrained less by the resource base than by poverty, trade barriers and maldistribution. Noting that the energy problem is more one of disposal than of supply, he points to the potential of virtually pollution-free sources of energy such as heat from the Earth's core, tidal energy and the sun. Turning to the issue of trade between North and South, Sagoff observes that the problems experienced by the South stem not so much from exploitation as from the North's becoming less reliant on raw materials from the South. He suggests that economic growth in the South may be 'the one thing that is sustainable', provided it is based on the production of appropriate crops and raw materials (such as tea, coffee, cocoa and palm oil).

Suppose his argument succeeds, and it is proved that technology can make the world safe both for, and from, development. A critic may insist that the real question is whether, in the light of social, economic and political realities, it is at all likely that it will do so. But Sagoff is certainly not about to go the stake for the right of the wealthy to consume more. Far from it. He writes as indignantly as others about the growing gap between rich and poor and of 'the assault that commerce makes upon the quality of our lives.' The twist of his piece comes in the tail. We – if we count ourselves among the wealthy – do consume too much. But he is adamant that the reasons for saying this are moral, religious and spiritual ones. We consume too much just and when we allow ourselves to become consumers. For then we shall have lost our bearings since, as Sagoff concludes, 'we take our bearings from the natural world.'

~ O ~

# 7 Can Technology Make the World Safe for Development? The Environment in the Age of Information

## Mark Sagoff

### – Introduction –

In 1994, when delegates from around the world gathered in Cairo for the International Conference on Population and Development, representatives from developing countries protested that a baby born in the United States will consume during its lifetime twenty times as much of the world's resources as an African or an Indian baby. The problem for the world's environment, they argued, is overconsumption in the North, not over-population in the South. Consumption in industrialised nations 'has led to overexploitation of the resources of developing countries,' a speaker from Kenya declared. A delegate from Antigua reproached the wealthiest 20 per cent of the world's population for consuming 80 per cent of the goods and services produced from the earth's resources.[1]

Do we consume too much? To some, the answer is self-evident. If there is only so much food, timber, petroleum, and other material to go around, the more we consume, the less must be available for others. The global economy cannot grow indefinitely on a finite planet. As populations increase and economies expand, natural resources must be depleted; prices will rise, and humanity – especially the poor and future generations at all income levels – will suffer as a result.[2]

Other reasons to suppose we consume too much are less often stated though also widely believed. Of these the simplest – a lesson we learn from our parents and from literature since the Old Testament – may be the best: although we must satisfy basic needs, a good life is not one devoted to amassing material possessions; what we own comes to own us, keeping us from fulfilling commitments that give meaning to life, such as those to family, friends, and faith. The appreciation of nature also deepens our lives. As we consume more, however, we are more likely to transform the natural world, so that less of it will remain for us to appreciate.

The reasons for protecting nature are often religious or moral. As the philosopher Ronald Dworkin points out, many Americans believe that we have an obligation to protect species which goes beyond our own well-being; we 'think we should admire and protect them because they are important in themselves, and not just if or because we or others want or enjoy them' (Dworkin 1994, pp. 72–3).[3] In a recent survey Americans from various walks of life agreed by large majorities with the statement 'Because God created the natural world, it is wrong to abuse it.' The anthropologists who conducted this survey concluded that 'divine creation is the closest concept American culture provides to express the sacredness of nature' (Kempton et al. 1995, pp. 91–2).

During the nineteenth century, preservationists forthrightly gave ethical and spiritual reasons for protecting the natural world. In 1912, John Muir condemned the 'temple destroyers, devotees of ravaging commercialism' who 'instead of lifting their eyes to the God of the mountains, lift them to the Almighty dollar' (1912, p. 256). This was not a call for better cost-benefit analysis: Muir described nature not as a commodity but as a companion. Nature is sacred, Muir held, whether or not resources are scarce.

Philosophers such as Emerson and Thoreau thought of nature as full of divinity. Walt Whitman celebrated a leaf of grass as no less than the journeywork of the stars: 'After you have exhausted what there is in business, politics, conviviality, love, and so on,' and 'found that none of these finally satisfy, or permanently wear – what remains? Nature remains' (1971, p. 61). These philosophers thought of nature as a refuge from economic activity, not as a resource for it.

Today those who wish to protect the natural environment rarely offer ethical or spiritual reasons for the policies they favour. Instead they say we are running out of resources or causing the collapse of ecosystems on which we depend. Predictions of resource scarcity appear objective and scientific, whereas pronouncements that nature is sacred or that greed is bad appear judgemental or even embarrassing in a secular society. Prudential and economic arguments, moreover, have succeeded better than moral or spiritual ones in swaying public policy.

These prudential and economic arguments are not likely to succeed much longer. It is simply wrong to believe that nature sets physical limits to economic growth – that is, to prosperity and the production and consumption of goods and services on which it is based. The idea that increasing consumption will inevitably lead to depletion and scarcity, as plausible as it may seem, is mistaken both in principle and in fact. It is based on four misconceptions.

## – Misconception No. 1: We are running out of raw materials –

In the 1970s Paul Ehrlich, a biologist at Stanford University, predicted that global shortages would soon send prices for food, fresh water, energy, metals, paper, and other materials sharply higher. 'It seems certain,' Paul and Anne Ehrlich wrote in 1974, 'that energy shortages will be with us for the rest of the century, and that before 1985 mankind will enter a genuine age of scarcity in which many things besides energy will be in short supply.' Crucial materials would near depletion during the 1980s, the Ehrlichs predicted, pushing prices out of reach: 'Starvation among people will be accompanied by starvation of industries for the materials they require' (Ehrlich and Ehrlich 1974, p. 33).

Things have not turned out as predicted. In the early 1990s real prices for food overall fell.[4] Raw materials – including energy resources – are generally more abundant and less expensive today than they were twenty years ago. When Ehrlich wrote, economically recoverable world reserves of petroleum stood at 640 billion barrels (1974, p. 48). Since that time reserves have increased by more than 50 per cent, reaching more than 1,000 billion barrels in 1989.[5] They have held steady in spite of rising consumption. The pre-tax real price of petrol was lower during the 1990s than at any other time since 1947.[6] The World Energy Council announced in 1992 that 'fears of imminent [resource] exhaustion that were widely held 20 years ago are now considered to have been unfounded' (World Bank 1994b, p. 9).

The World Resources Institute referred to 'the frequently expressed concern that high levels of consumption will lead to resource depletion and to physical shortages that might limit growth or development opportunity.' Examining the evidence, however, the Institute said that 'the world is not yet running out of most non-renewable resources and is not likely to, at least in the next few decades' (World Bank 1994b, p. 5). A 1988 report from the USA Office of Technology Assessment concluded: 'The nation's future has probably never been less constrained by the cost of natural resources' (Moore 1995, p. 137).

It is reasonable to expect that as raw materials become less expensive, they will be more rapidly depleted. This expectation is also mistaken. From 1980 to 1990, for example, while the prices of resource-based commodities declined (the price of rubber by 40 per cent, cement by 40 per cent, and coal by almost 50 per cent), reserves of most raw materials increased.[7] Economists offer three explanations.

First, with regard to subsoil resources, the world becomes ever more adept at discovering new reserves and exploiting old ones. Exploring for oil, for example, used to be a hit-or-miss proposition, resulting in a lot of dry holes. Today oil companies can use seismic waves to help them create precise computer images of the Earth.[8] New methods of extraction – for example, using bacteria to leach metals from low-grade ores – greatly increase resource recovery. Reserves of resources 'are actually functions of technology,' one analyst, Thomas H. Lee, has written; 'The more advanced the technology, the more reserves become known and recoverable' (Lee 1989, p. 116).

Second, plentiful resources can be used in place of those that become scarce. Analysts speak of an 'Age of Substitutability' and point, for example, to nanotubes, tiny cylinders of carbon whose molecular structure forms fibers a hundred times as strong as steel, at one sixth the weight.[9] As technologies that use more-abundant resources take the place of those needing less-abundant ones – for example, ceramics in place of tungsten, fiber optics in place of copper wire, aluminum cans in place of tin ones – the demand for and the price of the less-abundant resources decline.

One can easily find earlier instances of substitution. During the early nineteenth century, whale oil was the preferred fuel for household illumination.[10] A dwindling supply prompted innovations in the lighting industry, including the invention of gas and kerosene lamps and Edison's carbon-filament electric bulb.[11] Whale oil has substitutes, such as electricity and petroleum-based lubricants. Whales are irreplaceable.

Third, the more we learn about materials, the more efficiently we use them. The progress from candles to carbon-filament to tungsten incandescent lamps, for example, decreased the energy required for and the cost of a unit of household lighting by many times. Compact fluorescent lights are four times as efficient as today's incandescent bulbs and last ten to twenty times as long.[12] Comparable energy savings are available in other appliances: for example, refrigerators sold in 1993 were 23 per cent more efficient than those sold in 1990 and 65 per cent more efficient than those sold in 1980, saving consumers billions in electric bills.[13]

Amory Lovins, the director of the Rocky Mountain Institute, has described a new generation of ultralight automobiles that could deliver the safety and muscle of today's cars but with far better mileage – four times as much in prototypes and ten times as much in projected models.[14] Since in today's cars only 15 to 20 per cent of the fuel's energy reaches the wheels (the rest is lost in the engine and the transmission), and since materials lighter and stronger than steel are available or on the way, no expert questions the feasibility of the high-mileage vehicles Lovins describes.

Computers and cameras are examples of consumer goods getting lighter and smaller as they get better. The game-maker Sega is marketing a hand-held children's game, called Saturn, that has more computing power than the 1976 Cray supercomputer, which the United States tried to keep out of the hands of the Soviets.[15] Improvements that extend the useful life of objects also save resources. Platinum spark plugs in today's cars last for 100,000 miles, as do 'fill-for-life' transmission fluids. On average, cars bought in 1993 have a useful life more than 40 per cent longer than those bought in 1970.[16]

As lighter materials replace heavier ones, economies like the US continue to shed weight. The US per capita consumption of raw materials such as forestry products and metals has, measured by weight, declined steadily over the past twenty years. A recent World Resources Institute study measured the 'materials intensity' of the economy – that is, 'the total material input and the hidden or indirect material flows, including deliberate landscape alterations' required for each dollar's worth of economic output. 'The result shows a clearly declining pattern of materials intensity, supporting the conclusion that economic activity is growing somewhat more rapidly than natural resource use' (World Bank 1994b, p. 15).[17] Of course, we should do better. The Organisation for Economic Cooperation and Development, an association of the world's industrialised nations, has proposed that its members strive as a long-range goal to decrease their materials intensity by a factor of ten. (See ibid.)

Communications also illustrates the trend toward lighter, smaller, less materials-intensive technology. Just as telegraph cables replaced frigates in transmitting messages across the Atlantic and carried more information faster, glass fibres and microwaves have replaced cables – each new technology using a smaller amount of materials but providing greater capacity for sending and receiving information. Areas not yet wired for telephones (in the former Soviet Union, for example) are expected to leapfrog directly into cellular communications.[18] Robert Solow, a Nobel laureate in economics, says that if the future is like the past, 'There will be prolonged and substantial reductions in natural-resource requirements per unit of real output.' He asks, 'Why shouldn't the productivity of most natural resources rise more or less steadily through time, like the productivity of labor?' (1973, p. 49).

## – MISCONCEPTION No. 2:
### WE ARE RUNNING OUT OF FOOD AND TIMBER –

The United Nations projects that the global population, currently 5.7 billion, will peak at about 10 billion in the next century and then stabilise or even decline.[19] Can the earth feed that many people? Even if food crops increase sufficiently, other renewable resources, including many fisheries and forests, are already under pressure. Should we expect fish stocks to collapse or forests to disappear?

The world already produces enough cereals and oilseeds to feed 10 billion people a vegetarian diet adequate in protein and calories. If, however, the idea is to feed 10 billion people not healthful vegetarian diets but the kind of meat-laden meals that Americans eat, the production of grains and oilseeds may have to triple – primarily to feed livestock.[20] Is anything like this kind of productivity on the cards?

Maybe. From 1961 to 1994, global production of food doubled. Global output of grain rose from about 630 million tons in 1950 to about 1.8 billion tons in 1992, largely as a result of greater yields.[21] Developing countries from 1974 to 1994 increased wheat yields per acre by almost 100 per cent, corn yields by 72 per cent, and rice yields by 52 per cent.[22] 'The generation of farmers on the land in 1950 was the first in history to double the production of food,' the Worldwatch Institute has reported. 'By 1984, they had outstripped population growth enough to raise per capita grain output an unprecedented 40 per cent' (Brown et al. 1995, p. 7).[23] From a two-year period ending in 1981 to a two-year period ending in 1990, the real prices of basic foods fell 38 per cent on world markets, according to a 1992 United Nations report.[24] Prices for food have continually decreased since the end of the eighteenth century, when Thomas Malthus argued that rapid population growth must lead to mass starvation by exceeding the carrying capacity of the Earth.

Farmers worldwide could double the acreage in production, but this should not be necessary.[25] Better seeds, more irrigation, multi-cropping, and additional use of fertiliser could greatly increase agricultural yields in the developing world, which are now generally only half those in the industrialised countries. It is biologically possible to raise yields of rice to about seven tons per acre – about four times the current average in the developing world.[26] Super strains of cassava, a potato-like root crop eaten by millions of Africans, promise to increase yields tenfold.[27] American farmers can also do better. In a good year, such as 1994, Iowa corn growers average about 3.5 tons per acre, but farmers more than double that yield in National Corn Growers Association competitions.[28]

In drier parts of the world the scarcity of fresh water presents the greatest challenge to agriculture. But the problem is regional, not global. Fortunately, as Lester Brown of the Worldwatch Institute points out, vast opportunities exist for improving water efficiency in arid regions, ranging from installing better water-delivery systems to planting drought-resistant crops.[29] He adds, 'Scientists can help push back the physical frontiers of cropping by developing varieties that are more drought resistant, salt tolerant, and early maturing. The payoff on the first two could be particularly high.'[30]

As if in response, Novartis Seeds has announced a programme to develop water-efficient and salt-tolerant crops, including genetically engineered varieties of wheat.[31] Researchers in Mexico have announced the development of drought-resistant corn that can boost yields by a third. Biotechnologists are converting annual crops into perennial ones, eliminating the need for yearly planting. They also hope to enable cereal crops to fix their own nitrogen, as legumes do, minimising the need for fertiliser (genetically engineered nitrogen-fixing bacteria have already been test-marketed to farmers). Commercial varieties of crops such as corn, tomatoes, and potatoes which have been genetically engineered to be resistant to pests and diseases have been approved for field testing in the United States; several are now being sold and planted.[32] A new breed of rice, 25 per cent more productive than any currently in use, suggests that the Gene Revolution can take over where the Green Revolution left off.[33] Biotechnology, as the historian Paul Kennedy has written, introduces 'an entirely new stage in humankind's attempts to produce more crops and plants' (1993, p. 70).

Biotechnology cannot, however, address the major causes of famine: poverty, trade barriers, corruption, mismanagement, ethnic antagonism, anarchy, war, and male-dominated societies that deprive women of food. Local land depletion, itself a consequence of poverty and institutional failure, is also a factor.[34] Those who are too poor to use sound farming practices are compelled to overexploit the resources on which they depend. As the economist Partha Dasgupta has written, 'Population growth, poverty and degradation of local resources often fuel one another' (1995, p. 41). The amount of food in world trade is constrained less by the resource base than by the maldistribution of wealth.

Analysts who believe that the world is running out of resources often argue that famines occur not as a result of political or economic conditions but because there are 'too many people.' Unfortunately, as the economist Amartya Sen has pointed out, public officials who think in Malthusian terms assume that when absolute levels of food supplies are adequate, famine will not occur. This conviction diverts attention from the actual causes of famine, which has occurred in places where food output kept pace with population growth but people were too destitute to buy it.[35]

We would have run out of food long ago had we tried to supply ourselves entirely by hunting and gathering. Likewise, if we depend on nature's gifts, we will exhaust many of the world's important fisheries. Fortunately, we are learning to cultivate fish as we do other crops. Genetic engineers have designed fish for better flavour and colour as well as for faster growth, improved disease resistance, and other traits. Two farmed species – silver carp and grass carp – already rank among the ten most-consumed fish worldwide.[36] A specially bred tilapia, known as the 'aquatic chicken', takes six months to grow to a harvestable size of about one and a half pounds.[37]

Aquaculture produced more than 16 million tons of fish in 1993; capacity has expanded over the past decade at an annual rate of 10 per cent by quantity and 14 per cent by value. In 1993 fish farms produced 22 per cent of all food fish consumed in the world and 90 per cent of all oysters sold.[38] The World Bank reports that aquaculture could provide 40 per cent of all fish consumed and more than half the value of fish harvested within the next fifteen years.[39]

Salmon ranching and farming provide examples of the growing efficiency of aquacultural production. Norwegian salmon farms alone produce 400 million pounds of fish a year.[40] A biotech firm in Waltham, Massachusetts, has applied for government approval to commercialise salmon genetically engineered to grow four to six times as fast as their naturally occurring cousins.[41] As a 1994 article in Sierra Magazine noted, 'There is so much salmon currently available that the supply exceeds demand, and prices to fishermen have fallen dramatically' (Lord 1994, p. 63).

For those who lament the decline of natural fisheries and the human communities that grew up with them, the successes of aquaculture may offer no consolation. In the Pacific North-west of the USA, for example, over-fishing in combination with dams and habitat destruction has reduced the wild salmon population by 80 per cent. Wild salmon – but not their bio-engineered aquacultural cousins – contribute to the cultural identity and sense of place of the North-west. When wild salmon disappear, so will some of the region's history, character, and pride. What is true of wild salmon is also true of whales, dolphins, and other magnificent creatures – as they lose their economic importance, their aesthetic and moral worth becomes all the more evident. Economic considerations pull in one direction, moral considerations in the other. This conflict colours all our battles over the environment.

The transition from hunting and gathering to farming, which is changing the fishing industry, has taken place more slowly in forestry. Still there is no sign of a timber famine. In the United States forests now provide the largest harvests in history, and there is more forested US area today than there was in 1920.[42] Bill McKibben (1995) has observed that the eastern United States, which loggers and farmers in the eighteenth and nineteenth centuries nearly denuded of trees, has become reforested during this century. One reason is that farms reverted to woods. Another is that machinery replaced animals; each draft animal required two or three cleared acres for pasture.

Natural reforestation is likely to continue as biotechnology makes areas used for logging more productive. According to Roger Sedjo (1995), a respected forestry expert, advances in tree farming, if implemented widely, would permit the world to meet its entire demand for industrial wood using just 200 million acres of plantations – an area equal to only five per cent of current forest land. As less land is required for commercial tree production, more natural forests may be protected – as they should be, for aesthetic, ethical, and spiritual reasons.

Often natural resources are so plentiful and therefore inexpensive that they undercut the necessary transition to technological alternatives. If the US government did not protect wild forests from commercial exploitation, the timber industry would have little incentive to invest in tree plantations, where it can multiply yields by a factor of ten and take advantage of the results of genetic research. Only by investing in plantation silviculture can North American forestry fend off price competition from rapidly developing tree plantations in the southern hemisphere.[43] Biotechnology-based silviculture can in the near future be expected to underprice 'extractive' forestry worldwide. In this decade China will plant about 150 million acres of trees; India now plants four times the area it harvests commercially.[44]

The expansion of fish and tree farming confirms the belief held by Peter Drucker and other management experts that our economy depends far more on the progress of technology than on the exploitation of nature. Although raw materials will always be necessary, knowledge has become the essential factor in the production of goods and services. In other words, the limits to knowledge are the only limits to growth. 'Where there is effective management,' Drucker has written, 'that is, application of knowledge to knowledge, we can always obtain the other resources' (1993, p. 45).

The reasons to preserve nature are ethical more often than they are economic. Indeed, if we assume, along with Drucker and others, that resource scarcities do not exist or are easily averted, it is hard to see how economic theory, which after all concerns scarcity, can even provide a conceptual basis for valuing the environment.

## – MISCONCEPTION No. 3:
### WE ARE RUNNING OUT OF ENERGY –

Probably the most persistent worries about resource scarcity concern energy. 'The supply of fuels and other natural resources is becoming the limiting factor constraining the rate of economic growth,' a group of experts proclaimed in 1986. They predicted the exhaustion of domestic oil and gas supplies by 2020 and, within a few decades, 'major energy shortages as well as food shortages in the world' (Gever et al. 1986, pp. xxix, xxx and 9).

Contrary to these expectations, no global shortages of hydrocarbon fuels are in sight. 'One sees no immediate danger of "running out" of energy in a global sense', writes John P. Holdren, a professor of environmental policy at Harvard University. According to Holdren, reserves of oil and natural gas will last seventy to a hundred years if exploited at 1990 rates. (This does not take into account huge deposits of oil shale, heavy oils, and gas from unconventional sources.) He concludes that 'running out of energy resources in any global sense is not what the energy problem is all about' (Holdren 1992, p. 165).

The global energy problem has less to do with depleting resources than with controlling pollutants. Scientists generally agree that gases, principally carbon dioxide, emitted in the combustion of hydrocarbon fuels can build up in and warm the atmosphere by trapping sunlight. Since carbon dioxide enhances photosynthetic activity, plants to some extent absorb the carbon dioxide we produce. In 1995 researchers reported in *Science* that vegetation in the northern hemisphere in 1992 and 1993 converted into trees and other plant tissue 3.5 billion tons of carbon – more than half the carbon produced by the burning of hydrocarbon fuels worldwide.[45]

However successful this and other feedback mechanisms may be in slowing the processes of global warming, a broad scientific consensus, reflected in a 1992 international treaty, has emerged for stabilising and then decreasing emissions of carbon dioxide and other 'greenhouse' gases. This goal is well within the technological reach of the United States and other industrialised countries.[46] Amory Lovins, among others, has described commercially available technologies that can 'support present or greatly expanded worldwide economic activity while stabilising global climate – and saving money.' He observes that 'even very large expansions in population and industrial activity need not be energy-constrained' (1991, p. 95).

Lovins and other environmentalists contend that pollution-free energy from largely untapped sources is available in amounts exceeding our needs. Geothermal energy – which makes use of heat from the Earth's core – is theoretically accessible through drilling technology in the US in amounts thousands of times as great as the amount of energy contained in domestic coal reserves. Tidal energy is also promising.[47] Analysts who study solar power generally agree with Lester Brown of the Worldwatch Institute that 'technologies are ready to begin building a world energy system largely powered by solar resources' (Brown et al. 1991, p. 10). In the future these and other renewable energy sources may be harnessed to the nation's system of storing and delivering electricity.

Joseph Romm and Charles Curtis have described advances in photo-voltaic cells (which convert sunlight into electricity), fuel cells (which convert the hydrogen in fuels directly to electricity and heat, producing virtually no pollution), and wind power. According to these authors, genetically engineered organisms used to ferment organic matter could, with further research and development, bring down the costs of ethanol and other environmentally friendly 'biofuels' to make them competitive with gasoline.[48]

Environmentalists who, like Amory Lovins, believe that the US economy can grow and still reduce greenhouse gases, emphasise not only that one should be able to move to renewable forms of energy, but also that fossil fuels can be used more efficiently. Some improvements are already evident. In developed countries the energy intensity of production – the amount of fuel burned per dollar of economic output – has been decreasing by about two per cent a year.[49]

From 1973 to 1986, for example, energy consumption in the USA remained virtually flat while economic production grew by almost 40 per cent. Compared with Germany or Japan, this is a poor showing.[50] The Japanese, who tax fuel more heavily than the Americans do, use only half as much energy as the United States per unit of economic output. (Japanese environmental regulations are also generally stricter than American ones; if anything, this has improved the competitiveness of Japanese industry.) The United States still wastes hundreds of billions of dollars annually in energy inefficiency. By becoming as energy-efficient as Japan, the USA could expand its economy and become more competitive internationally.[51]

If so many opportunities exist for saving energy and curtailing pollution, why have the Americans not seized them? One reason is that low fossil-fuel prices remove incentives for fuel efficiency and for converting to other energy sources. Another reason is that government subsidies for fossil fuels and nuclear energy amounted to many billions of dollars a year during the 1980s, whereas support for renewables dwindled in the USA to $114 million in 1989, a time when it had been proposed for near elimination.[52] A vast array of subsidies and barriers to trade protects politically favoured technologies, however inefficient, dangerous, filthy, or obsolete. 'At heart, the major obstacles standing in the way [of a renewable-energy economy] are not technical in nature', the energy consultant Michael Brower has written, 'but concern the laws, regulations, incentives, public attitudes, and other factors that make up the energy market' (1992, p. 26).

In response to problems of climate change, the World Bank and other international organisations have recognised the importance of transferring advanced energy technologies to the developing world.[53] Plainly, this will take a large investment of capital, particularly in education. Yet the 'alternative for developing countries', according to José Goldemberg, a former Environment Minister of Brazil, 'would be to remain at a dismally low level of development which . . . would aggravate the problems of sustainability' (Golemberg 1995).

Technology transfer can hasten sound economic development world-wide. Many environmentalists, however, argue that economies cannot expand without exceeding the physical limits nature sets – for example, with respect to energy. These environmentalists, who regard increasing affluence as a principal cause of environmental degradation, call for economic retrenchment and retraction – a small economy for a small Earth. With Paul Ehrlich, they reject 'the hope that development can greatly increase the size of the economic pie and pull many more people out of poverty.' This hope is 'basically a humane idea', the Ehrlichs have written, 'made insane by the constraints nature places on human activity' (Enrlich and Ehrlich 1990, p. 269, n. 29). In developing countries, however, a no-growth economy 'will deprive entire populations of access to better living conditions and lead to even more deforestation and land degradation' as Goldemberg warns (1995, p. 1059). Moreover, citizens of developed countries are likely to resist an energy policy that they associate with poverty, discomfort, sacrifice, and pain. Technological pessimism, then, may not be the best option for environmentalists. It is certainly not the only one.

## – MISCONCEPTION NO. 4:
## THE NORTH EXPLOITS THE SOUTH –

William Reilly, when he served as administrator of the Environmental Protection Agency in the Bush Administration, encountered a persistent criticism at international meetings on the environment. 'The problem for the world's environment is your consumption, not our population', delegates from the developing world told him. Some of these delegates later took Reilly aside. 'The North buys too little from the South,' they confided. 'The real problem is too little demand for our exports.'[54]

The delegates who told Reilly that the North consumes too little of what the South produces have a point. 'With a few exceptions (notably petroleum)', a report from the World Resources Institute observes, 'most of the natural resources consumed in the United States are from domestic sources' (World Bank 1994b, p. 16). Throughout the 1980s the USA and Canada were the world's leading exporters of raw materials.[55] The USA consistently leads the world in farm exports, running huge agricultural trade surpluses. The share of raw materials used in the North that it buys from the South stands at a thirty-year low and continues to decline; industrialised nations trade largely among themselves.[56] The World Resources Institute has reported that 'the United States is largely self-sufficient in natural resources.' Again, excepting petroleum, bauxite (from which aluminum is made), 'and a few other industrial minerals, its material flows are almost entirely internal' (Adriannse et al. 1997, p. 13).

Sugar provides an instructive example of how the North excludes – rather than exploits – the resources of the South. Since 1796 the USA has protected domestic sugar against imports.[57] American sugar growers, in part as a reward for large contributions to political campaigns, have long enjoyed a system of quotas and prohibitive tariffs against foreign competition.[58] American consumers paid about three times world prices for sugar in the 1980s, enriching a small cartel of US growers. *Forbes* magazine has estimated that a single family, the Fanjuls, of Palm Beach, reaps more than $65 million a year as a result of quotas for sugar.[59]

The sugar industry in Florida, which is larger than that in any other state, makes even less sense environmentally than economically.[60] It depends on a publicly built system of canals, levees, and pumping stations. Fertiliser from the sugar cane fields chokes the Everglades. Sugar growers, under a special exemption from labour laws, import Caribbean labourers to do the grueling and poorly paid work of cutting cane.[61]

As the USA tightened sugar quotas (imports fell from 6.2 to 1.5 million tons annually from 1977 to 1987), the Dominican Republic and other nations with climates ideal for growing cane experienced political turmoil and economic collapse. Many farmers in Latin America, however, did well by switching from sugar to coca, which is processed into cocaine – perhaps the only high-value imported crop for which the USA is not developing a domestic substitute.[62]

Before the Second World War the USA bought 40 per cent of its vegetable oils from developing countries. After the war the United States protected its oilseed markets – for example, by establishing price supports for soybeans.[63] Today the USA is one of the world's leading exporters of oil and oilseeds, although it still imports palm and coconut oils to obtain laurate, an ingredient in soap, shampoo, and detergents. Even this form of 'exploitation' will soon cease. In 1994 farmers in Georgia planted the first commercial acreage of a high-laurate canola, genetically engineered by Calgene, a biotechnology firm.[64]

About 100,000 Kenyans make a living on small plots of land growing pyrethrum flowers, the source of a comparatively environmentally safe insecticide of which the USA has been the largest importer. The US Department of Commerce, however, awarded $1.2 million to a biotechnology firm to engineer pyrethrum genetically. Industrial countries will soon be able to synthesise all the pyrethrum they need and undersell Kenyan farmers.[65]

An article in Foreign Policy in December of 1995 observed that the biotechnological innovations that create 'substitutes for everything from vanilla to cocoa and coffee threaten to eliminate the livelihood of millions of Third World agricultural workers' (Broad and Cavanaugh 1995). Vanilla cultured in laboratories costs a fifth as much as vanilla extracted from beans, and thus jeopardises the livelihood of tens of thousands of vanilla farmers in Madagascar.[66] In the past, farms produced agricultural commodities and factories processed them. In the future, factories may 'grow' as well as process many of the most valuable commodities – or the two functions will become one. As one plant scientist has said, 'We have to stop thinking of these things as plant cells, and start thinking of them as new microorganisms, with all the potential that implies' – meaning, for instance, that the cells could be made to grow in commercially feasible quantities in laboratories, not fields (Curtin 1983, p. 657).

The North not only balks at buying sugar and other crops from developing countries; it also dumps its excess agricultural commodities, especially grain, on them. After the Second World War, American farmers, using price supports left over from the New Deal, produced vast wheat surpluses, which the USA exported at concessionary prices to Europe and then the Third World. These enormous transfers of cereals to the South, institutionalised during the 1950s and 1960s by US food aid, continued during the 1970s and 1980s, as the USA and the European Community vied for markets, each outdoing the other in subsidising agricultural exports.[67]

Grain imports from the United States 'created food dependence within two decades in countries which had been mostly self-sufficient in food at the end of World War II', the sociologist Harriet Friedmann has written. Tropical countries soon matched the grain gluts of the North with their own surpluses of cocoa, coffee, tea, bananas, and other export commodities. Accordingly, prices for these commodities collapsed as early as 1970, catching developing nations in a scissors. As Friedmann describes it, 'One blade was food import dependency. The other blade was declining revenues for traditional exports of tropical crops' (Friedmann 1994, pp. 102–3).

It might be better for the environment if the North exchanged the crops for which it is ecologically suited – wheat, for example – for crops easily grown in the South, such as coffee, cocoa, palm oil, and tea. Contrary to common belief, these tropical export crops – which grow on trees and bushes, providing canopy and continuous root structures to protect the soil – are less damaging to the soil than are traditional staples such as cereals and root crops.[68] Better markets for tropical crops could help developing nations to employ their rural populations and to protect their natural resources. Allen Hammond, of the World Resources Institute, points out that 'if poor nations cannot export anything else, they will export their misery – in the form of drugs, diseases, terrorism, migration, and environmental degradation' (personal communication, 2 April 1997).

Peasants in less-developed nations often confront intractable poverty, an entrenched land-tenure system, and a lack of infrastructure; they have little access to markets, education, or employment. Many of the rural poor, according to the environmental consultant Norman Myers, 'have no option but to over-exploit environmental resource stocks in order to survive' – for example, by 'increasingly encroaching onto tropical forests among other low-potential lands' (Myers 1994, p. 129). Myers observes that the principal agents of tropical deforestation are refugees from civil war and rural poverty, who are forced to eke out a living on marginal lands. According to Myers, slash-and-burn farming by displaced peasants accounts for far more deforestation than all commercial uses of forests combined. Most of the wood from trees harvested in tropical forests – that is, those not cleared for farms – is used locally for fuel. The likeliest path to protecting the rainforest is through economic development that enables peasants to farm efficiently, on land better suited to farming than to forest, and to puchase kerosene and other fuels.[69]

These poorest of the poor, Myers has written, 'are causing as much natural-resource depletion as the other three billion developing-world people put together' (1993, p. 306). Peasants who try to scratch a living from an inhospitable environment, according to Myers, 'are often the principal cause of deforestation, desertification, and soil erosion' as well as of the 'mass extinction of species' (ibid.). These people 'can be helped primarily by being brought into the mainstream of sustainable development, with all the basic needs benefits that would supply' (ibid.).

Many have argued that economic activity, affluence, and growth automatically lead to resource depletion, environmental deterioration, and ecological collapse. Yet greater productivity and prosperity – which is what economists mean by growth – have become prerequisite for controlling urban pollution and protecting sensitive ecological systems such as rainforests. Otherwise, destitute people who are unable to acquire food and fuel will create pollution and destroy forests. Without economic growth, which also correlates with lower fertility, the environmental and population problems of the South will only get worse. For impoverished countries facing environmental disaster, economic growth may be the one thing that is sustainable.

## – WHAT IS WRONG WITH CONSUMPTION? –

Any of us in the affluent North who attended college in the 1960s and 1970s took pride in how little we owned. Decades later, middle-aged and middle-class, many of us have accumulated an appalling amount of stuff. The quantity of resources, particularly energy, we waste and the quantity of trash we throw away (recycling somewhat eases our conscience) add to our consternation.

Even if predictions of resource depletion and ecological collapse are mistaken, it seems that they should be true, to punish us (Americans, for the purposes of this chapter) for our sins. We are distressed by the suffering of others, the erosion of the ties of community, family, and friendship, and the loss of the beauty and spontaneity of the natural world. These concerns reflect the most traditional and fundamental of American religious and cultural values.

Simple compassion instructs us to give to relieve the misery of others. There is a lot of misery worldwide to relieve. But as bad as the situation is, it is improving. In 1960 nearly 70 per cent of the people in the world lived at or below the subsistence level. Today less than a third do, and the number enjoying fairly satisfactory conditions (as measured by the United Nations Human Development Index) rose from 25 per cent in 1960 to 60 per cent in

1992.[70] Over the twenty-five years before 1992, average per capita consumption in developing countries increased 75 per cent in real terms.[71] The pace of improvements is also increasing. In developing countries in that period, for example, power generation and the number of telephone lines per capita doubled, while the number of households with access to clean water grew by half.[72]

What is worsening is the discrepancy in income between the wealthy and the poor. Although world income measured in real terms has increased by 700 per cent since the Second World War, the wealthiest people have absorbed most of the gains. Since 1960 the richest fifth of the world's people have seen their share of the world's income increase from 70 to 85 per cent. Thus one fifth of the world's population possesses much more than four fifths of the world's wealth, while the share held by all others has correspondingly fallen; that of the world's poorest 20 per cent has declined from 2.3 to 1.4 per cent.[73]

Benjamin Barber has described market forces that 'mesmerize the world with fast music, fast computers, and fast food – with MTV, Macintosh, and McDonald's, pressing nations into one commercially homogeneous global network: one McWorld tied together by technology, ecology, communications, and commerce' (Barber 1992, p. 53). Affluent citizens of South Korea, Thailand, India, Brazil, Mexico, and many other rapidly developing nations have joined with Americans, Europeans, Japanese, and others to form an urban and cosmopolitan international society. Those who participate in this global network are less and less beholden to local customs and traditions. Meanwhile, ethnic, tribal, and other cultural groups that do not dissolve into the McWorld often define themselves in opposition to it – fiercely asserting their ethnic, religious, and territorial identities.

The imposition of a market economy on traditional cultures in the name of development – for example, the insistence that everyone produce and consume more – can dissolve the ties to family, land, community, and place on which indigenous peoples traditionally rely for their security. Thus development projects intended to relieve the poverty of indigenous peoples may, by causing the loss of cultural identity, engender the very powerlessness they aim to remedy. Pope Paul VI, in the encyclical 'Populorum progressio' (1967), described the tragic dilemma confronting indigenous peoples: 'Either to preserve traditional beliefs and structures and reject social progress; or to embrace foreign technology and foreign culture, and reject ancestral traditions with their wealth of humanism' (p. 184).

The idea that everything is for sale and nothing is sacred – that all values are subjective – undercuts our own moral and cultural commitments, not just those of tribal and traditional communities. No one has written a better critique of the assault that commerce makes on the quality of our lives (in the North) than Thoreau provides in *Walden*. The cost of a thing, according to Thoreau, is not what the market will bear but what the individual must bear because of it; it is 'the amount of what I will call life which is required to be exchanged for it, immediately or in the long run' (in Krutch 1965, p. 128).

Many observers point out that as we work harder and consume more, we seem to enjoy our lives less. We are always in a rush – a 'Saint Vitus's dance' as Thoreau called it (ibid., p. 174). Idleness is suspect. Americans today spend less time with their families, neighbours and friends than they did in the 1950s. Juliet B. Schor, an economist at Harvard University, argues that 'Americans are literally working themselves to death' (1991, p. 11). A fancy car, video equipment, or a complex computer program can exact a painful cost in the form of maintenance, upgrading, and repair. We are possessed by our possessions; they are often harder to get rid of than to acquire.

That money does not make us happier, once our basic needs are met, is a commonplace overwhelmingly confirmed by sociological evidence. Paul Wachtel, who teaches social psychology at the City University of New York, has concluded that bigger incomes 'do not yield an increase in feelings of satisfaction or well-being, at least for populations who are above a poverty or subsistence level' (Wachtel 1994, p. 5). This cannot be explained simply by the fact that people have to work harder to earn more money; even those who hit jackpots in lotteries often report that their lives are not substantially happier as a result.[74] Well-being depends upon health, membership in a community in which one feels secure, friends, faith, family, love, and virtues that money cannot buy. Robert Lane, a political scientist at Yale University, using the concepts of economics, has written, 'If "utility" has anything to do with happiness, above the poverty line the long-term marginal utility of money is almost zero' (Lane 1994, p. 7).

Economists in earlier times predicted that wealth would not matter to people once they attained a comfortable standard of living. 'In ease of body and peace of mind, all the different ranks of life are nearly upon a level', wrote Adam Smith, the eighteenth-century English advocate of the free market (1926, p. 185). In the 1930s the British economist John Maynard Keynes argued that after a period of great expansion, further accumulation of wealth would no longer improve personal well-being.[75] Subsequent economists, however, found that even after much of the industrial world had attained the levels of wealth Keynes thought were sufficient, people still wanted more. From this they inferred that wants are insatiable.[76]

Perhaps this is true. But the insatiability of wants and desires poses a difficulty for standard economic theory, which posits that humanity's single goal is to increase or maximise wealth. If wants increase as fast as income grows, what purpose can wealth serve?[77]

Critics often attack standard economic theory on the ground that economic growth is 'unsustainable.' We are running out of resources, they say; we court ecological disaster. Whether or not growth is sustainable, there is little reason to think that once people attain a decent standard of living, continued growth is desirable. The economist Robert H. Nelson recently wrote that it is no longer possible for most people to believe that economic progress will 'solve all the problems of mankind, spiritual as well as material' (Nelson 1997, p. 188). As long as the debate over sustainability is framed in terms of the physical limits to growth rather than the moral purpose of it, mainstream economic theory will have the better of the argument. If the debate were framed in moral or social terms, the result might well be otherwise.

## – MAKING A PLACE FOR NATURE –

According to Thoreau, 'a man's relation to Nature must come very near to a personal one' (1949, p. 252). For environmentalists in the tradition of Thoreau and John Muir, stewardship is a form of fellowship; although we must use nature, we do not value it primarily for the economic purposes it serves. We take our bearings from the natural world – our sense of time from its days and seasons, our sense of place from the character of a landscape and the particular plants and animals native to it. An intimacy with nature ends our isolation in the world. We know where we belong, and we can find the way home.

In defending old-growth forests, wetlands, or species we make our best arguments when we think of nature chiefly in aesthetic and moral terms.[78] Rather than having the courage of our moral and cultural convictions, however, we too often rely on economic arguments for protecting nature, in the process attributing to natural objects more instrumental value than they have. By claiming that a threatened species may harbour lifesaving drugs, for example, we impute to that species an economic value or a price much greater than it fetches in a market. When we make the prices come out right, we rescue economic theory but not necessarily the environment.

There is no credible argument, moreover, that all or even most of the species we are concerned to protect are essential to the functioning of the ecological systems on which we depend. (If whales went extinct, for example, the seas would not fill up with krill.) David Ehrenfeld, a biologist, makes this point in relation to the vast ecological changes we have already survived: 'Even a mighty dominant like the American chestnut, extending over half a continent, all but disappeared without bringing the eastern deciduous forest down with it.' Ehrenfeld points out that the species most likely to be endangered are those the biosphere is least likely to miss. 'Many of these species were never common or ecologically influential; by no stretch of the imagination can we make them out to be vital cogs in the ecological machine' (Ehrenfeld 1988, p. 215).

Species may be profoundly important for cultural and spiritual reasons, however. Consider again the example of the wild salmon, whose habitat is being destroyed by hydroelectric dams along the Columbia River. Although this loss is unimportant to the economy overall (there is no shortage of salmon), it is of the greatest significance to the Amerindian tribes that have traditionally subsisted on wild salmon, and to the region as a whole. By viewing local flora and fauna as a sacred heritage – by recognising their intrinsic value – we discover who we are rather than what we want. On moral and cultural grounds, society might be justified in making great economic sacrifices – removing hydro dams, for example – to protect remnant populations of the Snake River sockeye, even if, as critics complain, hundreds or thousands of dollars are spent for every fish that is saved.

Even those plants and animals that do not define places possess enormous intrinsic value and are worth preserving for their own sake. What gives these creatures value lies in their histories, wonderful in themselves, rather than in any use to which they can be put. The biologist E. O. Wilson elegantly takes up this theme: 'Every kind of organism has reached this moment in time by threading one needle after another, throwing up brilliant artifices to survive and reproduce against nearly impossible odds' (Wilson 1992, p. 345). Every plant or animal evokes not just sympathy but also reverence and wonder in those who know it.

In *Earth in the Balance*, Al Gore, then a senator, wrote: 'We have become so successful at controlling nature that we have lost our connection to it' (1992, p. 225). It is all too easy 'to regard the earth as a collection of resources having an intrinsic value no larger than their usefulness at the moment' (ibid., p. 1). The question before us is not whether we are going to run out of resources. It is whether economics is the appropriate context for thinking about environmental policy.

Even John Stuart Mill, one of the principal authors of utilitarian philosophy, recognised that the natural world has great intrinsic and not just instrumental value. More than a century ago, as England lost its last truly wild places, Mill condemned a world with nothing left to the spontaneous activity of nature; with every rood of land brought into cultivation, which is capable of growing food for human beings; every flowery waste or natural pasture ploughed up; all quadrupeds or birds which are not domesticated for man's use exterminated as his rivals for food, every hedgerow or superfluous tree rooted out, and scarcely a place left where a wild shrub or flower could grow without being eradicated as a weed in the name of improved agriculture. (Mill 1987, p. 750)

The world has the wealth and the resources to provide everyone with the opportunity to live a decent life. We consume too much when market relationships displace the bonds of community, compassion, culture, and place. We consume too much when consumption becomes an end in itself and makes us lose affection and reverence for the natural world.

## – Notes –

1. See Struck 1994.
2. See, for example, Daly 1992, pp. 23–7.
3. For an application of this principle to the endangered species issue, see pp. 76–7.
4. Over the course of the twentieth century, according to a careful study conducted by the World Bank and published in 1988, the relative price of food grains dropped by over 40 per cent. For this and other supporting evidence, see Eberstad 1995, pp. 7–47.
5. World Bank 1996, p. 275 observes that estimates of global petroleum reserves have increased by 43 per cent between 1984 and 1994. Since 1989, new discoveries, additions, and recisions have broadly matched the world's production, leaving total reserves basically unchanged.
6. Moore, 1995, pp. 110–39.
7. See Moore 1995, pp. 126–7.
8. See Gianturco 1994, p. 120.
9. See Goeller and Weinberg, 1976; Suplee 1996.
10. See Yergin 1992, p. 122.
11. See Ausubel 1996b, pp. 1–19.
12. See Ausubel 1996a. For further information see Solstice: the Internet Information Service of the Center for Renewable Energy and Sustainable Technology, http://www.crest.org/.
13. See Energy Conservation News 1995.
14. Lovins and Hunter 1995.
15. See Huey 1994; Castro 1987.
16. See Brown and Hamilton 1997.
17. See also Adriannse et al. 1997, p. 2.
18. See Blomquist 1995.

19. See World Bank 1996, pp. 173–4.
20. See Waggoner 1994; World Bank 1994b, Ch. 6, especially pp. 107–8.
21. See Brown et al. 1996, p. 25; Bailey 1995, p. 409.
22. See *Washington Post* 1995.
23. See also Sen 1994a and 1994b.
24. UNCTAD VIII 1992, p. 235.
25. See Smil 1993, p. 46.
26. *Washington Post* 1995.
27. Briscoe 1996.
28. See Waggoner 1994, pp. 26–7, citing National Corngrowers Association 1993 Tabulation of the 1992 Maize Yield Contest. Annual yields of biomass up to 550 tons per hectare are theoretically possible for algal cultures; yields half as great have been achieved. See also Radmer and Kok 1977.
29. Brown et al. 1991, p. 87.
30. Brown 1989, pp. 17–18.
31. See Moran 1994. For a useful survey of developments in agricultural biotechnology, see Krimsky and Wrubel 1996.
32. Cooke (1994) describes corn genetically engineered to be 40 per cent more productive and to withstand drought and poor soil conditions; see also Goldberg 1996; World Bank 1994b, pp. 118–21.
33. Rensberger 1994. For a thorough study of the prospects of improvement in rice yields in Asia and Latin America, see Lang 1996.
34. World Bank 1992, esp. pp. 30–3. The Bank states: 'Land-hungry farmers resort to cultivating unsuitable areas – steeply sloped, erosion-prone hillsides; semiarid land where soil degradation is rapid; and tropical forests where crop yields on cleared fields frequently drop sharply after just a few years . . . Poor families often lack the resources to avoid degrading their environment' (p. 30).
35. Sen, among other scholars, points out that insistence on the Malthusian belief that overpopulation and global food scarcity are the causes of famine, by diverting attention from the real causes of malnutrition, namely, poverty and powerlessness, have caused the deaths of many millions of people.

    First, by focusing on such misleading variables as food output per unit of population, the Malthusian approach profoundly mis-specifies the problems facing the poor of the world . . . Since global food supplies are more than adequate to meet human needs, the Malthusian is then led to complacency. It is often overlooked that what may be called "Malthusian optimism" has actually killed millions of people. (Sen 1984, p. 524)

    See also Dreze and Sen 1989, pp. 26–8.
36. Brown et al. 1995, p. 30.
37. Dinsmore 1995.
38. Brown et al. 1994, p. 32.
39. Harding 1995.
40. Lord 1994, p. 64.
41. Goldberg 1996, p. 63.

42. See Sedjo 1991, esp. p. 110.
43. See Sedjo 1991, p. 111.
44. World Bank 1994b, pp. 79 and 134.
45. Ciais et al. 1995.
46. For a discussion of the extent to which industrialised nations are developing non-carbon based sources of energy (thus moving to a hydrogen economy), see Nakicenovic 1996.
47. For discussion of the promise of geothermal, tidal, and other alternative forms of energy, see Kelly et al. 1993; Brower 1992; *Sierra Magazine* 1991.
48. Romm and Curtis 1996.
49. See Ellerman 1996.
50. See Brower 1992, esp. pp. 13–15.
51. For data comparing energy efficiency in the US with that of its trading partners and relevant analysis and recommendations, see Romm and Lovins 1992. For further evidence and argument, see Porter and van der Linder 1995.
52. Brower 1992, p. 22.
53. World Bank 1992, esp. pp. 17–19.
54. In a phone interview, 21 December 1994, Mr. Reilly vouched for these remarks, noting that this incident happened more than once.
55. World Bank 1994b, p. 291.
56. World Bank 1994b, pp. 13–16.
57. See *The Economist* 1992.
58. Holton 1990.
59. Berman and Alger 1995.
60. See Maskus 1989.
61. Holton 1990.
62. For an excellent account of the political costs of the sugar programme internationally, see Krueger 1990.
63. See Llambi 1994.
64. See *Sacramento Bee* (1994); *BIOTECH Patent News* (1994); *Genetic Engineering News* (1995).
65. For this and other examples, see de Selincourt 19993a and 1993b. The *Washington Post* reports that Agridyne is spending $3 million on getting genetically engineered microbes to express pyrethrum – see Lehrman 1992.
66. Lehrman 1992.
67. For documentation and further analysis, see Gardner 1996; Biyearly 1987.
68. Dasgupta et al. 1994, p. 31.
69. Myers 1991, esp. p. 243.
70. UNDP 1994, p. 2.
71. World Bank 1992, p. 29.
72. World Bank 1994a, p. 1.
73. UNDP 1994, esp. p. 35.
74. See Argyle 1986.
75. See Keynes 1963, pp. 366, 369–70, 372.

76. See Nelson 1991, esp. ch. 6.
77. See Stein 1994.
78. Aesthetic, cultural, and moral terms, of course, may also have economic and prudential significance. For an insightful discussion of normative terms such as health and integrity as applied to ecological communities and systems, see Westra 1994.

## – BIBLIOGRAPHY –

Adriaanse, Albert (1997), *Resource Flows: The Material Basis of Industrial Economies*, Washington DC: World Resources Institute, Wuppertal Institute.

Argyle, Michael (1986), *The Psychology of Happiness*, New York: Methuen.

Ausubel, Jesse (1996a), 'Can technology spare the earth?', *American Scientist* 84, pp. 166–78.

Ausubel Jesse (Summer 1996b), 'The liberation of the environment', *Daedelus* Summer 1996, 125:3, pp. 95–112.

Bailey, Ronald (1995) ed., *The True State of the Planet*, New York: Free Press.

Barber, Benjamin R. (1992), 'Jihad vs. McWorld', *The Atlantic Monthly* March 1992, pp. 53–65.

Berman, Phyllis, and Alexandra Alger (1995), 'The set-aside charade', *Forbes*, 13 March 1995.

BIOTECH Patent News (1994), 'Calgene begins world's first commercial planting of genetically engineered plant oil, November 1994.'

Biyearly, Derek (1987), 'The political economy of Third World food imports: the case of wheat', *Economic Development and Cultural Change* 35, pp. 307–28.

Blomquist, Peter (1995), 'Fighting poverty in the information age', *Seattle Times*, B5, 18 October 1995.

Briscoe, David (1996), 'Can the world feed 8 billion more people by 2025?', *The Charleston Gazette*, 1A, 28 October 1996.

Broad, Robin, and John Cavanaugh (1995), 'Don't neglect the impoverished South's developng countries', *Foreign Policy*, 22 December 1995, pp. 18–27.

Brower, Michael (1992), *Cool Energy: Renewable Solutions to Environmental Problems*, Cambridge, MA: MIT Press.

Brown, Lester R. (1989), 'The grain drain', *The Futurist* 23:4, pp. 17–8.

Brown, Lester R., Christopher Flavin, and Sandra Postel (1991), *Saving the Planet*, New York: Norton.

Brown, Lester R., Hal Kane, and David M. Roodman (1994), *Vital Signs*, New York: W. W. Norton.

Brown, Lester R., Christopher Flavin and Sandra Posted (1995), *The State of the World*, New York: W. W. Norton.

Brown, Lester R., Christopher Flavin, and Hale Kane (1996), *Vital Signs*, New York: W. W. Norton.

Brown, Warren and Martha M. Hamilton (1997), 'Running on, and on, and on:

better cars are changing the economics of driving for consumers and firms', *The Washington Post*, H1, 9 March 1997.

Castro, Janice (1987), 'Tussle over high technology', *Time Magazine*, 26 January 1987, p. 48.

Ciais, P., P. Tans, M. Torlier, J. W. C. White, and R. J. Francey (1995), 'A large northern hemisphere terrestrial $CO_2$ sink indicated by the 13C/12C ratio of atmospheric $CO_2$, *Science*, 25 August 1995, pp. 1098–1100.

Cooke, Robert (1994), 'Aw shucks, this here's great corn', *Newsday*, 9 August 1994, p. 25.

Curtin, Mary Ellen (1983), 'Harvesting profitable products from plant tissue culture', *BioTechnology* 1.

Daly, Herman E. (1992), 'From empty-world economics to full-world economics: recognizing an historical turning point in economic development', in Robert Goodland, Herman E. Daly and Salah El Serafy (eds), *Population, Ecology, and Lifestyle*, Washington DC: Island Press.

Dasgupta, Partha S. (1995), 'Population, poverty and the local environment', *Scientific American*, February 1995.

Dasgupta, Partha S., Carl Folke, and Karl-Goren Malal (1994), 'The environmental resource base of human welfare', in Kerstin Lin (ed.), *Population, Economic Development and the Environment*, New York: Oxford University Press.

Dinsmore, Christopher (1995), 'Tilapia fish farm, new in Suffolk, aims toward a growing market', *Virginian Pilot*, D2, 8 September 1995.

Dreze, Jean, and Amartya Sen (1989), *Hunger and Public Action*, Oxford: Clarendon Press.

Drucker, Peter (1993), *Post Capitalist Society*, New York: Harper Business.

Dworkin, Ronald (1994), *Life's Dominion*, New York: Vintage Books.

The Economist (1992), 'America's farm subsidies', 27 June 1992.

Eberstadt, Nicoholas (1995), 'Population, food and income: global trends in the twentieth century', in Ronald Bailey (ed.), *The True State of the Planet*, New York: Free Press.

Ehrenfeld, David (1988), 'Why put a value on biodiversity?', in E. O. Wilson (ed.), *Biodiversity*, Washington DC: National Academy Press.

Ehrlich, Paul R., and Anne H. Ehrlich (1974), *The End of Affluence*, New York: Ballantine Books.

Ehrlich, Paul R., and Anne H. Enrlich (1990), *The Population Explosion*, New York: Simon and Schuster.

Ellerman. A. Denny (1996), 'Energy polices, R&D, and public policy', in Davis Lewis Feldman (ed.), *The Energy Crisis: Unresolved Issues and Enduring Legacies*, Baltimore: Johns Hopkins Press.

Energy Conservation News (1995), 'Appliance standards are getting results', 1 September 1995.

Friedmann, Harriet (1994), 'The international relations of food: the unfolding crisis of national regulation', in Barbara Hariss-White and Sir Raymond Hoffendberg (eds), *Food: Multidisciplinary Perspectives*, Oxford: Blackwell.

Gardner, Bruce L. (1996), 'The politcal economy of US export subsidies for wheat', in Anne Krueger (ed.), The Political Economy of American Trade Policy, Chicago: University of Chicago Press.

Genetic Engineering News (1995), 'Calgene completes talks with FDA on laurate canola', 15 April 1995.

Gever, John, Robert Kaufmann, David Skole, and Charles Vorosmartz (1986), Beyond Oil: The Threat to Food and Fuel in the Coming Decades, Cambridge, MA: Ballinger.

Gianturco, Michael (1994), 'Seeing into the Earth', Forbes, 20 June 1994.

Goeller, H. E., and Alvin M. Weinberg (1976), 'The age of substitutability', Science, 20 February 1976, pp. 683–9.

Goldberg, Rebecca (1996), 'Novel crops and other transgenics: how green are they?', in Ralph W. F. Hardy and Jane Baker Segelken (eds), Agricultural Biotechnology: Novel Products and New Partnerships Ithaca, NY: National Agricultural Biotechnology Council.

Goldemberg, José (1995), 'Energy needs in developing countries and sustainability', Science, 25 August 1995, pp. 1058–9.

Gore, Al (1992), Earth in the Balance: Ecology and the Human Spirit, Boston: Houghton Mifflin Company.

Harding, James (1995), 'World Bank sees big future of fish farming', Financial Times, 15 May 1995, p. 4.

Holdren, John (1992), 'The energy predicament in perspective', in Irving M. Mintzer (ed.), Confronting Climate Change: Risks, Implications and Responses, New York: Cambridge University Press.

Holton, Sean (1990), 'Sugar growers reap bonanza in glades', Orlando Sentinel Tribune, 18 September 1990.

Huey, John (1994), 'Waking up to the new economy', Fortune Magazine, 27 June 1994, p. 36.

Kelly, Henry, Thomas Johansson, Robet H. Williams and Amulya K. Ready (1993), eds, Renewable Energy: Sources for Fuel and Electricity, Washington DC: Island Press.

Kempton, Willet, James S. Boster, and Jennifer A. Hartley (1995), Environmental Values in American Culture, Cambridge, MA: MIT Press.

Kennedy, Paul (1993), Preparing for the Twenty-first Century, New York: Vintage Books.

Keynes, John Maynard [1930] (1963), 'Economic possibilities for our grandchildren', in Keynes' Essays in Persuasion, New York: W. W. Norton.

Krimsky, Sheldon, and Roger Wrubel (1996), Agricultural Biotechnology and the Environment: Science, Policy, and Social Issues, Urbana: University of Illinois Press.

Krueger, Anne O. (1990), 'The political economy of controls: American sugar', in Maurice Scott and Deepak Lal (eds), Public Policy and Economic Development: Essays in Honor of Ian Little, New York: Oxford University Press.

Krutch, Joseph Wood (1965), Thoreau: Walden and Other Writings, New York: Bantam Books.

Lane, Robert E. (1994), 'The road not taken: giving friendship priority over commodities', paper presented at a conference on Consumption, Global Stewardship and the Good Life, University of Maryland.

Lang, James (1996), *Feeding a Hungry Planet: Rice, Research and Development in Asia and Latin America*, Chapel Hill: University of North Carolina.

Lee, Thomas H. (1989), 'Advanced fossil fuel systems and beyond', in Jesse H. Assubel and Hedy E. Sladovich (eds), *Technology and Environment*, Washington, DC: National Academy Press.

Lehrman, Sally (1992), 'Splicing genes or slicing exports? US firms' bio-engineered tropical plants may threaten Third World farmers', *Washington Post*, H1, 27 September 1992.

Llambi, Luis (1994), 'Opening economies and closing markets: Latin American agriculture's difficult search for place in the emerging global order', in Alessandro Bonanno, Lawrence Bush, William Friedland, Lourdes Gouveia and Enzio Mingione (eds), *From Columbus to ConAgra*, Lawrence, KA: University of Kansas Press.

Lord, Nancy (1994), 'Born to be wild', *Sierra Magazine*, November–December 1994.

Lovins, Amory B. (1991), 'Energy, people and industrialization', in Kingsley Davis and Nikhail S. Bernstam (eds), *Resources, Environment and Population: Present Knowledge, Future Options*, New York: Oxford University Press.

Lovins, Amory B., and L. Hunter Lovins (1995), 'Reinventing the wheels', *The Atlantic Monthly*, January 1995.

Maskus, Keith (1989), 'Large costs and small benefits of the American sugar programme', *World Economy* 12, pp. 85–104.

McKibben, Bill (1995), 'An Explosion of Green', *The Atlantic Monthly*, April 1995, pp. 61–83.

Mill, John Stuart (1987) [1848] *Principles of Political Economy with Some of Their Applications to Social Philosophy*, Fairfield, NJ: Augustus M. Kelley Publishers.

Moore, Stephen (1995), 'The coming age of abundance', in Ronald Bailey (ed.), *The True State of the Planet*, New York: Free Press.

Moran, Nuala (1994), 'Scientists engineer a fruitful harvest', *The Independent*, 24 July 1994, p. 4.

Muir, John (1912), The Yosemite, New York: Century Press.

Myers, Norman (1991), 'The world's forests and human populations', in Kingsley Davis and Nikhail S. Bernstam (eds), *Resources, Environment and Population: Present Knowledge, Future Options*, New York: Oxford University Press.

Myers, Norman (1993), 'The question of linkages in environment and development', *Bioscience* 43:5, pp. 302–10.

Myers, Norman (1994), 'Population and biodiversity', in Sir Francis Graham-Smith (ed.), *Population: The Complex Reality*, Golden, CO: North American Press.

Nakicenovic, Nebojsa (1996), 'Freeing energy from carbon', *Daedalus*, Summer 1996; pp. 95–112.

Nelson, Robert H. (1991), *Reaching for Heaven on Earth: The Theological Meaning of Economics*, Lanham, MD: Rowman and Littlefield.

Nelson, Robert H. (1997), 'In memoriam: on the death of the "market mechanism" ', *Ecological Economics* 20, pp. 187–97.

Pope Paul VI (1967), 'Encyclical of Pope Paul VI on the Development of Peoples', in Claudia C. Ihm (ed.), *The Papal Encyclicals 1958–1981*, pp. 183–5.

Porter, Michael E., and Claas van der Linder (1995). 'Green and competitive: ending the stalemate', *Harvard Business Review*, September–October 1995, pp. 120–30.

Radmer, Richard and Bessel Kok (September 1977), 'Photosynthesis: limited yields, unlimited dreams', *Bioscience* 27:9, 599–604.

Rensberger, Royce (1994), 'New "super rice" nearing fruition', *Washington Post*, A1, 24 October 1994.

Romm, Joseph, and Charles B. Curtis (1996), 'Mideast oil forever?', *The Atlantic Monthly*, April 1996, 57–74.

Romm, Joseph, and Amory B. Lovins (1992), 'Fueling a competitive economy: profiting from energy', *Foreign Affairs*, Winter 1992, pp. 46–60.

Sacramento Bee (1994), 'Calgene get canola OK', 2 November 1994.

Schor, Juliet B. (1991), *The Overworked American*, New York: Basic Books.

Sedjo, Roger A. (1991), 'Forest resources: resilient and serviceable', in Kenneth Frederick and Roger Sedjo (eds), *America's Renewable Resources*, Washington, DC: Resources for the Future.

Sedio, Roger A. (1995), 'Forests: conflicting signals', in Ronald Bailey (ed.) *The True State of the Planet*, New York: Free Press.

de Selincourt, Kate (1993a), 'Future shock; effects of biotechnology on developing countries', *New Statesman & Society*, 3 December 1993.

de Selincourt, Kate (1993b), *Genetic Engineering Targets Third World Crops*, London: Panos Institute.

Sen, Amartya (1984), *Resources, Values and Development*, Cambridge, MA: Harvard University Press.

Sen, Amartya (1994a), 'Population: delusion and reality', *New York Review of Books*, 22 September 1994, pp. 62–7.

Sen, Amartya (1994b), 'Population and reasoned agency: food, fertility and economic development', in Kerstin Lindahl-Kiessling and Hans Landberg (eds), *Population, Economic Development and the Environment*, New York: Oxford University Press.

Sierra Magazine (1991), 'Positive Energy', March–Aprtil 1991.

Smil, Vaclav (1993), *Global Ecology*, London: Routledge.

Smith, Adam (1976) [1790], *The Theory of the Moral Sentiments*, ed. D. D. Raphael and A. L. Macfie, Oxford: Clarendon Press.

Solow, Robert M. (1973), 'Is the end of the world at hand?', in Andrew Weintraub, Eli Schwarz and J. Richard Aronson (eds), *The Economic Growth Controversy*, White Plains, NY: Institute of Arts and Science Press.

Stein, Herbert (1994), '*The Washington Economist*: the end of economics as we know it', *The American Enterprise*, September–October 1994, pp. 6–9.

Struck, David (1994), 'Rich nations challenged on resource consumption', *The Baltimore Sun*, 9 September 1994.

Suplee, Curt (1996), 'Infinitesimal carbon structures may hold gigantic potential', *Washington Post*, A3, 2 December 1996.

Thoreau, H. D. (1949) [1837–1862], *The Journal of Henry David Thoreau*, Vol. 10, ed. Bradford Torrey and Francis H. Allen, Boston: Houghton Mifflin Co.

UNCTAD VIII (1992), *Analytical Report by the UNCTAD Secretariat*, New York: United Nations.

UNDP (1994), Human Development Report 1994, New York: Oxford University Press.

Wachtel, Paul (1994), 'Consumption, satisfaction and self-deception', paper presented at a conference on Consumption, Stewardship and the Good Life, University of Maryland.

Waggoner, Paul (1994), 'How much land can 10 billion people spare for nature?', *Task Force Report* No. 121. Ames, IA: Council for Agricultural Science and Technology.

*Washington Post* (1995), 'Feeding a hungrier world', A3, 13 February 1995.

Westra, Laura (1994), *An Environmental Proposal for Ethics: The Principle of Integrity*, Lanham, MD: Rowman and Littlefield.

Whitman, Walt (1971) [1882], *Specimen Days*, Boston: David R. Godine, Publisher.

Wilson, Edward O. (1992), *The Diversity of Life*, Cambridge, MA: Harvard University Press.

The World Bank (1992), *World Development Report 1992*, New York: Oxford University Press.

The World Bank (1994a), *World Development Report 1994*, New York: Oxford University Press.

The World Bank (1994b), *World Resources 1994–95*, New York: Oxford University Press.

The World Bank (1996), *World Resources 1996–97*, New York: Oxford University Press.

Yergin, Daniel (1992), *The Prize: The Epic Quest for Oil, Money, and Power*, New York: Simon and Shuster.

COMMENTARY ON CHAPTER 8

# Economic development: women's worst enemy?

Discussions of the 'special relationship' between women and nature have been a commonplace of feminist writings. A persistent theme in those discussions has been the notion that 'development' tends towards both the destruction of nature and the subordination of women. Against this background, Mary Mellor seeks to bring ecofeminist insights to bear on the question of sustainability and, like Enrique Leff in an earlier chapter, identifies the basis for an alternative vision of sustainable development.

She begins by noting that women's experience of the 'development' process is markedly different in the North and in the South. She documents the ways in which the global market economy has undermined the role of women in the informal and subsistence-based agricultural economies of the South, and how even well-intentioned schemes have served to deny them access to the basic necessities of life, besides making them prime targets for population control policies. A new threat has emerged as multinational companies move in to appropriate seeds and other genetic resources. This undermines the crucial role that women play in maintaining both the social and ecological diversity of rural economies.

The Chipko movement of the 1970s – the action of Himalayan villagers, many of them women, to prevent the felling of trees – seems to epitomise the 'special relationship' between women and nature; but some critics strike a warning note, pointing to the irony that 'the forest that the Chipko women protected is now a bio reserve from which they are excluded', and criticising the tendency to universalise women's conditions and interests. Mellor treads a middle path. She departs from Maria Mies and Vandana Shiva in her belief that women's interests may be equally at risk in indigenous subsistence cultures as in the global market economy, but she also believes that the persistent subordination of women cannot be ascribed to mere historical and social contingency. She takes the view that the link between women and nature is not a determined relation, but is a real enough product of a structure of exploitation engendered by the global market economy.

The role and treatment of women as bearers of local ecological knowledge is a case in point, and links also to our next chapter. The instruments of global development tend to involve context-free practices and methods which are divorced from responsibilities and responsiveness to peoples and to environments; they drive out and marginalise local skills, crafts and wisdom, to the detriment of both women and environment. As Mark Sagoff, too, has said, development projects can thus 'dissolve the ties to family, land, community and place on which indigenous peoples . . . rely for their security.'

~ O ~

# 8 Women, Development and Environmental Sustainability

## *Mary Mellor*

### – Introduction –

In order to discuss the position of women in relation to sustainable development, it is necessary to address some wider debates about women and environmental sustainability and the relationship of women to the development process. The case for seeing women as having a special relationship to 'nature' has been made by ecofeminists for more than two decades (Ruether 1975; Plant 1989; Merchant 1996). However, conceptions of the nature of this link vary from asserting a physiological connection between women and nature (women as birth givers, the menses following the lunar cycle) to a more socially based view linked to women's social role (as mothers, farmers, water carriers, carers). I have discussed the different approaches of ecofeminism elsewhere and will not rehearse them in detail here (Mellor 1992; 1997a).

One argument that does link all ecofeminists is a critique of the Western model of industrial/capitalist/technological development which is seen as leading to the destruction of the environment and the continued, and even enhanced, subordination of women. Subordination here does not necessarily mean outright impoverishment; the emphasis is more on the subordination of the feminine (for those who stress a direct women/nature link) or of women's work and lives (for those who stress women's social position). Subordination of women/nature reflects the superordination of the masculine in modern industrial/capitalist societies. Modern society is seen as prioritising men, culture, science and technology over women, nature, local knowledge and non-industrial technologies. It is in this sense that women and nature are linked. They are both the subordinated other in a pattern of hierarchical dualisms (Plumwood 1993). Insofar as the development process aims to bring the 'benefits' of the Western model to the rest of the world it is of central concern to ecofeminists.

Although there is a tendency in ecofeminist literature to use the word 'women' generically, it is clear that women from 'developed' and 'developing' countries stand in very different relation to the development process. Equally, there are differences between women in both contexts. However, since the development process is male-dominated, as are the economic, political and military systems that accompany it, it could be argued that women share a common experience of marginalisation within the development process around which they can unite. Further, it could be argued that women generally have less invested in the development process and, consequently, would be less committed to it. They are likely, therefore, to be more sympathetic to critiques of the development process, and more willing to take action to oppose it and to advocate alternative sustainable approaches. This logic could be taken even further to argue that where women exist largely outside the development process, they could offer solutions to the ecological crisis based on their own lives and experience. This logic has led to many ecofeminists extolling (as do many male Greens) the relevance of the experience of indigenous peoples (Salleh 1997) and those in subsistence economies that have not yet been absorbed into the global market system (Shiva 1989; Mies and Shiva 1993). Although there has been considerable attention paid to the adverse impact of development on women and indigenous peoples in the South, particularly in rural communities, development has also been challenged by women in the North through grassroots and other social movements (Seager 1993; Sturgeon 1997). I will use South and North as collective nouns rather than the more clumsy 'so-called developing/developed countries', although these are by no means accurate geographically.

In this chapter I shall look first at the debates around women's experience of development in the South and the claims that ecofeminists have made based on that experience. I shall then link this discussion with ecofeminist debates in the North. I shall argue that while the ecofeminist position is open to many criticisms it can form the basis of an analysis that provides insights into the question of sustainability.

## – DEVELOPMENT: THE CRITIQUE FROM THE SOUTH –

A large number of studies have detailed the hardship that the introduction of the global market economy, and particularly the commercialisation of agriculture and land, has visited on women in what were previously subsistence-based rural communities (Sen and Grown 1987; Dankelman and Davidson 1988; Shiva 1989; Sontheimer 1991; Kabeer 1994; Sachs 1996; Visvanathan et al. 1997). One of the earliest studies; *Women's Role in Economic Development*, was published in 1970 by Ester Boserup. Her research revealed the extent to which women in sub-Saharan Africa were engaged in agricultural work. This directly challenged the prevailing Western patriarchal assumption, based on the idealised industrial model, that men were the workers/breadwinners while women carried out domestic work within the home. This was not the case for many working-class families in industrial societies and certainly not true of women in subsistence economies. As Haleh Afshar (1985) has remarked, 'male extension workers often carry an ideological image of households with male heads, the man tilling the land and the woman rocking the cradle and keeping the home fires burning' (p. xiii). Development policies based on this erroneous notion not only did not aid women, but often made their lives more difficult. In many cases they increased their burden of work as they were forced to take on new activities from which they would not necessarily benefit. In others, it meant loss of access to land as male heads of household were encouraged to produce commercial crops. Evidence grew that women's agricultural work (paid and unpaid) was being substantially under-reported (Waring 1989). National statistics for Egypt in 1970 showed women as representing only 3.6 per cent of the agricultural labour force, whereas interviews revealed that 55–70 per cent of women were involved in agricultural production (Pietila and Vickers 1990, p. 14). Census figures for Peru in 1972 showed women as 2.6 per cent of the rural labour force, whereas 86 per cent of women were actually involved in agriculture (ibid., p. 15).

Traditionally women's access to resources was often secured by usufruct, that is rights to use common or family land and resources without individual ownership. The commercialisation of agriculture and forestry led to the 'privatisation' or 'statisation' (state ownership/control) of land (Agarwal 1997). Privatisation usually meant ownership of land by the male head of household or local landlords. Even if land was redistributed it tended to be given to landless men rather than landless women. Women's access to livelihood became increasingly dependent on the goodwill of their male relatives. As Agarwal has pointed out, development agencies tend to relate to the notion of a 'unitary household' with a failure to understand intra-household dynamics. This perpetuates the 'popular fiction' of 'harmonious households with altruistic male heads' (ibid., p. 1378). Even joint title disadvantages women as they are still reliant on the goodwill of men and are forced to stay in oppressive relationships in order to secure their access to land.

Commercialisation of agriculture and forestry also meant that there was less attention paid to subsistence needs, traditionally women's area of agricultural and domestic work. Lack of ready access to land and natural resources such as water led to women becoming increasingly impoverished and vulnerable. As Rocheleau et al. note: 'access to resources . . . proves to be an important environmental issue for women virtually everywhere' (1996, p. 291). Loss of readily accessible common land meant that women were forced to go further to look for water and fuel or risk destroying local tree cover. This, and their need to grow food on marginal land, led in some cases to women being blamed for the loss of trees and erosion of land. With men being inclined, or forced by economic circumstances, to take waged work, women were left to meet subsistence needs. Without access to adequate land, women were also forced into waged work at very low rates of pay that Maria Mies (1986) has referred to as 'super-exploitation.' As Beneria and Sen have pointed out, this process follows the logic of capitalism: 'the single most powerful tendency of capitalist accumulation is to separate direct producers from the means of production and to make their conditions of survival more insecure and contingent' (1997, p. 47). Devaki Jain, a founder member of DAWN (Development Alternatives with Women for a New Era), summed up the position in 1984:

> Economic development, that magic formula, devised sincerely to move poor nations out of poverty, has become women's worst enemy. Roads bring machine-made ersatz goods, take away young girls and food and traditional art and culture; technologies replace women, leaving families even further impoverished. Manufacturing cuts into natural resources (especially trees), pushing fuel and fodder resources further away, bringing home-destroying floods or life-destroying drought, and adding all the time to women's work burdens. (quoted in Pietila and Vickers 1990, p. 35)

The designation of 1975 as International Women's Year and the launch of the United Nations Decade for the Advancement of Women became a focus for protest about the lack of women's involvement in development programmes. The initial approach to women's marginalisation was the demand that women's economic needs be taken into account and that their voices be heard in the development process. Claims that women's involvement would increase efficiency and effectiveness led development agencies gradually to acknowledge the role that women play in informal, rural and market economies. This approach became known as Women in Development (WID). However, during the next decade it became clear that the problems of gender relations in the development process were far more complex. As the social and environmental consequences of development became more clear, the WID approach was criticised for endorsing development (Kabeer 1994; Harcourt 1994; Braidotti et al. 1994). It was also argued that women were being used in an instrumental way by development agencies to secure the implementation of their programmes rather than to further the interests of women themselves (Jackson 1994). This was particularly the case for population control policies.

One of the earliest concerns raised by the environmental movement was the issue of world population and the 'carrying capacity' of the planet. Predictably the finger was pointed at the growing population of the South, ignoring the fact that population in the North had only just stabilised after more than a century of rapid growth and spread of population through colonisation (Hynes 1993). The United States had gone so far as to tie its development programme to population control. Women were the target for authoritarian population control policies often involving invasive forms of birth control or forced abortion. Birth control became one of the most important arms of the struggle between women in the South and the imposed 'solutions' from the North, so much so that one feminist report concluded that women's 'bodies have become a pawn in the struggles among states, religions, male heads of households, and private corporations' (Sen and Grown 1987, p. 49). They called for women to have the right to control their own fertility and for recognition that the so-called population problem was largely the result of poverty and lack of resources.

The Cairo summit on population in 1994 seemed to offer some hope for women when it was agreed that encouraging women's economic and social progress (and particularly education) was the most effective way of encouraging birth control. However, as Hynes has argued, instrumentalism is still the primary motivation. Women are being offered social progress as a means to the end of population reduction: 'a woman's rights agenda has been a rhetorical means for a populationist end' (Hynes 1993, p. 47). She goes on to argue that population control policies aim for 'a reduction of the poorest people on Earth' while avoiding the need to confront the political problem of tackling the question of over-consumption in population-stable countries. Nor do population control policies address the problem of how women in patriarchal cultures are going to give effect to the empowerment that the Cairo solution promises. Most importantly, they do not engage with the problem of the education of men in the need to take their share of responsibility for birth control (Sen 1994).

The hardship the poorest women and communities were facing led to a move away from the aim of women's involvement in the development process, far from WID, a critique emerging from the whole development process. In preparation for the 1985 UN Decade for Women meeting in Nairobi, a group of twenty-two activists, researchers and policy-makers from Africa, Asia and Latin America met in Bangalore, India, to prepare an independent report on the position of women in the South. The group called themselves DAWN. The report which they presented, *Development Crises and Alternative Visions*, was published in 1987 (Sen and Grown 1987).

DAWN's survey of women's position at the end of the UN Decade for the Advancement of Women showed that women's position had considerably worsened: 'with few exceptions, women's relative access to economic resources, income, and employment has worsened, their burdens of work have increased, and their relative and even absolute health, nutritional, and educational status has declined' (ibid., p. 16).

The crises that they saw in development were impoverishment, food insecurity and non-availability, financial and monetary 'disarray', environmental degradation and demographic pressure. In particular, women's role in the provision of basic needs was being severely undermined. Equally the interlocking of women's social and economic marginalisation and the degradation of the environmental was becoming clear. Commercial development had failed to take account not only of the basic needs for survival of poor women but of the interdependence of ecosystems. Loss of fertile land, damming of water courses and tree-felling all contributed to the crisis of survival for women and for the natural environment. DAWN argued that, as rural women were at the centre of the food fuel water crisis, a coherent and integrated policy to meet that crisis would need to have women, particularly poor landless women, at its centre. Carolyn Sachs, writing nearly ten years later, found that the situation had not improved and that 'rural women in most regions of the world can no longer rely completely on subsistence activities and male wages to support their families.' In fact women were leaving rural areas, driven out by 'patriarchal authority, increased workloads, confined sexuality, heightened poverty' (Sachs 1996, p. 178).

In the 1990s, new dangers have emerged for traditional rural communities in the growth of biotechnology (Abramovitz 1994). International companies are patenting seeds and other genetic material in a process that Salleh has called cellular bio-prospecting (1996, p. 145). Campaigns against genetic and reproductive engineering have been launched by organisations such as FINRRAGE (Feminist International Network of Resistance to Reproductive and Genetic Engineering). From an ecofeminist perspective, Maria Mies and Vandana Shiva have condemned the new technologies of reproductive and genetic engineering outright: 'We can no longer argue about whether reproductive or genetic technology as such is good or bad; the very basic principles of this technology have to be criticised no less than its methods' (1993, p. 175). Shiva sees the new technologies as a fundamental threat to the freedom of humanity and nature: 'Biotechnology . . . makes it possible to colonise and control that which is autonomous free and self-regenerative . . . the seed, women's bodies as sites of regenerative power are, in the eyes of capitalist patriarchy, among the last colonies' (Shiva 1994, p. 129). Such 'colonisation', she argues, will necessarily lead to loss of biodiversity and this will in turn destroy cultural diversity as they go hand in hand: 'Diversity is the characteristic of nature and the basis of ecological stability. Diverse ecosystems give rise to diverse life forms and to diverse cultures. The co-evolution of cultures, life forms and habitats has conserved the biological diversity on this planet' (Mies and Shiva 1993, p. 65).

The evidence of rural depopulation presented by Carolyn Sachs (1996) would seem to show that ecological, economic and social diversity is being lost in the South in the same way that it has been destroyed in the North. Shiva (1994) sees women playing a particularly important role in the maintenance of diversity, particularly of knowledge through their subsistence work in rural communities. Abramovitz has also argued for recognition of 'the vital role women play in understanding and managing the living diversity of their surroundings, and the importance of that diversity to sustaining women and the families they support' (1994, p. 198). A similar point is made by Sachs (1996).

## – WOMEN AND ENVIRONMENT IN THE SOUTH –

Following growing evidence of women's increasingly marginal position in rural areas and the problems of a deteriorating environment, these concerns were brought together by activist groups such as DAWN under the banner of Women, Environment and Development (WED). For some ecofeminists this took the form of a claim that women in rural subsistence communities had a knowledge and awareness which could provide a focus for a radical critique of Western development. A particularly strong case is made by Vandana Shiva (1994), supported by Maria Mies (Mies and Shiva 1993). Shiva's argument is partly based on the assertion of an essentialised 'Feminine' that women embody, and partly on women's social responsibility for subsistence work. Mies and Shiva draw their inspiration on both aspects from women's involvement in grassroots campaigns over development issues that have been taking place for more than twenty years. In particular, they draw upon their experience of the Chipko movement:

These oak trees,
save and worship them,
because
their roots store water,
their leaves have milk and fodder,
the breeze blows cool
over the beautiful rhododendron flower.
(Song of the women of Gadkharkh village in the Himalayas, in Dankelman and Davidson 1988, p. 58)

From the mid-1970s the women (and men) of the Himalayas have voiced their concern about the impact of commercialisation upon their communities in what became known as the Chipko movement. Chipko, meaning hugging in Hindi, gained worldwide publicity in the mid 1970s through the action of Himalayan villagers (mainly women) hugging trees to prevent them from being felled. Shiva has argued that the role of women in the movement was vital: 'environmental movements like the Chipko have become historical landmarks because they have been fuelled by the ecological insights and political and moral strengths of women' Shiva 1989, p. 67). She claims that for poor rural women of the South, their link with the natural world is the reality of their daily lives; all struggle is ecological struggle. At the heart of the women's campaign in the Chipko movement was not only a protest against commercial felling, but the fact that while commercial pine or eucalyptus plantations provided work for some villagers (mainly men), they did not meet the needs of women who were almost all involved in cultivation and relied on trees for fuel-wood and fodder for animals. This difference between men's and women's interests is for Shiva what makes women's involvement in Chipko both 'ecological *and* feminist' (ibid., p. 76; italics in the original).

For Joni Seager the Chipko 'symbolizes Third World resistance to misdirected "international development" . . . [and] has come to symbolize a struggle for autonomy from the stranglehold that Western reductionist science has come to have on resource management' (1993, pp. 266–7). As Bina Agarwal points out, 'it is women of poor, rural households who are most adversely affected and who have participated actively in ecology movements' (1992, p. 150). She notes a spreading grass-roots resistance to inequality and environmental destruction and argues that women's militancy is more linked to family survival issues than that of men (ibid., p. 151).

However, although Agarwal shares with Mies and Shiva an appreciation of the commitment of the women of the Chipko movement, she is concerned about some of the implications of Mies and Shiva's approach. Shiva has argued that rural women have a particular understanding of their ecosystem and that this knowledge is in danger of being destroyed. With Mies she argues strongly against the incursion of the global market economy and argues instead for a preservation of subsistence economies to preserve both cultural and biological diversity. This approach has raised concerns for other feminists for a number of reasons. It puts considerable responsibility onto rural women; it is in danger of uncritically upholding traditional patriarchal societies and it appears to essentialise women (Jackson 1994; 1995).

Like the WID approach which saw women as making a substantial contribution to the development process, the WED approach is also in danger of seeing women as the saviours of the environment. WED has challenged the idea of women as 'victims' and pointed instead to the strengths and resilience of women at the grass roots and the benefits of the special knowledge and experience that they have. Women, having ceased to be seen as victims, are coming to be seen as the solution: 'The prevailing image of women as agents fighting the effects of the global ecological crisis casts them as *the* answer to the crisis: women as privileged knowers of natural processes, resourceful and "naturally" suited to provide the "alternative" ' (Hausler 1994, p. 149).

Cecile Jackson claims that 'for the World Bank women have become the means by which environmental ends are achieved' (1994, p. 114). She sees women's burden of work being increased by the assumption that women will altruistically look after trees or carry out soil conservation work. Jackson argues strongly against the assumption that the interests of women and the environment are compatible; in fact there is likely to be 'a clash more frequently than a complementarity of environmental interests and women's gender interests' (ibid., p. 116). She points to evidence of rural women opposing conservationist strategies and asks why it is the poor who are targeted in sustainable development programmes. She fears that there is a 'romanticization of poverty' in ecofeminist thinking and points to the irony that the forest the Chipko women protected is now a bio reserve from which they are excluded (1996, p. 153).

Concerns about the romanticisation of women in the South is also expressed by Braidotti et al. (1994) who have also criticised the tendency to treat all women in the South as having the same experience and potential.

From a postmodern perspective, they argue that a new totalising image of the valiant 'Third World Woman' is being presented that deflects attention from divisions between women. Agarwal (1992) and Jackson (1995) have expressed a similar concern that an overemphasis on women's involvement in movements like the Chipko will give a false impression of an explicitly feminist commitment rather than reflecting women's involvement in peasant movements generally. Agarwal (1992) is also concerned that a critique of class and property relations will become lost in the emphasis on gender.

Braidotti et al. join Jackson and Agarwal in being concerned that an uncritical celebration of grass-roots movements would deflect attention from the inequality and oppressiveness, particularly towards women, in traditional communities. They criticise 'the tendency to idealize everything local and traditional while glossing over indigenous structures of exploitation and domination that were in place before the advent of development' (Braidotti et al. 1994, p. 112). Cecile Jackson points to the fact that 'eco-order' can be constructed on structures of inequality such as caste (1994, p. 136).

The ecofeminist claim of a link between the subordination of women and the destruction of nature is potentially undermined by such critiques. Jackson accuses ecofeminism of gender-blindness, the failure to see that masculinity and femininity are 'relational, socially constructed, culturally specific and negotiated categories' (ibid., p. 125). She argues that ecofeminism feminises nature while naturalising women, and she shares the postmodernist concern that this falsely universalises women's conditions and interests. For Jackson, 'poor women may be more or less environment-friendly in their behaviour than poor men or rich men/women depending on their rights, responsibilities, knowledges and bargaining positions within households and communities' (ibid., p. 129). To avoid what she sees as the essentialist and orientalist assumptions about peoples and nature that seem to be implicit in the notion of 'women' in the development context (ibid., p. 115), Jackson argues for a gender analysis that reflects the distribution of gender relations and activities in particular historical and social circumstances.

While I have some sympathy with this view, Jackson's preference for gender analysis has the effect of removing the specificity of women's position in the development process. It also has the effect of disembodying the analysis; sex is taken out of gender. While it is important not to naturalise gender relations in any determinist way, the notion that they are socially constructed and culturally specific cannot explain why gender inequality is, and has been, so universally subordinating of women. Gender inequality as a process demands an explanation that is more structurally and materially based than the notion of 'negotiated categories.'

Maria Mies (1986) has shown in her classic study of global economic relations that an analysis of the structural inequality of women is central to capital accumulation. Her ecofeminism developed with Shiva (Mies and Shiva 1993) grows out of this materialist analysis. Their concern is that 'maldevelopment' is violating the integrity of the global ecosystem as well as increasingly undermining the position of women in subsistence economies. While having great sympathy for Mies and Shiva's campaign for the retention of indigenous subsistence societies in order to sustain cultural and biological diversity, I share the concern of Jackson and others that women's interests may be sacrificed in the process. Traditional societies are no less patriarchal than 'developed' ones.

## – WOMEN, ENVIRONMENT AND THE GLOBAL AGENDA –

What is common to women's grass-roots campaigns, North and South, is women's vulnerability to environmental problems and their lack of access to the centres of decision-making which cause them. While women are disproportionately represented in poor and vulnerable communities, men are disproportionately represented in positions of power and influence. This point has been made by women from the North and from the South at national and international conferences, forums and seminars (Merchant 1992; Women's Environmental Network 1989; Shiva 1994). Campaigns and conferences linking women, environment and development have increasingly brought together grass-roots activists from North and South as well as researchers, academics, radical development and environment campaigners and political activists. The concerns of women about environment and development issues were brought to the attention of international agencies during the run-up to the Rio Summit in 1992. Two conferences took place in Miami in 1991. The first, 'Global Assembly of Women for a Healthy Planet', brought over 200 women from all over the world to present their experiences of managing and protecting the environment to 500 invited delegates from development organisations. The second called 1,500 women together from eighty-three countries to prepare a Women's Action Agenda for the 'Earth Summit.' Braidotti et al. argue that the Miami Conferences represent a 'major breakthrough' because 'for the first time ever women across political/geographical, class, race, professional and institutional divides came up with a critique of development and a collective position on the environmental crisis, arrived at in a participatory and democratic process' (1994, p. 103).

In parallel to the Summit itself in June 1992, the Brazilian Women's Coalition organised a women's conference, Planeta Femea, at the NGO forum in Rio de Janeiro. The result of these meetings was an input to Agenda 21 in which the position of women was addressed, specifically in Chapter 24, where the need for the active involvement of women in economic and political decision-making was acknowledged. However, in practice little has come of the Rio process. Sabine Hausler sees the Rio Summit as 'a failure of global proportions' (1994, p. 146). She argues that the notional acknowledgement of women in UN texts means that women are now likely to become the targets for further policies of 'sustainable development' and population programmes, and concludes: 'The past experience of such development projects has shown that they put more strain on already overworked rural women without necessarily leading to much-needed wider legal and political changes' (ibid., p. 151). Achieving these changes requires a challenge to the gendered nature of human societies, North and South.

## – WOMEN AND SUSTAINABILITY –

Our traditional roles as mothers, nurses and guardians of the home and community have placed us at the receiving end of an increasingly sophisticated technology, the implications of which have become alarming in the threat they pose to health and life on this planet. The time has come for women to take a leading role in rectifying the balance. (Caldecott and Leland 1983, p. 5)

Caldecott and Leland's 1983 work *Reclaim the Earth* brought together a range of ecofeminist writings and descriptions of women's actions around the environment and peace movements. Fifteen years later the theoretical development of ecofeminist thought has deepened and expanded (Plumwood 1993; Mies and Shiva 1993; Warren 1996; Merchant 1996; Sturgeon 1997; Salleh 1997; Mellor 1997a). All are exploring the notion that the subordination of women and the degradation of the environment are linked, and that a political analysis starting from women's lives may provide a route to sustainability. However, while women-based grass-roots and activist campaigns around environmental issues are emerging across the world, not all explicitly make connections between women and the environment. The growing environmental justice movement in the United States, for example, reflects campaigns on the issue of toxic waste and dangerous production by the poor, Black, Hispanic and native American neighbourhoods in which they are sited (Hofrichte 1993). Even if women are over-represented among the poor, and disproportionately take part in these grass-roots struggles, does this mean gender should be prioritised above class and race?

Joni Seager, who has expressed doubts about some of the excesses of ecofeminism, notes that women are the 'backbone' of virtually all environmental organisations in the US. They account for 60–80 per cent of members in paid-up groups are and even more highly represented in grass-roots groups (Seager 1996, p. 271). She also argues that 'women's participation often changes the nature of environmental discourse by introducing new concerns and ways of expressing them' (ibid., p. 273). Seager also notes that most women who get involved in grass-roots movements have often not been active before and have to run the gauntlet of accusations of ignorance and hysteria from 'experts' and officials, and even their own male relatives: 'the grassroots environmental movement expands our sense not only of what is possible, but of what is necessary. It is a movement that is fuelled by persistence, resistance, stubbornness, passion and outrage. Around the world, it is the story of "hysterical housewives" taking on "men of reason" – in the multitude of guises in which they each appear' (1993, p. 280).

Within industrialised societies, feminists have focused upon the gendered assumptions that lie behind the scientific and technological claims of the 'men of reason.' Science and reason are seen as superior to folk knowledge, feelings and personal experiences; love and knowledge are seen as incompatible (Rose 1994). Human artefacts are valued over natural processes and the separateness of humanity from its natural context is emphasised. Humanity becomes associated with a disembodied notion of 'Man.' Human societies are disembedded from their ecological hinterland. Economic systems are represented by the disembedded notion of the corporation and the disembodied 'economic man' (Mellor 1997b). Corporations only take account of costs that are integral to their own functioning. Wherever possible, the consequences of production are externalised, from waste products to the need to care for old or sick workers. The case for acknowledging environmental externalities has been well made within the Green movement, although it has yet to become a serious political reality. The position for women is less acknowledged. The construction of the 'public' world of work and consumption, politics and leisure, ignores the problems of human embodiment. There is little room for the young, the old, the sick, people with disabilities or the daily and routine activities of human life. These are all ushered into the private world of domestic and personal life. Sex/gender is at the heart of the public/private divide. Failure to see the needs of the privatised individual leads to societies where children cannot play out of doors because the design of communities and the predominance of work-oriented transport make the external world too dangerous.

For Seager, women as 'close observers of their local environments' (1996,

p. 281) have a gut feeling if things are going wrong, as their knowledge is based on 'lived expertise' (ibid., p. 283). Aware of the issue of women's differences, Seager does still see a commonality at the heart of women's experience: 'if there is a universalism of "women's voice" on the environment this may reflect a certain universalism in women's social location' (ibid., p. 280). Women have common experiences of unremunerated and obligated work whether in the household, in subsistence agriculture or in the wider family or community. Elsewhere I have called this 'imposed altruism' (Mellor 1992, p. 252). Women's work tends to be supportive, caretaking, replenishment work. It is this low-level labouring work that creates the opportunity for those less encumbered to explore social time and space. At the same time women by their association with this work are denied social opportunity. As Rocheleau et al. observe in a subsistence context: '(W)omen have a disproportionate share of responsibility for procuring resources for the household, and for maintaining the environment with limited formal rights' (1996, p. 291).

The failure to see the reality of human existence and the way it is gendered is at the heart of the damage done to women and the environment in the development process. Western conceptions of 'development' rest on notions of individual autonomy and self-determination, disembeddedness from immediate awareness and responsibility for environmental processes, instrumentalism in the treatment of people and environment, and the imposition of Western models on a global scale. The fact that women and 'nature' are marginalised by these processes is of material significance. However, to link women and the environment structurally does not have to assume that they have an identity of interests or a physiological connection. Nor does an exploration of women's distinct social roles imply an essentialist revaluation of them as somehow associated with 'women's natures.' However, if women's subordination is structurally related to the ecological destructiveness of the development process then it would be culpably remiss not to explore the woman-nature relation. Noel Sturgeon has described the collective struggles of women around environmental issues as 'strategic essentialism' (1997).

Carolyn Sachs has argued for the importance of a materialist analysis of the connection of women and nature, particularly for poor rural women (1996, p. 18). She argues that rural women are the first to experience increased workloads and health problems as the environment declines. If women's position is to be improved, development processes must lose their urban and Northern bias. Women's knowledge must be seen as important in terms of seed diversity, multiple uses of plants, multi-cropping and so on (ibid., p. 179). Rocheleau et al. also stress the importance of local knowl-

edge, of 'perspectives from the margins' based on 'experience, responsibilities and daily practice' (1996, p. 292). They argue for a feminist political
ecology that acknowledges that ecological, economic and political issues are
linked and that environment issues are survival issues (ibid., p. 289). For
women, the problem is finding the economic, political and environmental
resources to resist, and find alternatives to, destructive processes where
'command over space and gendered rights of control and access are sources
of social and political power' (ibid., p. 293).

Sex/gender is not the only dimension upon which a challenge to
unsustainable development can be made. Racism and capitalism are as
much a cause of ecological destruction. However, to identify more than one
dimension of inequality is not to deny the existence of any one of them.
Similarly, to assert the differences between women should not lead to the
denial of any structural commonalities. Materialist ecofeminism argues that
the structural inequalities between men and women create a ME-world
(male-experience world) that allows some men and women to distance
themselves and the social structures they create from the limits imposed by
natural processes and needs. These are represented by the WE-world
(women's-experience world) (Mellor 1992, p. 250). The ME-world and
the WE-world are partly ideological constructs peopled by both men
and women. However they also represent structural relations of inequality
where the subordinate groups based on sex/gender (but the analysis could
equally be extended to 'race' or class) mediate the escape from their
embodiment and the embeddedness of the superordinate groups (Mellor
1997a, pp. 188–90). These are structures of exploitation which also displace
the burdens and consequences of human aggrandisement onto the ecosystem. This is the link between 'women' and 'nature.' It is not a determined
relation, but it is not just a historical and social contingency. Without a
material and materialist analysis of the gendered nature of the relationship
between 'humanity', as represented by dominant social forces, and the
natural world, environmental sustainability is unlikely to be achieved.

## – BIBLIOGRAPHY –

Abramovitz, Janet M. (1994), 'Biodiversity and gender issues: recognising common
    ground', in Wendy Harcourt (ed.), Feminist Perspectives on Sustainable Develop-
    ment, London: Zed Press.
Afshar, Haleh (1985), Women, Work and Ideology in the Third World, London:
    Tavistock.
Agarwal, Bina (1992), 'The gender and environment debate: lessons from India',
    Feminist Studies 18:1, pp. 119–58.

Agarwal, Bina (1997), 'Re-sounding the alert – gender, resources and community action', *World Development* 25:9 pp. 1373–80.

Beneria, Lourdes, and Gita Sen (1997), 'Accumulation, reproduction and women's role in economic development: Boserup revisited', in Nalini Visvanathan, Lynn Duggan, Laurie Nisonoff and Nan Wiegersma (eds), *The Women, Gender and Development Reader*, London: Zed Press.

Boserup, Ester (1970), *Women's Role in Economic Development*, New York: St Martins Press.

Braidotti, Rosi, Ewa Charkiewicz, Sabine Hausler, and Saskia Wieringa (1994), *Women, the Environment and Sustainable Development*, London: Zed Press.

Caldecott, Leonie and Stephanie Leland (1983) eds, *Reclaim the Earth*, London: The Women's Press.

Dankelman, Irene, and Joan Davidson (1988), *Women and Environment in the Third World*, London: Earthscan.

Harcourt, Wendy (1994) ed., *Feminist Perspectives on Sustainable Development*, London: Zed Press.

Hausler, Sabine (1994), 'Women and the politics of sustainable development', in Wendy Harcourt (ed.), *Feminist Perspectives on Sustainable Development*, London: Zed Press.

Hofrichter, Richard (1993) ed., *Toxic Struggles*, Philadelphia: New Society Publishers.

Hynes, Patricia (1993), *Taking Population Out of the Equation*, Amherst: Institute of Women and Technology.

Jackson, Cecile (1994), 'Gender analysis and environmentalisms', in Michael Redclift and Ted Benton (eds), *Social Theory and the Global Environment*, London: Routledge.

Jackson, Cecile (1995), 'Radical environmental myths: a gender perspective', *New Left Review* 210, pp. 124–40.

Jackson, Cecile (1996), 'Still stirred by the promise of modernity', *New Left Review* 217: 148-54.

Kabeer, Naila (1994), *Reversed Realities*, London: Verso.

Mellor, Mary (1992), *Breaking the Boundaries*, London: Virago.

Mellor, Mary (1997a), *Feminism and Ecology*, Cambridge and New York: Polity Press and New York University Press.

Mellor, Mary (1997b), 'Women, nature and the social construction of "economic man" ', *International Journal of Ecological Economics* 20, pp. 129–40.

Merchant, Caroly (1992), *Radical Ecology*, London: Routledge.

Merchant, Carolyn (1996), *Earthcare*, London: Routledge.

Mies, Maria (1986), *Patriarchy and Accumulation on a World Scale*, London: Zed Press.

Mies, Maria, and Vandana Shiva (1993), *Ecofeminism*, London: Zed Press.

Pietila, Hilkka, and Jeanne Vickers (1990), *Making Women Matter*, London: Zed Press.

Plant, Judith (1989) ed., *Healing the Wounds: The Promise of Ecofeminism*, London: Green Print.

Plumwood, Val (1993), *Feminism and the Mastery of Nature*, London: Routledge.

Rocheleau, Dianne, Barbara Thomas-Slayter, and Ester Wangari (1996) eds, *Feminist Political Ecology*, London: Routledge.

Rose, Hilary (1994), *Love, Power and Knowledge*, Cambridge: Polity Press.

Ruether, Rosemary Radford (1975), *New Woman, New Earth*, New York: The Seabury Press.

Sachs, Carolyn (1996), *Gendered Fields*, Boulder: Westview.

Salleh, Ariel (1996), 'An ecofeminist bio-ethic and what post-humanism really means', *New Left Review* 217, pp. 138–47.

Salleh, Ariel (1997), *Ecofeminism as Politics*, London: Zed Press.

Seager, Joni (1993), *Earth Follies*, London: Earthscan.

Seager, Joni (1996), 'Hysterical housewives and other mad women', in Dianne Rocheleau, Barbara Thomas-Slayter and Ester Wangari (eds), *Feminist Political Ecology*, London: Routledge.

Sen, Gita (1994), 'Women, poverty and population: issues for the concerned environmentalist', in Wendy Harcourt (ed.), *Feminist Perspectives on Sustainable Development*, London: Zed Press.

Sen, Gita, and Carem Grown (1987), *Development crises and alternative visions*, New York: Monthly Review.

Shiva, Vandana 1989), *Staying Alive*, London: Zed Press.

Shiva, Vandana (1994), 'The seed and the earth: biotechnology and the colonisation of regeneration', in Vandana Shiva (ed.), *Close to Home*, Philadelphia: New Society Publishers.

Sontheimer, Sally (1991) ed., *Women and the Environment: A Reader*, London: Earthscan.

Sturgeon, Noel (1997), *Ecofeminist Natures*, London: Routledge.

Visvanathan, Nalini, Lynn Duggan, Laurie Nisonoff, and Nan Wiegersma (1997) eds, *The Women, Gender and Development Reader*, London: Zed Press.

Waring, Marilyn (1989), *If Women Counted*, London: Macmillan.

Warren, Karen J. (1994) ed., *Ecological Feminism*, London: Routledge.

Warren, Karen J. (1996) ed., *Ecological Feminist Philosophies*, Bloomington: Indiana University Press.

Women's Environmental Network (1989) *Women, Environment, Development Seminar Report*, London: WEN.

# Local knowledge:
## no basis for universal prescriptions

Local or indigenous knowledge is commonly referred to, but rarely explained. Roy Ellen makes good the omission in full measure. He begins by charting the various ways in which the term 'local' or 'indigenous' knowledge is used and identifies some of its leading characteristics. Thus, it is oral and empirical rather than written and theoretical, and tends to reside not so much in individual people as in the practices and interactions in which they engage. Before the rise of modern science, Ellen records, the boundaries between 'science' and folklore were permeable, and even after its rise, official science made extensive if unacknowledged use of local and indigenous knowledge. Only in the twentieth century, when science had become institutionalised in laboratories and universities, did the attitude develop that 'folk' knowledge was to be superseded and put aside.

Ellen dates the rediscovery and resurgence of interest in indigenous knowledge to the 1960s, when it was at first portrayed in an idealised and romantic form. The harnessing of indigenous knowledge to the sustainability agenda belongs to the subsequent period but still, in his view, harbours a 'depleted vision.' He is critical of the way in which indigenous cultures are held up as models of sustainable living, and of the way that indigenous knowledge is mistaken for a set of insights or techniques capable of being universally applied, instead of being recognised as what Ellen calls a 'performance', suited to a particular occasion (and location).

Moving through examples of forest-fallow cultivation, the gathering of forest products, fishing regimes and the farming of starch staples, Ellen demonstrates the highly context-specific character and varied effectivenesss of traditional practices. He identifies, as the most important lesson to be learned from his discussion, that the contrast commonly drawn between Western science and indigenous knowledge – usually to the advantage of the former – is misconceived. It treats indigenous knowledge as if it were all of a piece, and obscures the fact that Western science is itself a form of indigenous knowledge, anchored in its own socio-economic milieu.

A parting thought is that if indigenous knowledge has a role to play in achieving sustainable development at a global level, and if codifications and abstractions of such knowledge precisely negate its special significance, then the indigenous peoples themselves had better have a role to play.

~ O ~

# 9 LOCAL KNOWLEDGE AND SUSTAINABLE DEVELOPMENT IN DEVELOPING COUNTRIES

## *Roy Ellen*[1]

### – INTRODUCTION –

Official valuations placed on the local knowledge of rural peoples in developing countries have changed considerably over a period of 500 years. From the sixteenth century onwards, Europeans depended extensively on such knowledge to create viable colonial economies, and much of it was absorbed into the Western tradition of science and medicine. However, particularly from the second half of the nineteenth century onwards, the regard for such knowledge became increasingly negative, and by the middle of the twentieth century – through a combination of ignorance and arrogance – 'top-down' development paradigms and educational agendas were routinely bereft of local expertise and relevance. The 1960s began to see a change in this, both for ideological and for pragmatic reasons. An alternative green politics enthused about the environmental wisdom locked in traditional eco-cosmologies, while hard-headed technocrats espoused 'farmer-first' and participatory rural development in the hope that these approaches would succeed where previous ones had palpably failed.

This chapter begins by addressing the difficulties in defining 'local knowledge', or any of its commonly-met cognates, such as 'indigenous knowledge.' It continues by exploring, first, the historical denial of the value of local knowledge and, then, its subsequent resurgence. It examines the difficulties of blanket endorsement of local knowledge as an appropriate means of achieving sustainable development and, in particular, the desire to identify entire cultural traditions as unambiguously consistent with the goals of sustainability. It argues that what counts is the practical experience of people in particular places rather than generic knowledge-bearing institutions, the selective tapping of potential embodied in traditional practices rather than the wholesale codification of abstract knowledge as a transferable solution to diverse development problems (about which we should be sceptical), as well as the preservation of diversity and flexible response in the face of environmental change, market pressure, official moralising and regimentation. These arguments are supported in relation to the literature on 'shifting cultivation', the extraction of non-timber forest products, the regulation of marine resources, and the landrace diversity of some major starch staples.

## – The terms 'local' and 'indigenous' as applied to knowledge –

What is meant by 'local knowledge' is by no means clear, and it makes some sense at the outset to draw attention to the variable terminologies, definitions and cognate concepts through their geographical, local-global and various historic and disciplinary refractions. The words we use are not insignificant, since whether we speak of 'indigenous knowledge' (IK), 'indigenous technical knowledge (ITK)', ethnoecology, 'local knowledge', 'folk knowledge', 'traditional knowledge', 'traditional environmental (or ecological) knowledge' (TEK), 'people's science', or intuitive knowledge, says something of the direction from which we approach the subject and the assumptions we make about it. However, these terms are often used interchangeably, and there is arguably enough overlap between their meanings to recognise the existence of a shared intersubjective understanding. However, if we are to move beyond the level of describing particular empirical bodies of such knowledge and their applications, we cannot proceed far without a more rigorous attempt to deconstruct the subject.

Given its conflicting, ambiguous and strong moral load, 'indigenous' might seem the least useful way to describe a particular kind of knowledge.[2] 'Native' and 'aboriginal' have similar connotations; 'tribal' is too restrictive and confuses a political condition with a distinct kind of knowledge; 'folk' and 'traditional' are less morally loaded, though 'folk' still has rather quaint associations in some quarters. Of them all 'traditional' seems to have more credibility, and is among the most common ways of describing a particular kind of cultural other. Like the rest of the terms, it derives its meanings from variations on the modern/traditional, scientific/folk dualisms, which we have quite rightly learned to treat with suspicion. Although 'local' may seem to be the most acceptable appellation, apparently devoid of moral content, politically neutral, and referring only to a population in a specific place, it is problematic because it fails to make certain distinctions which those academically and practically concerned with such knowledge take for granted, and because the power of discourse fails to maintain its neutrality. Thus, the knowledge used by a local population might well combine the insights of ancestral knowledge, practical experience, the knowledge of other neighbouring local peoples, regional scholarly traditions, or scientific or official knowledge acquired through, say, agricultural extension officers, government departments, television, or whatever. Just how local does local knowledge have to be? Alternatively, 'local' may simply be used as a politically correct euphemism, in which case no clarity is achieved. In the discourse on sustainable development, part of the issue is precisely that local knowledge has a particular set of qualities – those we associate with tradition, folk, indigenous, intuition, informality – in contrast with that formal knowledge which emanates from laboratories, research stations, government offices and NGOs.[3]

At this stage, it is convenient to have some standard by which to operationalise a few arguments. To this end we can at least provisionally list some of the more commonly asserted characteristics of what I shall call here 'indigenous knowledge' (IK for short), aware of the drawbacks of the term and of all possible alternatives.

IK is local: it is rooted to a particular place and set of experiences, and generated by people living in those places; it is orally transmitted, or transmitted through imitation and demonstration; it is the consequence of practical engagement in everyday life, and is constantly reinforced by experience and trial and error; it is empirical rather than theoretical knowledge. To some extent, its oral character hinders the kind of organisation necessary for the development of true theoretical knowledge; it is characteristically repetitious, though such redundancy aids retention and reinforces ideas; it is fluid, constantly changing, being created as well as replicated, discovered as well as lost; it is characteristically shared to a much greater degree than other forms of scientific knowledge, though its distribution is socially clustered within a population, divided by gender and age, for example, and preserved through the memories of different individuals. Specialists may exist by virtue of experience, but also by virtue of ritual or political authority. Although it may be focused on particular individuals and may achieve a degree of coherence in rituals and other symbolic constructs, the distribution of IK is always fragmentary; it does not exist in its totality in any one place or individual. Indeed, to a considerable extent it is devolved not in individuals at all, but in the practices and interactions in which people themselves engage. Despite claims for the existence of culture-wide (indeed universal) abstract classifications of knowledge based on non-functional criteria, where IK is at its densest and directly applicable, its organisation is essentially functional. Finally, IK is character-istically situated within broader cultural traditions; separating the technical from the non-technical, the rational from the non-rational is problematic.

## – A SHORT HISTORY OF
### INDIGENOUS ENVIRONMENTAL KNOWLEDGE –

Using this rather crude checklist of characteristics, we are now in a position to examine a number of features of critical relevance.

First of all we need to note that the distinctions between the West and the rest, scientific and folk, are historically permeable. Much Western science and technology, for example, finds its origins in European folk knowledge (such as herbal cures), while from the earliest times ideas and practices have flowed into Europe from other parts of the world, and *vice versa*. By the later middle ages, however, and the beginnings of modern European global expansion, there emerged a self-consciousness about the desirability of obtaining new knowledge. We can see this process at work in recent scholarship relating to European scientific interests in India and Indonesia.[4]

During the nineteenth and twentieth centuries, local knowledge was increasingly systematically tapped and codified by Europeans. Such 'rou-tinisation' resulted in the publication of scientific accounts of new species and revisions of classifications which, ironically, depended upon a set of diagnostic and classificatory practices which though represented as Western science, had been derived from earlier codifications of indigenous knowl-edge. Numerous encyclopedic inventories began to appear, such as George Watt's *Dictionary of the Economic Products of India* (1889–96). In this way the European relationship with local non-Western knowledge was, paradoxi-cally, to acknowledge its importance through scholarly and technical appropriation, and yet somehow to deny it by reordering it in cultural schemes which linked it to an explanatory system proclaimed as Western. While on a personal level, scientists may have acknowledged the contribu-tions of their local informants, at the professional level the cultural influences which those same informants represented were mute.

If, in the context of late European colonial scientific fieldwork, traditional knowledge was evident but mute, it became, with the inexorable rise of modernity, 'a kind of ignorance.'[5] Tradition was something to be overcome rather than encouraged, and several generations of 'top-down' development experts, and organisations engaged in resource extraction and management in the underdeveloped world, have either deliberately avoided it on the grounds that their own models were superior, or simply never realised that it might be a resource to be tapped. The dominant model of development has been for some fifty years or more based on useful knowledge generated in laboratories, research stations and universities, and only then transferred to ignorant peasants.[6] Such attitudes are now very much on record thanks to the work of, for example, Paul Richards (see Richards 1985). However, not only has IK been grossly undervalued by Western-trained 'scientific' managers in terms of its potential practical applications, but when it was at last absorbed into 'scientific' solutions it was – curiously – insufficiently 'real' to merit any certain legal status or protection from the battery of patents and copyrights which give value and ownership to Western scholarly knowledge and expertise. Even when the knowledge was clearly being utilised, it was often redescribed in ways which eliminated any credit to those who had brought it to the attention of science in the first place. This view was reinforced by perceptions that traditional peoples often adopted wasteful, even delinquent, patterns of resource extraction, as classically exemplified in the literature on shifting cultivation (see below); and that when subsistence practices were evidently damaging, this was a matter of preference rather than an outcome of poverty.

## – THE REDISCOVERY AND REINVENTION OF INDIGENOUS KNOWLEDGE –

Since about the mid-1960s, the process of marginalising IK as outlined above has been put into reverse, and its reversed progress is indeed accelerating to a remarkable degree.[7] There are both romantic and practical reasons for this.

The romantic reasons have their immediate political renaissance in the 1960s counter-culture,[8] with the notion that traditional, indigenous or 'primitive' peoples are in some kind of idyllic harmony with nature. Such a view was initially prompted by a crisis in the modernist project of science and technology, both in terms of the increasing remoteness and arcane character of science and its perceived arrogance and negative technological outcomes, as well as its inability to explain much about the world which ordinary people sought explanations for. What this sometimes involved was the selective remodelling of exotic traditions to suit the needs of a Western environmentalist rhetoric drawn from an intellectual pedigree which favoured idealised native images.

In this new vision, indigenous peoples are given central focus because of, rather than in spite of, their cultural differences. But, as Conklin and Graham point out (1995, p. 696), this perception and consequent alliance between indigenous peoples and science is a fragile one, based upon an assumed ideal of (indigenous) realities which contrasts with the realities experienced by the local people themselves. Such assumptions are in danger of leading to 'cross-cultural misperceptions and strategic misrepresentations.' The selective reconstitution of local knowledge has often drawn together both the great and the little traditions (the scholarly and the tribal), often failed to distinguish between the two, and confused ideal symbolic representations with hard-headed empirical practice. In this vision entire cultural traditions are treated as being unambiguously consistent with the goals of sustainability. It is not altogether surprising, therefore, that this muddle has confirmed some scientists in their worst prejudices and led to the inevitable backlash, summed-up in phrases such as 'the environmentalist myth' (Conklin and Graham 1995).

Nevertheless, with the discarding of the more idealistic portrayals of the wisdom of traditional peoples, a more practical approach has emerged. This has been encouraged by anthropologists and other development professionals eager to make IK palatable to technocratic consumers and by technocrats themselves already predisposed to see a role for IK. The dissemination of this approach has been part of a rhetoric extolling the virtues of 'participation', 'empowerment', 'bottom up', and 'farmer-first.' Some measure of the institutionalisation of this version of IK is the number of networking organisations and research units.[9] One of the difficulties with this approach, however, is that we seem to end up with a theory which misrepresents the context in which certain knowledges occur and are experienced. Hobart (1993) has pointed to the limitations of development and scientific knowledge in that they ignore or undervalue contexts. By uncritically placing local knowledge systems under the umbrella concept 'indigenous knowledge', decontextualisation is necessarily implied, and the unique and important knowledge of specific groups becomes subject to the same limitations and criticisms that we make on behalf of Western science and development theories. Moreover, the tendency to define indigenous knowledge in relation to Western knowledge is problematic in that it raises Western science to a level of reference, ignoring the fact that all systems are culture-bound, and thereby excluding Western knowledge itself from scrutiny. This limits analysis of indigenous systems by narrowing the parameters of understanding through the imposition of Western categories. Fairhead and Leach (1994, p. 75) draw attention to this problem, particularly regarding the tendency to isolate bits of knowledge which are fitted into a 'mirror set of ethno-disciplines' for the purposes of analysis and documentation. By examining local knowledge in relation to scientific disciplinary distinctions, they point to how this can lead to the construction of certain aspects of local knowledge as important, while excluding or ignoring other areas and possibilities of knowledge which do not fall within the selective criteria of Western science. They argue, moreover, that this risks overlooking broadly held understandings of agroecological knowledge and social relations. So, for example, research and extension agents examining Kouranko farmers, tree-management practices in Guinea fail to take into account the farmers' tree-related knowledge, which involves knowledge and management of crops, water and vegetation succession, as well as the ecological and socioeconomic conditions which influence them. By failing to include the broader constitutive processes surrounding Kouranko tree management, extension workers risk obscuring and decontextualising local knowledge, and jeopardise the potential it may have for development on specific and general levels.[10]

Thus, in this depleted vision, IK becomes a major concept within development discourse, a convenient abstraction, consisting of bite-sized chunks of information that can be slotted into Western paradigms, fragmented, decontextualised: a kind of quick fix if not a panacea. Such approaches are in danger of repeating the same problems of simplification and over-generalisation that Richards and Hobart identify as major limitations in development theory and in science applied to development, ignoring specific and local experience in favour of a generalisable and universal solution. Furthermore, in the hands of NGOs – which in the last few decades have become significant 'knowledge-making institutions' – and within the 'universalising discourse' of environmentalism, IK has become further reified. Because environmentalist and indigenous NGOs are now an influential moral and social force, stimulating public awareness, acting as whistle-blowers and watch-dogs, and moving from the role of critics to offering policy proposals to governments, and since they often use the rhetoric of science, they gain enormous authority.[11] This process has evidently yielded results in terms of projecting a more positive image of IK.

If indigenous knowledge is inherently scattered, local and 'embedded', then the attempt to essentialise, isolate, archive and transfer it can only seem contradictory. If Western science is to be condemned for being non-responsive to local demands, and divorced from people's lives, then centralised storage and management of indigenous knowledge lays itself open to the same criticism.

Richards' analysis of knowledge as performance challenges the very idea of practices being grounded in an 'indigenous knowledge' (1993, p. 62), suggesting rather that the range of skills and strategies employed by farmers extends beyond simple applied knowledge into a 'set of improvisational capacities called forth by the needs of the moment.' He posits a 'theory of performance' which challenges the assumption that cultivation practices are evidence of a stock of knowledge from which techniques are drawn, and suggests that farmers adjust and adapt their techniques and skills according to the needs which arise at a particular moment. Thus, Hausa farmers in northern Nigeria make a series of adjustments to drought by planting and replanting different seed mixes until germination is secured, or until available resources are exhausted. The end result or cropping pattern is not, he argues, a necessarily predetermined design, but rather:

> each mixture is a historical record of what happened to a specific farmer on a specific piece of land in a specific year. It is not the outcome of a prior body of 'indigenous technical knowledge' in which farmers are figuring out variations on a local theory of inter-species ecological complementarity. (Richards 1993, p. 67)

Codifying and documenting indigenous knowledge systems could be a worthwhile endeavour if it were not for the tendency to present such systems as models or blueprints for general use, and under the broad heading 'indigenous knowledge.' Furthermore, these kinds of analyses present little more than decontextualised inventories of people's knowledge. From an anthropological perspective, such contributions are inadequate because they ignore the social and cultural context in which knowledge is generated and put to practical use,[12] and as local knowledge is analysed and documented for use it undergoes changes which necessarily result from the specific orientations, strategies and agendas of those using it, as well as the transformations which inevitably occur through translation. For example, Zerner (1994b, p. 1104; 1994a) discusses the introduction of an awards scheme by the Indonesian government for villages who observe idealised sasi customs in the central Moluccan islands. Sasi are ritualised arrangements for controlling access to natural resources on a temporal and spatial basis, including closed seasons for particular species – often those of commercial value – enforced through traditional sanctions. Zerner notes that the effect of this is to put villages in the public eye, and under the direction of local officials who are now able to get villagers to make changes regarding the management of their resources. In the same way, support groups and NGOs have been set up to observe and ensure that sasi law is adhered to.

Thus, the status of such knowledge may alter depending on whether we adopt the point of view of indigenous peoples themselves, or those of their non-Western compatriots and national political leaders. In the modern period, reliance on indigenous knowledge has been a combination of economic necessity and tradition. Many scientists, decision-makers and administrators in developing countries have internalised an essentially Western model in frequently rejecting IK as backward, something which has to be replaced. Others have always recognised the efficacy of some kinds of IK but have seen it as strictly complementary knowledge, which has little to do with science-driven development. In recent years, however, the state sector and NGOs in many countries have moved from colonial hegemonic denial towards the positive acceptance of the utility of local knowledge in medicine and sustainable development, partly for political and partly for economic reasons. IK is being rediscovered and 'reinvented', as we have seen in the case of the sasi institution described above. As partly explained above, sasi are arrangements for ritually protecting resources by imposing prohibitions on harvesting at a critical period in the growth or reproduction of the resource. In many areas, Moluccan sasi had become moribund by the 1980s, but experienced a revival through endorsement by NGOs. They were integrated into state development plans, celebrated at a national level in the discourse on development (linking, as they conveniently did, ancestral with historic resistance to colonial Dutch depradations on livelihoods), and redefined as 'people's science', as a form of resource management and conservation that was wholly beneficial.[13]

Explicit and full recognition – in developing countries and in the West – together with the rights which are deemed to accompany this, has only come with the failure of top-down approaches, with the quest for appropriate and cheap technologies for development, with the rise of ethnobotany in the pharmaceutical industry, and at a time when the environmental movement has become morally committed to the notion of indigenous environmental wisdom. No wonder then that at this precise historical moment, when IK (through the assertion of intellectual property rights) and the rights of 'indigenous' peoples in more general terms are higher on the political agenda than they have ever been before, 'indigenous' as a label is being reclaimed by the protagonists themselves in pursuance of their own interests. Individual native peoples have seen indigenous knowledge as part of their own cultural identity, and as a very concrete and politically appropriate way of asserting it. Part of the reason for this is because although the guardians of such knowledge are traditionally oriented individuals and groups, those who wish to document it are from Westernised elites or are outsiders. Thus, a very important relationship of unequal power is articulated.[14]

In this way, IK is almost placed outside culture. Thus, in their analysis of farmer experimentation in the Andes, Rhoades and Bebbington (1995, p. 298) present local knowledge as a sort of free-floating science based on individual creativity. In an effort to liberate small-scale farmers from previous assumptions which presented them as passive and culture-bound, the authors are concerned to illustrate that farmer knowledge is as much a science as that of laboratory scientists, and to separate what is 'useful' from what is not. This approach has the effect of redefining what is useful in a narrow and ethnocentric way, and externalising culture (separating it from what good farmers do), and recasting it as an impediment to successful development. Such experimental techniques are no less cultural than anything else farmers may do or believe. The failure to take into account the coexistence, of and interconnections between, both empirically and symbolically motivated criteria within any system of knowledge inevitably leads to limited understandings and perhaps even a fundamental failure of understanding about how IK operates and how it is successful.

## – LOCAL KNOWLEDGE AND
### THE ACHIEVEMENT OF SUSTAINABILITY –

I have tried to illustrate in the preceding sections of this chapter the way in which IK is constantly changing, being produced as well as reproduced, discovered as well as lost; a performative art wielded by individuals in the context of experience, shared and transmitted knowledge and informed guesses, often contradictory but always flexible and embedded. Scientific and moral attitudes towards IK are part of a history in which Western science has by turns absorbed local knowledge (both non-Western and folk European) into its own, then rejected it as inferior, only to rediscover its practical benefits. This is reflected in competing definitions and conceptions of IK in the context of contemporary theory and practice in development and conservation. The confusion in our attitudes towards local or indigenous knowledge is nowhere better illustrated than with respect to the concept of sustainability.

The concept of sustainability as we currently find it applied to development is discussed thoroughly from different angles in other chapters of this volume.[15] As applied to small-scale societies treated holistically, it effectively emerged firstly out of an empirical ethnographic literature in the 1950s which sought to redress the balance of observations which criticised the subsistence patterns of such societies as primitive, wasteful and unsophisticated,[16] and secondly – and rather later – out of a theoretical literature which attributed changeless, steady-state qualities to local cultures, stressing their adaptiveness to local conditions, and strategies which enabled them to keep within carrying capacity.[17] This latter, in turn, was founded on the equilibrium models of functionalist anthropology. Both approaches acknowledged that local peoples were in some sense aware that there were 'limits to growth', and that they adopted strategies to cope with this. Thus, with the emergence of a concept of sustainable development as a world political and environmentalist ideal, there was an understandable merging of thinking.

Recent work has tended to emphasise the active as opposed to the passive role of local decision-making with respect to resource maintenance, stressing how local peoples have increased the usefulness of their environment, not merely changed it,[18] and how cultural diversity appears to be causally associated with biological diversity.[19] At the same time – disturbed by the simplistic blanket endorsement of indigenous knowledge by some, and its reflection in the popular imagination – some studies have shown that we must be wary of enthusiasm fuelled by ideology.[20] The same studies have provided evidence to show that the actions of many local populations have historically led to resource depletion, indeed – in some cases – to system collapse.[21]

As the concept of sustainable development is intrinsically vague, elusive, overused and much abused, in relation to local knowledge it requires special critical interrogation as to whether the concept incorporates ecological, economic, social and cultural variables, or some combination of each. Economic sustainability can be achieved at the expense of ecological sustainability, cultural sustainability at the expense of economic sustainability and so on. If we are speaking of cultural sustainability then to say that IK sustains it is a tautology – that is, it is to say that culture sustains culture. Inevitably, the notion of sustainability requires negotiation over values before agreement on the best objective way to measure it can be reached, while it is always relative in the sense that no human system is completely sustainable, only more or less so. Thus, sustainable agriculture is agriculture which is relatively more conservationist, more economical, more equitable, than some other system. Moreover, globalisation and growing resource competition has increased conflict over who controls the definitions and discourse of sustainability.[22] For biotechnology multinationals investing in research on genetically modified crops, or for Green Revolution technologists before them, it is global and regional food production which has to be sustained, not the livelihoods of individual peasant families. By contrast, much literature now assumes a synergy between environmental conservation and social justice.[23] Modifying James Scott's notion of a moral economy, Dove and Kammen, for example, have attempted to give precision to this idea by proposing a 'moral ecology', which 'guarantees the basic sustainability of both society and environment through investment in exchange relations of great time-depth and spatial-breadth' (Dove and Kammen 1997, p. 91).

But although there is growing evidence concerning the rationality of indigenous farming, the anthropological literature in particular has sometimes led to the assumption that IK is always well-adapted, and the conflation of ecological and economic rationalities is increasingly common in programmes to improve sustainability.[24] Some NGOs, frustrated with the opportunistic and imprecise use of the term 'sustainable development', avoid it altogether, and prefer to speak in terms of specific goals. For others, sustainable development is a vector of 'desirable social objectives', and sustainability is 'the general requirement that a vector of development characteristics be non-decreasing over time.' Thus, 'what constitutes development and the time horizon to be adopted are both ethically and practically determined' (Pearce et al. 1990, pp. 2–3, 4). The key necessary condition here is the 'constancy (or increase) of the natural capital stock.' Such a definition is, I suppose, as good as any, but in discussing the four examples which follow I distinguish between sustainable use and sustainable development. After all, most local knowledge is concerned with short-term planning horizons, even if decisions are taken in the context of well-understood long-term ecological cycles, and has evolved in social contexts which are changing much more slowly than most do today. In terms of practical advocacy, the transition from applying local knowledge to achieve sustainable extraction in a known context, to advising on its applicability to reach a vague goal with many unknown variables, is immense.

– SHIFTING CULTIVATION –

The history of our understanding of shifting cultivation is an interesting one. Early, colonial, accounts gave it a bad reputation as an inefficient and wasteful form of agriculture which had no virtues and, it was argued, should be superseded by intensive monocrop farming as soon as possible. Its reputation began to change, at least amongst anthropologists, as a result of the work of Harold Conklin (1957),[25] who was able to show that far from being wasteful it was often the most appropriate form of agriculture for the environmental and social circumstances in which people found themselves, involving the optimal use of resources and achieving appropriate levels of output. Although Conklin did not use the language of 'sustainability', he was clearly saying that this was what the shifting cultivators of his acquaintance were engaged in. The lead set by Conklin inspired others to develop his observations. For example, Michael Dove (1983; 1985) has been able to show not only that colonial agricultural and forestry agencies had misunderstood such practices, but that there was often an inbuilt local prejudice against rain-fed forest-fallow farming by the wet-rice cultivators at the core of traditional centralised states and their modern successors. With the international Green political agenda being increasingly set by environmentalist and conservationist NGOs, emphasis in recent years has tended to shift onto the inherent biodiversity maintenance quotient of this kind of farming, the way in which shifting cultivation actively contributes towards the creation of forest and the enhancement of its ecological richness.[26]

Such arguments, however, do need to be carefully qualified. The use of the term 'shifting agriculture' itself is avoided by many because it implies that the peoples who conduct it habitually move around, and because – like 'slash-and-burn' – it has been closely associated with a negative stereotype. An alternative term, 'swiddening', is often preferred to describe forest-fallow systems, but amongst traditional swidden populations there is enormous variation in practices. The basic technique is always slash-and-burn or slash-and-mulch, followed by between one and three years of cultivation, followed by long-term forest or bush fallow. Nevertheless, distinctions need to be made between pioneer aggressive swiddeners such as the Iban of East Malaysia, and those who self-consciously recycle land over a given time period, allowing for the rejuvenation of soil nutrients and the maturing of forest cover. Differences also depend on crops grown, patterns of movement, and the extent to which farming is subsidised by other subsistence strategies.

The major problem, however, is that in a modern context the term 'shifting cultivation' is often used to describe not only the practices of traditional forest peoples, but also the slash-and-burn techniques employed by land settlers, whose use of forest is not informed by the same body of ethnoecological knowledge, and whose lives are guided by different economic rationalities.[27] Also, traditional swidden cultivators are themselves subject to market and governmental pressures which increase the amount of land under cultivation, and which replace crop diversity with specialised reliance on single cash crops and reduce the length of the fallow period. This in turn is aggravated by deforestation through logging, land clearance, and plantation establishment, all of which means that farming practices, which were once sustainable in a general sense, are no longer necessarily so.

In many places traditional swiddening practices are no longer viable because of a reduction in the population-forest ratios to levels which do not allow sufficient regrowth. However, in some areas swiddening remains the most effective use of forest and soil. In places, the cultivation of crops such as pepper and rubber, the gathering of non-timber forest products (NTFPs) such as rattan, and the possibility of adopting other starch staples, enable people to manage periodic swidden failure, and to participate sustainably in a wider market economy. Indeed, it is possible to introduce techniques to enhance swidden viability, as with Baduy planting of the leguminous tree *Albizzia* (*Paserianthes falcataria*)[28] as a fallow crop in highland West Java. This not only restores fertility to the soil rapidly, and therefore makes possible a shorter recultivation cycle, but also provides fuel, and a cash crop in the form of marketable timber. The paradox, however, is that by so doing, the Baduy are altering the ecological conditions of their own existence, reducing biodiversity, and becoming reliant on a wider market economy in order to maintain their cultural autonomy and traditional pattern of agriculture.

## – THE EXTRACTION OF NON-TIMBER FOREST PRODUCTS –

Swidden cultivators and non-agriculturalists in the tropics have long relied upon the extraction of forest products for their own subsistence. Some small populations have been able to rely solely on forest products, usually involving some modification and domestication of species, such as the planting of semi-domesticated palms, and the inadvertent distribution of other useful food trees. The collection of evidence for such practices has been fostered by the emerging approach of historical ecology, and the observation that much lowland forest on which such populations rely is effectively anthropogenic. Despite such evidence, most forest peoples have had to subsidise their diet by either growing crops in dryfields or by exchanging forest products for starch staples.[29] This dependency, whatever its historical origins, is often linked with long-standing involvement in extraction of forest products for trade, sometimes products which do have local uses, such as bushmeat, but often products which have no local value other than as trade objects, such as bird-nests or ambergris. The scale of such trade in past centuries has been highly significant,[30] and there is no particular reason for assuming that extraction was ever deliberately sustainable overall. Indeed, there is good evidence for the local depletion of resources due to over-extraction in pre-modern times. One traditional buffer against over-extraction in particular localities has been the delinreating of protected sacred forest, along the lines of the sasi principle described above, and prohibitions on particular species by particular groups in a community.[31] Sustainable extraction has also been achieved through modification of the forest, for example by planting useful trees, such as *Canarium*, *Tectona* or *Agathis*, in eastern Indonesia, transplanting sago suckers in Melanesia, or replanting the heads of harvested tubers such as *Dioscorea* in the southern Philippines.

Recent work has shown that the effective extraction of forest products in the ways described, which minimise negative environmental impacts, is only achievable given a sophisticated level of knowledge of individual organisms, of the general principles of physiology, autoecology and reproductive behaviour, and of systems of interconnected organisms.[32] Such knowledge is not abstract, but culturally embedded and linked to long-term and spatially conscious conceptions of environmental variability. Dove and Kammen (1997, p. 92) show how forest-dwelling peoples of Borneo understand the dynamics of mast-fruiting of dipterocarps, triggered by slight climate fluctuation, in places attributable to the phenomen known as the El Niño Southern Oscillation (ENSO). These events are irregular and local, but result in the mass flowering and then fruiting of different dipterocarp species, which provides a windfall source of food for humans through the direct consumption and marketing of edible nuts, and indirectly through the additional food released for game animals upon which humans are dependent. In the language of sustainability, the value of such long-term, though irregular, sources of food, which supplement normal subsistence practices, is greater than that of short-term timber extraction which destroys the possibility of the mast altogether. In recent years, market pressure has often led to the over-extraction of NTFPs, despite the existence of local knowledge and apparently ecofriendly value systems. It must always be the case that small-scale producers are periodically compelled by short-term imperatives to extract at levels beyond what their experience dictates can be maintained over the longer term.

## – Regulation of marine resources –

The use of indigenous knowledge in the regulation of marine resources was perhaps the earliest to be systematically explored, and has arguably been the most effective in its influence on policy. The earliest studies (Davenport, 1960; Morrill 1967) are more concerned with the empirical knowledge of fishing peoples relating to reproductive cycles, migration patterns and local ecology, which demonstrated that such peoples were acting in ways which were economically rational and productive given the circumstances in which they found themselves. A second generation of studies – for example, Johannes 1978 – were more concerned with how traditional practices conserved local ecologies. A third generation of studies have more to do with rational commons management, responding to Hardin's grim hypothesis in 'The tragedy of the commons' (Hardin 1968) that, left to their own devices, individuals were bound to overextract from common resources, since they had no incentive not to do so. Traditional fishing practices appeared to offer a mid-level mechanism for controlling access to collective resources, with lessons for other artisanal and commercial fisheries.[33] Some local institutions, such as central Moluccan ritualised closed seasons (sasi) have acquired such a reputation for their effectiveness that they are encouraged as models for conservation elsewhere.[34]

## – LANDRACE DIVERSITY OF MAJOR STARCH STAPLES –

Agricultural change has usually been associated with the increasingly specialised production of high-yield cultivars. Indeed, it has widely been argued that, only with the adoption of such cultivars and the technology which goes with them (fertiliser, pesticides, cost-effective equipment for land preparation, harvesting and processing) is sustainable agriculture possible in the high-density population heartlands of the Third World. However, such strategies for sustainability assume a steady economic situation, a predictable climate and a highly controlled cultivation environment. They also bring with them radical transformations in social organisation and culture. The history of the Green Revolution is testimony to this. The recent Asian economic crisis and the El Niño Southern Oscillation have thrown such assumptions back into contention. By contrast, we now find that enclaves which have maintained a range of diverse traditional landraces have often been better at buffering instability.[35] Indeed, diversification of crops in general, and varied patterns of management, tend to keep pest populations relatively low,[36] even under conditions of intensive cultivation.[37]

## – CONCLUSION –

The limits to sustainable extraction through forest-fallow cultivation, the gathering of forest products, fishing and the farming of starch staples in developing countries, are, ultimately, defined by local population density and market demand. Where internal and external factors combine to increase these to critical levels, no amount of indigenous knowledge is able to maintain sustainability. What might make sense in terms of traditional rates and patterns of extraction does not necessarily make sense with modern rates of extraction and intensification, even if this is what local people seek. However, sustainability of a productive system must not be confused with conservation of a particular habitat, and sustainable productive systems have historically often been achieved where local populations have deliberately altered pre-existing ecologies over a period of many decades, and longer, amplifying and deviating certain valued features of a system. The rice-terraced landscapes of Bali and northern Luzon are excellent examples of this.[38] Moreover, adherence to a hard concept of indigenous knowledge linked to the politicised category of 'indigenous people' often seems to imply that non-indigenous people do not have valid knowledge of the environment, and diverts attention away from IK's inherently processual and embedded character. The dangers of the reification of IK, often through codification, in some cases with the active consent of indigenous people themselves, have been stressed in this chapter; however, we also need to recognise that the underlying categorisation of knowledge as 'local', 'traditional' and 'indigenous' does nothing to address problems of power and control,[39] and may even be counterproductive.

Although IK is not the solution to all problems of sustainable extraction, it can provide us with many useful lessons. We have seen how early studies were entirely concerned with asserting the extensiveness and efficiency of local knowledge and practice against a backdrop of assumptions that West was best. A second generation of studies have tried to demonstrate what we would now describe as sustainability in traditional systems, such as shifting cultivation; while a third generation have gone even further to argue that local knowledge has actively promoted biodiversity, ecological richness, and healthy living, and that cultural diversity and biological diversity are mutually reinforcing. In a contemporary, and essentially pragmatic, context, local knowledge has been shown to be vital in conserving and preserving resources, often because it is the quickest way of knowing what there is which is worth sustaining. At a global political level this is acknowledged in the IUCN World Conservation strategy, the Bruntland Commission Report *Our Common Future*, and the United Nations Conference on Environment and Development (UNCED) Agenda 21. Agencies such as the UK DIFID (formerly the ODA) and UNDP actively promote participatory and community-based approaches and the recognition of human rights. But although Agenda 21 says that indigenous people have a role to play by contributing their knowledge to conservation and development, the UNCED process reaffirmed a strategy of global science-led sustainable development and has effectively marginalised local and indigenous peoples themselves.

And this brings us to what is arguably the most important lesson of all, namely, that the pernicious and arrogant – but often unarticulated – assumption that scientific knowledge is inherently superior to local knowledge, and must therefore inevitably replace, rather than complement and support it, is just wrong. Without detracting from what is methodologically powerful in science, or demeaning its ability to discover what is universally valid, it is – in one important sense – no more than a particular form of local knowledge. Both traditional and Western knowledge are anchored in their own particular socio-economic milieu; they are all indigenous to a particular context. We need to ask whether a hard distinction between science and folk knowledge, reflected in the failure of scientific solutions due to ignorance concerning particular cultural circumstances, is in any way helpful in terms of finding workable solutions.[40] Global-local distinctions are now blurring, and we are told that we inhabit a world of 'transcultural discourse' (Milton 1996, p. 170). If it is implausible to regard local knowledges in past epochs as discrete and pristine phenomenal entities, then it is even more implausible for the contemporary world. Should we continue to try to separate local knowledge from global knowledge on the assumption that one or other is superior in a particular context, or should we give preference to 'hybrid technologies', the mixtures of local and non-local (including scientific) knowledge upon which most indigenous peoples now rely?[41] Whatever our view on this, hybridisation is happening, and is often the immediate and realistic solution adopted by many.

But however much the boundary may erode between global and local, scientific and folk, there will continue to be a dynamic local knowledge which is informal, tacit, intuitive, uncodified, which arises directly from peoples' practical experiences. It may not have been tested with scientific rigor nor be underpinned by particular scientific theories, but its strength lies specifically in the fact that it can be applied, as well as in the fact that it is by definition embedded and, therefore, presumably not irretrievably disharmonic with other features of local culture. The most valuable thing about IK, claims Chambers (1983, p. 91) is that it is local. And if sustainability is to extend beyond narrow technical practices, it must seek to embrace cultural and social systems more generally. Furthermore, reliance on local knowledge reduces dependency, and for this reason, and because it places value on what people understand, practice and own, it is also empowering.

## – Notes –

1. The paper has been written as part of the programme of work funded by the European Commission D-G 8, Avenir des Peuples des Forêts Tropicales (APFT). It draws extensively on Ellen and Harris 1997 (*Concepts of Indigenous Environmental Knowledge in Scientific and Development Studies Literature*), the first version of which appeared as an APFT Working Paper. I would like to register the important contribution of Holly Harris to this earlier work and, therefore, to the present chapter.
2. The difficulty is usually articulated in this way: those to whom we attribute indigenous knowledge must be 'indigenous' people, and yet the terminological difficulties we confront in saying as much uncover a veritable semantic, legal, political and cultural minefield. Moreover, it is impossible to use 'indigenous'

in any morally neutral or apolitical way. Peoples identify themselves as indigenous to establish rights and to protect their interests, NGOs are established to support them, and government departments to administer them. At the same time, governments claim that peoples so labelled are no more or less indigenous than other minorities or majorities under their jurisdiction. This, for example, is the very clear view of the Indonesian government. Although it may be convenient to seek a technical definition of indigenousness in terms of prior occupancy, length of occupancy, a capacity to remain unchanged, or whatever, such matters are seldom politically neutral. Additionally, the distinction indigenous/non-indigenous has many highly specific regional and historical connotations which are not always appropriate to particular cultural or political contexts. Some, indeed, argue that the term 'indigenous' forces us into an oppositional logic of 'us and them', while others assert that the category of IK is wholly compromised by the 'hegemonic opposition' of the privileged 'us' to the subordinated 'them', and therefore is morally objectionable as well as being practically useless. For Posey, indigenous people are 'indigenous and local communities embodying traditional lifestyles' (1996, p. 7), thus indicating the inevitable immanence of tautology.

3. See also Sillitoe 1998.
4. Ellen and Harris 1997.
5. Hunn 1993, p. 13.
6. Chambers and Richards 1995, p. xiii.
7. Consider, for example, a selection of just the most recent collections in this genre (including four with an identical main title): Berkes 1992 (*Traditional Ecological Knowledge*); Inglis 1993 *Traditional Ecological Knowledge*; Johannes 1989 (*Traditional Ecological Knowledge*); Johnson 1992 (*Lore*); Warren et al. 1995 (The Cultural Dimension of Development); Williams and Baines 1993 (*Traditional Ecological Knowledge*).
8. Ellen 1986; also Conklin and Graham 1995. For one example of the many books promoting generic images of 'primitive environmental wisdom' or 'ecological edens', see Hughes 1983.
9. See Warren et al. 1995, pp. xv–xviii, 426–516.
10. See Fairhead and Leach 1994, p. 75.
11. See Yearly 1996, p. 134.
12. See, for example, Fairhead and Leach 1994.
13. See Zerner 1994b, pp. 1101–4.
14. See Healey 1993.
15. But see, for example, Redclift 1989; Lele 1991.
16. See, for instance, Conklin 1954.
17. See, for instance, Rappaport 1984.
18. See, for example, Balée 1994.
19. See Hyndman 1994; Oldfield and Alcorn 1991.
20. See Ellen 1998.
21. See, for instance Abrams et al. 1996, pp. 55–75.

22. See Cleveland 1998, p. 325.
23. See Gadgil and Guha 1992; Allen and Sachs 1993.
24. For example, those of The World Bank. See Srivastava et al. 1996.
25. See also Geertz 1963, chap. 2. For more recent work critical of these simple earlier models of shifting cultivation see, for example, *Human Ecology* 1983.
26. See Padoch 1995; Fairhead and Leach 1996.
27. See, for instance, Sunderlin 1997; Brown and Schreckenberg 1998, pp. 1–4.
28. See Iskandar and Ellen (in press: b).
29. For example, Peterson 1978. On the controversy surrounding the extent to which non-agricultural populations can survive on the basis of tropical rainforest bounty alone, see Headland 1987 and Bahuchet et al. 1991. On anthropic rainforest, see Balée 1994.
30. See, for example, Dunn 1975.
31. See, for example, Fairhead and Leach 1998, pp. 261–3.
32. See Ellen 1998, pp. 89–91; Godoy and Bawa 1993.
33. See, for instance, Carrier 1987; McCay and Acheson 1987 generally for wider coverage.
34. See Zerner 1994b.
35. See, for example, Iskandar and Ellen (in press: a). On ecological instability arising from Green Revolution technology see, for example, Lansing 1991.
36. See Dove and Kammen 1997, p. 97.
37. See Lansing 1991.
38. See Conklin 1980; Lansing 1991.
39. See Agrawal 1995.
40. See Agrawal 1995, p. 4.
41. See Cleveland 1998, p. 335.

## – Bibliography –

Abrams, Elliot M., AnnCorinne Freter, David J. Rue, and John D. Wingard (1996), 'The role of deforestation in the collapse of the late classic Copan Maya state', in Leslie E. Sponsel, Thomas N. Headland and Robert C. Bailey (eds), Tropical Deforestation: the Human Dimension, New York: Columbia University Press, pp. 55–75.

Agrawal, Arun (1995), 'Indigenous and scientific knowledge: some critical comments', Indigenous Knowledge and Development Monitor 3:3 pp. 1–9. Elaborated as (1995), 'Dismantling the divide between indigenous and scientific knowledge', Development and Change 26, pp. 413–9.

Allen, P., and C. Sachs (1993), 'Sustainable agriculture in the United States: engagements, silences, and possibilities for transformation', in P. Allen (ed.), Food for the Future: Conditions and Contradictions of Sustainability, New York: John Wiley, pp. 139–67.

Bahuchet, S., D. McKey, and I. de Garine (1991), 'Wild yams revisited: is independence from agriculture possible for rainforest hunter-gatherers?, *Human Ecology* 19, pp. 213-44.

Balée, William (1994), Footprints of the Forest: Ka'apor Ethnobotany – The Historical Ecology of Plant Utilization by an Amazonian People, New York: Columbia University Press.

Berkes, Fikret (1992) ed., *Traditional Ecological Knowledge in Perspective*, Winnipeg: Natural Resources Institute.

Brown, David, and Kathrin Schreckenberg (1998), 'Shifting cultivators as agents of deforestation: assessing the evidence', *Natural Resource Perspectives* 29, pp. 1-4.

Carrier, James G. (1987), 'Marine tenure and conservation in Papua New Guinea: problems in interpretation', in Bonnie M. McCay and James M. Acheson (eds), *The Question of the Commons: The Culture and Ecology of Communal Resources*, Tucson: The University of Arizona Press, pp. 142-67.

Chambers, R. (1983), *Sustainable Rural Development: Putting the Last First*, London: Longman.

Chambers, Robert, and Paul Richards (1995), 'Preface', in D. Michael Warren, L. Jan Slikkerveer and David Brokensha (eds), *The Cultural Dimension of Development: Indigenous Knowledge Systems*, London: Intermediate Technology Publications, pp. xiii-xiv.

Cleveland, David A. (1998), 'Balancing on a planet: toward an agricultural anthropology for the twenty-first century', *Human Ecology* 26:2, pp. 323-40.

Colfer, C. J. Pierce, N. L. Peluso, and Chin See Chung (1997), *Beyond Slash and Burn: Building on Indigenous Knowledge in Managing Borneo's Tropical Rain Forests*, New York: New York Botanical Gardens Press.

Conklin, B., and L. Graham (1995), 'The shifting middle ground: Amazonian indians and eco-politics', *American Anthropologist* 97:4, pp. 695-710.

Conklin, Harold C. (1954), 'An ethnoecological approach to shifting agriculture', *Transactions of the New York Academy of Sciences* (Second series) 17, pp. 133-42.

Conklin, Harold C. (1957), *Hanunoo Agriculture in the Philippines*, Rome: Food and Agricultural Organization of the United Nations.

Conklin, Harold C. (1980), *Ethnographic Atlas of Ifugao: A Study of Environment, Culture and Society in Northern Luzon*, New Haven and London: Yale University Press.

Davenport, W. (1960), 'Jamaican fishing: a game theory analysis', in S. W. Mintz and D. Hall (eds), *The Origins of the Jamaican Internal Marketing System* (Yale University Publications in Anthropology, No. 57), New Haven: Yale University Press.

Dove Michael R. (1983), 'Theories of swidden agriculture and the political economy of ignorance', *Agroforestry Systems* 1:3, pp. 85-99.

Dove, Michael R. (1985), 'The agroecological mythology of the Javanese, and the political economy of Indonesia', *Indonesia* 39, pp. 1-35.

Dove, Michael R., and Daniel M. Kammen (1997), 'The epistemology of sustainable resource use: managing forest products, swiddens, and high-yielding variety crops', *Human Organization* 56:1, pp. 91-101.

Dunn, F. (1975), *Rainforest Collectors and Traders: A Study of Resource Utilization in Modern and Ancient Malaya*, Monograph of the Malaysian Branch of the Royal Asiatic Society.

Ellen, R. F. (1986), 'What Black Elk left unsaid: on the illusory images of Green primitivism', *Anthropology Today* 2:6, pp. 8–12.

Ellen, R. F. (1998), 'Indigenous knowledge of the rainforest: perception, extraction and conservation', in Bernard K. Maloney (ed.) *Human Activities and the Tropical Rainforest: Past, Present and Possible Future*, Dordrecht: Kluwer.

Ellen, R. F., and H. Harris (1997), *Concepts of Indigenous Environmental Knowledge in Scientific and Development Studies Literature: A Critical Assessment*, Canterbury: APFT Working Paper 2. Revised version (in press) as 'Introduction', in R. F. Ellen, P. S. C. Parkes and A. Bicker (eds), *Indigenous Environmental Knowledge and its Transformations: Critical Anthropological Approaches* (Studies in Environmental Anthropology, No. 5), Amsterdam: Harwood.

Farrhead, James, and Melissa Leach (1994), 'Declarations of difference', in I. Scoones and J. Thompson (eds), *Beyond Farmer First*, London: Intermediate Technology Publications.

Farrhead, James, and Melissa Leach (1996), *Misreading the African Landscape: Society and Ecology in a Forest-savannah Mosaic*, Cambridge: Cambridge University Press.

Fairhead, James, and Melissa Leach (1998), 'Representatives of the past: trees in historical dispute and socialised ecology in the forest zone of the Republic of Guinea, West Africa', in Laura Rival (ed.), *The Social Life of Trees: Anthropological Perspectives on Tree Symbolism*, Oxford: Berg, pp. 253–71.

Gadgil, M. and R. Guha (1992), *This Fissured Land: An Ecological History of India*, Delhi: Oxford University Press.

Geertz, C. (1963), *Agricultural Involution: The Processes of Ecological Change in Indonesia*, Berkeley and Los Angeles: University of California Press.

Godoy, R. A., and K. S. Bawa (1993), 'The economic value and sustainable harvest of plants and animals from the tropical forest: assumptions, hypotheses and methods', *Economic Botany* 47:3, pp. 215–19.

Hardin, G. (1968), 'The tragedy of the commons', *Science* 62, pp. 1243–8.

Headland, T. N. (1987), 'The wild yam question: how well could independent hunter-gatherers live in a tropical rainforest ecosystem?', *Human Ecology* 15:4, pp. 463–92.

Healey, C. (1993), 'The significance and application of TEK', in N.Williams and G. Baines (eds), *Traditional Ecological Knowledge: Wisdom for Sustainable Development*, Canberra: Centre for Resource and Environmental Studies, Australia National University, pp. 21–6.

Hobart, Mark (1993), 'Introduction: the growth of ignorance?', in M. Hobart (ed.), *An Anthropological Critique of Development*, London: Routledge, pp. 1–30.

Hughes, D. J. (1983), *American Indian Ecology*, University of Texas: Texas Western Press.

*Human Ecology* 11:1, 1–101. [Special issue on *Does the Swidden Ape the Jungle?*]

Hunn, Eugene (1993), 'What is traditional ecological knowledge?', in N. Williams and G. Baines (eds), *Traditional Ecological Knowledge: Wisdom for Sustainable Development*, Canberra: Centre for Resource and Environmental Studies, Australian National University, pp. 13-5.

Hyndman, D. (1994), 'Conservation through self-determination: promoting the interdependence of cultural and biological diversity', *Human Organization* 53:3, pp. 296-302.

Inglis, J. T. (1993), *Traditional Ecological Knowledge: Concepts and Cases*, Ottawa: International Development Research Centre.

Iskandar, J., and R. Ellen (in press: a), 'In situ conservation of rice landraces among the Baduy of West Java', *Journal of Ethnobiology*.

Iskandar, J., and R. Ellen (in press: b), 'The contribution of *Albizzia* to sustainable swidden management practices among the Baduy of West Java', *Human Ecology*.

Johannes, R. E. (1978), 'Traditional marine conservation methods in Oceania and their demise', *Annual Review of Ecology and Systematics* 9, pp. 349-64.

Johannes, R. E. (1989) ed., *Traditional Ecological Knowledge*, Cambridge: International Union for the Conservation of Nature, The World Conservation Union.

Johnson, M. (1992), *Lore: Capturing Traditional Environmental Knowledge*, Ottawa: International Development Research Centre.

Lansing, J. S. (1991), *Priests and Programmers: Technologies of Power in the Engineered Landscape of Bali*, Princeton, NJ: Princeton University Press.

Lele, S. M. (1991), 'Sustainable development: a critical review', *World Development* 19, pp. 607-21.

McCay, B. M., and J. M. Acheson (1987) eds, *The Question of the Commons: The Culture and Ecology of Communal Resources*, Tucson: University of Arizona Press.

Milton, Kay (1996), *Environmentalism and Anthropology: Exploring the Role of Anthropology in Environmental Discourse*, London: Routledge.

Morrill, W. (1967), 'The ethnoicthyology of the Cha-Cha', *Ethnology* 6, pp. 405-16.

Oldfield, M. L., and J. Alcorn (1991) eds, *Biodiversity: Culture, Conservation and Ecodevelopment*, Boulder: Westview.

Padoch, C. (1995), 'Creating the forest: Dayak resource management in Kalimantan', in Jefferson Fox (ed.), *Society and Non-timber Forest Products in Tropical Asia* (East-West Center Occasional Papers : Environmental Series, No. 19), Honolulu: East-West Center.

Pearce, David, Edward Barbier, and Anil Markandya (1990), *Sustainable Development: Economics and Environment in the Third World*, London: Earthscan.

Peterson, J. T. (1978), *The Ecology of Social Boundaries: Agta Foragers of the Philippines* (Illinois Studies in Anthropology, No. 11), Urbana, Chicago and London: University of Illinois Press.

Posey, Darrell A. (1996), *Provisions and Mechanisms of the Convention on Biological Diversity for Access to Traditional Technologies and Benefit Sharing for Indigenous and Local Communities Embodying Traditional Lifestyles* (OCEES, Research Paper No. 6), Mansfield College, Oxford: Oxford Centre for Environment, Ethics and Society.

Rappaport, Roy A. (1984) [revised edition of 1968], *Pigs for the Ancestors: Ritual in the Ecology of a New Guinea People*, New Haven and New York: Yale University Press.

Redclift, M. (1989), *Sustainable Development: Exploring the Contradictions*, London: Routledge.

Rhoades, R., and Anthony Bebbington (1995), 'Farmers who experiment: an untapped resource for agricultural research and development', in D. Michael Warren, L. Jan Slikkerveer and David Brokensha (eds), *The Cultural Dimension of Development: Indigenous Knowledge Systems*, London: Intermediate Technology Publications, pp. 296–307.

Richards, Paul (1985), *Indigenous Agricultural Revolution: Ecology and Food-crop Farming in West Africa*, London: Hutchinson.

Richards, Paul (1993), 'Cultivation: knowledge or performance?', in Mark Hobart (ed.), *An Anthropological Critique of Development*, London: Routledge.

Sillitoe, P. (1998), 'The development of indigenous knowledge: a new applied anthropology', *Current Anthropology* 39:2, pp. 223–52.

Srivastava, J., N. J. H. Smith, and D. Forno (1996), *Biodiversity and Agriculture: Implications for Conservation and Use* (World Bank Technical Paper 321), Washington DC: World Bank.

Sunderlin, William D. (1997), *Shifting Cultivation and Deforestation in Indonesia: Steps Toward Overcoming Confusion in the Debate* (Rural Development Forestry Network, Paper 21b), London: Overseas Development Institute, pp. 1–20.

Warren, D. Michael, L. Jan Slikkerveer, and David Brokensha (1995) eds, *The Cultural Dimension of Development: Indigenous Knowledge Systems*, London: Intermediate Technology Publications.

Williams, N., and G. Baines (1993) eds, *Traditional Ecological Knowledge: Wisdom for Sustainable Development*, Canberra: Centre for Resource and Environmental Studies, Australian National University.

Yearly, Steven (1996), *Sociology, Environmentalism, Globalization: Reinventing the Globe*, London: Sage.

Zerner, Charles (1994a), 'Transforming customary law and coastal management practices in the Maluku islands, Indonesia, 1870–1992, in David Western, R. Michael Wright and S. C. Strum (eds), *Natural Connections: Perspectives in Community Based Conservation*, Washington DC: Island Press, pp. 80–112.

Zerner, Charles (1994b), 'Through a green lens: the construction of customary environmental law and community in Indonesia's Maluku islands', *Law and Society Review* 28:5, pp. 1079–1122.

# Population control:
# the key to a sustainable future?

In an earlier chapter, Mark Sagoff has challenged the view that in order to achieve global sustainable development, we need to reduce the volume of consumption. But if it were required, how should we set about it? There are, as Avner de-Shalit observes, two ways to bring about a reduction in the volume of consumption. One is to reduce the number of consumers. The other is for those who consume more than their fair share to reduce the amount that they consume. De-Shalit boldly argues that the former option – population control – is (i) inefficient and (ii) immoral.

The efficiency argument: In the UK, at any rate, we have become accustomed to weather forecasters announcing a sudden increase in pollution levels in major cities, and attributing the phenomenon to the extremely warm weather. (No mention is made of the lorries and cars that are clogging the streets.) De-Shalit quotes a similar liberty with the facts from *The WWF Environment Handbook*, where starvation and illness in the Sahel are attributed, without ceremony, to the population increase. Citing examples where populations have risen without any concomitant ill-effects, and where threats to welfare have come from quite other causes, de-Shalit's claim is that other factors such as technological development, just institutions and access to education have a far more significant impact than mere numbers on human welfare and the state of the environment.

The morality argument: de-Shalit's first point about the morality of population policies is that they pose a *prima facie* threat to human liberty which stands in need of justification. If the right to have children were a mere right of possession (the right to the possession of some 'good'), then the fact that its exercise might harm the rights of others could provide such a justification. But there is, he suggests, another way to construe the right to 'have' children: not as a right of possession, but as a right to self-fulfilment. So understood, it amounts to a fundamental and basic freedom that one cannot reasonably ask people to give up. Why has the strength of the argument against population policies gone unrecognised? His answer is that the language in which the issue is typically discussed disguises the true nature of what is at stake: 'births' become 'reproduction', 'babies' become 'mouths to feed', 'the joy of children' becomes 'the marginal utitlity of every next child.' In short, human experience is de-humanised.

~ O ~

# 10 SUSTAINABILITY AND POPULATION POLICIES:

## MYTHS, TRUTHS AND HALF-BAKED IDEAS

## *Avner de-Shalit*

'Our duty to future persons is to see to it that there are not too many of them.' (Annette Baier 1980, p. 181)

'Historically, human societies have been pro-child; modern society is unique in that it is profoundly hostile to children. We in the west do not refrain from childbirth because we are concerned about the population explosion or because we feel we cannot afford children, but because we do not like children.' (Germain Greer 1984, p. 2)

## – INTRODUCTION –

It is widely believed among politicians, academics, environmental activists, and the general public, that if we want a sustainable environment we need to limit the over-use of resources and prevent the extinction of species. It is often claimed that this necessitates a reduction in the 'volume of consumption.' It is then argued 'population' is a key concept in understanding environmental degradation and ecological disasters. In particular, it is suggested, population size is a key factor in the impact of human beings on the environment. On the face of it, the theory is rather simple: the greater the number of people inhabiting the planet, the greater the pollution, waste and consumption and resource depletion.

So if, as many environmentalists see it, the goal is to reduce the 'volume of consumption', then a good way to achieve this is by reducing the volume of consumers. An alternative, to which I shall return below, is to deliberate collectively, openly and publicly about needs and, perhaps, to redefine them. If we as a society learn to live with less, or learn to enjoy what we have rather than be frustrated with not having more, then production and consumption will be reduced.[1] This, however, should be accompanied with a policy of redistribution of access to power and goods, to meet the newly defined needs. Which is why many – who have a lot to lose if redistribution takes place – object to this alternative, and insist that population policies are the right solution. On the face of it, this is another simple theory. So who is right?

My argument is twofold. First, one cannot deny that the population lobby's theory is reasonable, arithmetically speaking. If, say, an 'average' person consumes $X$, consumption will be smaller if it is the multiplication of $X$ by $n$ rather than by $n+m$. However, while the mathematics is right, the sociology is wrong. I would therefore argue that the impact of human beings on the environment is a function of three parameters, the least significant of which is the size of the population. The two other parameters – technological development and distributive justice, including distribution of knowledge and access to education – are far more significant. According to this view, population policies are an inefficient means of achieving the sought-after reduction in 'volume of consumption.' Secondly, I argue that population policies cannot be justified on moral grounds. While this claim is not novel – it has been asserted by many people, especially among the religious right wing – I shall suggest a liberal-leftist argument to support it. I conclude that the theory according to which population size is the biggest threat to the environment is partly a myth and partly a half-baked idea. I call it 'half-baked' because its advocates have, I think, failed to grasp the essence of their opponents' arguments.

## – ARE POPULATION POLICIES EFFICIENT? –

Let me introduce you to two families. The first is the Bermans. They live in a relatively large house covering an area of 160m, in a suburb, ten miles outside Jerusalem. The father, Mr. Berman, owns a firm dealing with the export of high-tech communications equipment. His products are internationally renowned, particularly in Europe, but also in the USA. To set up deals, he flies to Europe about twenty-five times a year, covering some 70,000 miles a year. He also needs to keep in touch with scientists and with what is going on in the field, and therefore he travels twice a year to America. He drives a 1.8-litre car, owned by the firm (petrol is free, as far as he is concerned). The mother, Dr. Berman, is a university lecturer, specialising in marine biology. She has her own car, since they live in a suburb. She flies abroad four times a year, to conferences, workshops and seminars. Her last paper was an analysis of the impact of fishermen's boats and their pollution on eel behaviour and populations. The expenses of these flights are covered by the university and grants, which are often funded by international firms. The Bermans' furniture is modern and mostly of wood imported from Finland. In the winter it is rather cold where they live, and so they heat the whole house with oil-fired central heating. Since they do not have enough time to take care of the garden, they decided last year to pave a third of the garden. As a result less rain water penetrates the soil. Including the house, altogether $250m^2$ are paved.

The Bermans are well-educated and care about the environment, hence they have only two children. The eldest, Ms. Berman, is twenty-eight years old, single and lives in Tel Aviv. Since her boyfriend lives in Jerusalem, she goes to see him four times a week. Being a very talented and famous architect, her time is valuable and so she takes the car rather than the bus, which would double the time of this journey. Her younger brother is twenty-four years old. He has just finished his studies and is off travelling around the world. His itinerary includes trekking in the Himalayas, where he intends to have a bath every evening, using wood from local forests to boil the water. I could elaborate even further and describe the party the Bermans organised for a friend who has just turned fifty (there were more than eighty people, and they all used disposable, plastic dishes; they all bought this friend presents which he will never need or use, because he already has more than he really needs), and so on.

The second family is the Abrams. This is a religious orthodox family of ten persons who live in a 70m flat. According to their religious conviction, contraception is forbidden, and they consider it a blessing to have as many children as possible. The Abrams feel very fortunate to have ten children. Mr. Abrams teaches in a local elementary school. He walks to work. Mrs. Abrams works part-time at the post office. She takes the bus to work. They earn very little, hence they cannot afford fancy (often imported) food, not to mention a car, foreign travel, or holidays in general. Three of their children are still in nappies. Since plastic nappies are very expensive, they use cotton nappies. Boiling them uses a lot of energy; and the cost of energy is increasing. However, as there are many households with small infants in the neighbourhood, these families decide to solve the problem by setting up a firm which collects the nappies, cleans and boils them and delivers them back by the afternoon. Meat is expensive, so the Abrams' diet consists of mainly vegetables and cereals. This makes their food consumption more environment-friendly than that of the Bermans, who eat a lot of meat. I could go on and on. The bottom line is that poor families often consume and pollute less than rich families even if they have more children per family.[2]

'But then,' you may insist, 'is there no basis to the argument that it would be better for the environment if fewer, rather than more people were alive?'

The answer is that of course, everything being equal, a larger number of people will pollute and consume more than a smaller number. But this does not mean that population is an environmental problem. In fact, the data and statistics released about populations and their environmental impact are often either exaggerated or simply misleading. Consider, for example the following information disclosed by the WWF (Cardwardine 1990, p. 70): the population in the Sahel has risen from 47 million in 1950 to a current 159 million, and for this reason the area suffers from starvation and illness. The innocent reader will of course accept the data and its interpretation as truth. However, if we take the data to be true and compare it with similar information about other countries, such as Israel, we find that the percentage rise in population was much higher for the same period than it was in the Sahel (from 700,000 to over 5 million), and yet not only is there no hunger, but the general welfare of the population is much greater than before the period in question. So the size of the population does not necessarily affect the welfare, not to mention well-being, of people. The same may be said for environmental impact; technology, the distribution of goods, welfare, and knowledge have a greater impact on the state of the environment than does population size. In Switzerland, for example, the amount of toxic waste produced, divided by the number of people (what is often referred to as 'use by the average person') is 2,000 times the amount produced by Sahelian farmers.[3]

Similarly one can show that distributive justice also has a greater impact on the environment than the number of people. For example, there was a time in Central America when the land was concentrated in the hands of a small number of very rich landlords who, supported by the military and the Church, enjoyed great prosperity; but during that time, the land was exploited and the forests were plundered. In Africa, prior to the 1990s, the powerful classes in Ivory Cost and Liberia sanctioned the import of hazardous chemical waste, produced by Europe and North America, for burial on land inhabited by disadvantaged tribes. This practice was halted only with the burgeoning of relative democratisation in these countries in the early 1990s. Such firms and their governments are now forced to find better and safer solutions for their wastes, if not to stop producing them altogether. It is clear then that even as the populations of these African countries grew, this form of environmental degradation ended.

## – ARE POPULATION POLICIES MORALLY JUSTIFIED? –

As far as I know, no one – except, perhaps, misanthropes – believes that population policies do not pose moral problems. All theorists acknowledge that such policies – be they in the form of sterilisation or incentives to reduce the size of families – tend to undermine individual liberties in one way or another. Hence, to support them, we need to show that they are morally defensible against the claim that *prima facie* they appear incompatible with upholding certain individuals' rights. Thus, in reply to the claim that population polices are morally wrong because we must respect human rights and individuals' liberties, supporters of population policies suggest that it is naive to believe that individual rights should always overrule any other moral consideration. For example, a person cnnot justify doing something detrimental to other individuals by claiming to be protecting her own rights. Many from the population lobby claim that the same rationale applies to the case of population policies: if we protect individuals' rights against all population policies, we might harm other individuals' rights.

Now, when examined carefully, these arguments can be divided into two sub-groups. Firstly, it is sometimes claimed that the environmental consequences of the 'population time bomb' are so severe that they justify restriction of individuals' rights and liberties.[4] I believe that the previous section has shown that there is no strong empirical ground for this claim. Secondly, other authors have suggested that if we do not control or limit population growth (limit 'procreation') because we want to defend the right of Johns to procreate, we might harm the rights of Smiths, for example, their right to sufficient nutrition. Recently, Marcel Wissenburg (1998, pp. 146–54) has identified twelve such arguments and effectively demolished each one of them.

So it seems on the face of it that the two rationales – the environmental impact of population growth, and the importance of other individuals' rights – given to support population policies *vis-a-vis* individuals' rights, are wrong. And yet, even Wissenburg believes that there should be another way to justify population policies. He seeks to provide yet another rationale. He writes:

> In sum, even an amended version of liberal democracy cannot be compatible with legal restriction to procreative liberties, nor with incentives or propaganda. This leaves the antinatalist with one and only one admissible policy: to appeal, as a citizen, to other citizens' feelings of responsibility. This policy can be supported by one that actually empowers individuals, i.e., that enlarges rather than limits the procreative liberties by making contraceptives and other alternatives to procreation available to those who, as yet, do not actually have the freedom to choose. (Wissenburg 1998, p. 157)

Giving birth to children – procreation, in Wissenburg's term – is seen as intercourse which happens to end up in pregnancy. Indeed, this points to the possibility that behind this stance taken by those in favour of population policies lies a misunderstanding of the claim made by those who defend their right to have children. There appear to be two ways of understanding the concept of the 'right to have children.' One is to see it as belonging to a group of liberty rights, in particular the right to possess property. The right to have a child is then related to sexual intercourse, and is seen as a series of several acts (each with its own right to liberty or property) which leads to having children. As such, the right to have children is viewed as a set of rights, each relating to a different stage of the process of sexual intercourse. Wissenburg lists four such stages and rights.

1. We are free to use or not use our sexual parts for 'normal' intercourse. No necessary prior act is required, and alternative forms of intercourse are imaginable.
2. Women are free to be or not be fertilised by means of 'normal' intercourse. There is nowadays an alternative called artificial insemination. Note that there is no such distinct basic act for men: they have only one means of fertilising.
3. Women are free to carry or not carry a child; an alternative to fertilisation as prior cause is implantation of an already fertilised egg from another source.
4. Women are free to carry a child through to birth or not; an alternative is abortion. (Wissenburg 1998, p. 144)

According to this standpoint, 'having a child' is consistent with the right to liberty in two ways: it consists, firstly, of the right to be autonomous, to decide whether to be 'fertilised' or not and whether to abort or not; and secondly, of the right to property – the (potential) child being one's property – and hence the right to dispossess oneself of one's property (that is, to abort) or the right to retain one's possession (that is, not to abort). As such, 'having children' is just like having other 'goods.' This is why Wissenburg goes on to argue that it could conflict with another person's right to the use of resources (p. 143): one person may limit the other by insisting on his or her right – for example, if I insist on my right to have four children, your right to have sweet water may be affected or limited.

There is, however, another way of understanding the right to have a child. 'Having' a child does not necessarily point to possessive relations but instead may be regarded as a metaphor. Rather than seeing the parent and the child as two distinct entities, one 'having' the other, a parent and a child can be seen as one. Thus the right to have children is a fundamental right to strive freely towards self-fulfillment.[5] This is especially true about women, but also, in many cases, about men.

Let me elaborate on this. In a lifetime, one passes through several stages: childhood, youth, adulthood, maturity. In each stage one can 'become' something. One becomes a child, one becomes a grown-up, one becomes an adult. Becoming this or that is therefore a fulfillment of a natural potential.[6] The same applies to parenthood. One has the potential to be a parent, and to many, becoming a parent is a sought-after fulfillment of a potential. 'I have always wanted to be a mother' is a remark we often hear. Recently, fathers have begun to feel the same way and have genuinely expressed a similar sentiment. Mothers and fathers confess to experiencing a wonderful feeling of radical change which adds significance to their lives, and leads to a reappraisal of things considered, up to the point of parenthood, to be important and meaningful in their lives. This is exactly the 'becoming' process: it involves a new, refreshing perspective on the previous period in one's life, a perspective which changes the meaning of previous periods of life. The right to have children is, in that sense, a person's right to self-fulfillment.[7]

But before I continue, I should modify my claim. It is true that not all parents regard their children as part of themselves or see being a parent as self-fulfillment. Some parents have children because they would like to have cheap labour at home, or because they would like their children's support when they become older. This is unfortunately part of life. I would, therefore, like to distinguish my claim from cases in which children are brought into the world to help sustain the family economically. In such cases children are nothing but a source of income (or sometimes prestige). In countries where there is no (efficient) system of welfare or redistribution, many parents find that the more children they have, the more likely they are to enjoy economic security when they grow too old or ill to work, as they will be supported by their children. The calculation is simple: each child would support them with X per cent of his or her income. The more children they have, the higher this aggregate support would be. In addition, there is a considerable amount of anthropological research indicating that in traditional societies, where women lack status and access to power, they tend to find comfort in having as many children as possible, partly because this is their way of gaining some status and respect.[8] These families would not benefit from the defence of procreation mentioned above because the parents' attitude to their children is instrumental. Having said that, we should remember that such parents are pressured with such consideration owing to the lack of welfare systems and the ensuing economic insecurity prevalent in these societies. Such attitudes can be replaced with a less instrumental attitude towards children if welfare systems, and redistribution mechanisms and institutions, were introduced into these societies, and if women were empowered with economic, human and political rights. Environmentalists cannot, therefore, be indifferent towards the injustice and poverty prevalent in these societies. They should therefore argue not only for ecological stability, but also for sustainable development within a society which is politically democratic and economically just.

Now let me return to the distinction between being a parent as self-fulfillment, and 'having a child.' The question arises: why do so many people engaged in the population debate misinterpret the claim made by those who oppose population policies and defend the right to have children? There are two explanations for this. One is sociological; the other relates to the use of 'clean language' which makes it possible to transfer the essential focus from having children as self-fulfillment to having children as a right to possession.

It can be argued that the population scare is very much a matter of an emotional aversion to and a dislike of the 'other', whose culture is different. Among other things, the other's culture consists of having many children, whether for economic reasons as described above, or for cultural and religious ones, or simply because of a love of children. I believe that Germaine Greer is a strong advocate of this explanation. In *Sex and Destiny* (Greer 1984, pp. 402–3) she quotes and challenges Paul Ehrlich's description of his travels through India, which appears in his book, *The Population Bomb* (Ehrlich 1968). Ehrlich writes:

> I have understood the population problem intellectually for a long time. I came to understand it emotionally one stinking hot night in Delhi a few years ago. My wife and daughter and I were returning to our hotel in an ancient taxi. The seats were hopping with fleas. The only functional gear was third. As we crawled through the city, we entered a crowded slum area. The temperature was well over 100°F; the air was a haze of dust and smoke. The streets seemed alive with people. People eating, people washing, people sleeping. People visiting, arguing and screaming, people thrusting their hand through the taxi window begging, people defecating and urinating. People clinging to buses. People herding animals. People, people, people. As we moved slowly through the mob, hand horn squawking, the dust, noise, heat and cooking fires gave the scene a hellish aspect. Would we ever get to our hotel? All three of us were frankly, frightened. It seemed that anything could happen . . . (Ehrlich 1968, p. 15)

In fact, all that is necessary to support the counter-theory is to quote this passage. Ehrlich is shown to be someone who simply dislikes Indians, especially when they are poor, and who believes that they are there only to obstruct his speedy return to his hotel. Faced with the tragic overwhelming poverty, all we hear is a concern about ever reaching his hotel. And why was he frightened? Was it a fear of the stranger? As Greer (1984) so pointedly puts it, perhaps those who find it so difficult to travel in hot countries should simply avoid such journeys (and, may I add, save the pollution of air travel).

Greer argues that the poverty in countries such as India may be traced back to a colonial past. At that time, poor people were a source of cheap labour for the emerging industrialised world. And so poverty and misery were forced upon them by the ancestors of those who now, after benefiting from this exploitation, demand that their societies lower their rate of reproduction. But exploitation in colonial times apart, it remains true that the demand for population policies is made in a deeply unequal world upon the disadvantaged and often exploited, by the dominant and the prosperous, fuelled by their fear, anxiety, dislike or even, sometimes, hatred of the numerous poor.

However, the explanation of why people like Ehrlich raise their demands for population policies – a powerful explanation as it is – does not go far enough. While it does explain why politicians and the industrial elite support population policies, it does not answer an argument that may be raised against my claim: if indeed population policies are immoral and inefficient, why then do so many philosophers and environmentalists support them? For them, Greer's reasoning is irrelevant since they obviously do not seek power nor do they benefit personally (at least not significantly) from the exploitation of women, Third World populations, and so on. I would therefore like to move on to an alternative explanation which relates to how the use of certain concepts helps to shape the debate. I argue that this population policy 'newspeak' tends to de-humanise the human experience.

Rather than discussing 'persons', these authors discuss 'populations.' Instead of 'births', they talk about 'multiplication' and 'reproduction'; instead of 'babies' or 'children' they talk about 'mouths to feed';[9] instead of 'communities' they write about 'the mob.'[10] Instead of 'not allowing people to give birth', they talk about 'population control' and rather than saying that they bribe people (for exampe by tax reduction) not to do what they would like to do – give birth to more children – and even to get sterilised, they talk about 'incentives' as a means of 'population policy', as if the matter concerned is consumption policies. Instead of 'the joy of children', they discuss 'the marginal utility of every next child' (Wissenburg 1998, p. 156), as if living with children is like owning several cars. Terms such as the 'carrying capacity' of the land are used, as if the number of people who can live on a given piece of land is a function of their density, rather than their culture, the technology they use, their attitudes to nature, and so on. Notice the policy implications of such changes in language. Rather than educating people and teaching them the pros and cons of having smaller families, population policy authorities assume that it is enough to sterilise people – an irreversible change in an individual's body and mind – without properly explaining why. The desperate need of the poor to survive is exploited to change them in an irreversible way which they might deeply regret later. Thus, in a society which worships freedom, the most basic freedom – to follow one's natural instincts and have children – is controlled and manipulated in an Orwellian style.[11]

## – Notes –

1. Note that I use the phrase 'we as a society' rather than 'people.' The difference is that if we talk of people, the inference is that individuals should be satisfied with what they have, hinting, perhaps, at a conservative and right-wing economy where poor people are expected to come to terms with, and accept their lot. While I would like to see an egalitarian redistribution of goods, I would suggest that society as a whole could learn to be satisfied with what it has.

2. This should come as no surprise. North Americans eat a lot of meat, and as the production of a pound of meat takes several pounds of grain, grain consumption per person in a year is 860kg in the USA and 974kg in Canada, whereas it is 145kg in Tanzania and 176kg in Bangladesh. In 1989, 20 per cent of the world's population (the richest) absorbed 83 per cent of the world's income, while the poorest 20 per cent absorbed less than 2 per cent. (Source: UNDP 1992, quoted in S. Postel, 1994, p. 5)

3. P. Predaverand 1991, p. 115.

4. Perhaps the two most often-quoted works claiming this are Garrett Hardin's 'The tragedy of the commons' (Hardin 1968) and William Ophuls' *Ecology and the Politics of Scarcity* (Ophuls 1977). (But see also the latter's more recent book, *Requiem for Modern Politics* (Ophuls 1997).)

5. However, I do not wish to present it as a right to self-fulfillment *simpliciter*. It should also be emphasised immediately that the right to have children is not a positive right, that is there is no duty on a third party to supply children or do all they can to help a woman to have children; rather it is a right not to be stopped from having children. I explain this below.

6. 'Natural' in the sense that it is very common. But this does not imply that those who chose not to become this or that act against nature, in the normative sense.

7. It is interesting to note that 'deep ecologists' and Spiritualists who often write about enlarging the self cannot grasp this attitude and, instead, call for population policies.

8. Shiva writes:

> In a society in which a woman has no choice about when and to whom she gets married, when and how many times she conceives, or even how much she should eat while she is pregnant or lactating, and in which she is in no position to avail herself of minimal rest from strenuous work in the terminal states of her pregnancy, does she have any choice regarding contraceptive methods? (Shiva 1991, p. 113)

Accordingly, it is useless to try and persuade women to use contraception when the social structure remains unchanged.

9. 'This means an extra 1.3 million mounts to feed every year' (Cardwardine 1990, p. 70).

10. See, for instance, Ehrlich 1968.

11. In Orwell's *1984*, drastic policies are always accompanied by a change in language use.


## – BIBLIOGRAPHY –

Baier, Annette (1980), 'The rights of past and future people', in E. Partridge (ed.), *Responsibilities to Future Generations*, Buffalo, NY: Prometheus Books.

Cardwardine, Mark (1990), *The WWF Environment Handbook*, London: Optima.

Ehrlich, Paul (1968), *The Population Bomb*, New York: Ballantine Press.

Greer, Germaine (1984), *Sex and Destiny*, London: Picador.

Hardin, Garrett (1968), 'The tragedy of the commons', *Science* 162, pp. 1243–8.

Ophuls, William (1977), *Ecology and the Politics of Scarcity*, San Francisco: W. H. Freeman.

Ophulus, William (1997), *Requiem for Modern Politics*, Oxford and Boulder: Westview.

Postel, S. (1994), 'Carrying capacity: earth's bottom line', in Lester Brown, Christopher Flavin and Sandra Postel (eds), *State of the World*, Washington DC: World Watch Institute.

Predaverand, P. (1991), 'The interaction of population and natural resources', in J. Kirkby, Phil O'Keefe and Lloyd Timberlake (eds), *Sustainable Development*, London: Earthscan.

Shiva, M. (1991), 'The politics of population policies', in J. Kirkby, Phil O'Keefe and Lloyd Timberlake (eds), *Sustainable Development*, London: Earthscan.

UNDP (1992), *Human Development Report*, New York: Oxford University Press.

Wissenberg, M. (1998), *Green Liberalism*, London: University College of London Press.

# Participation and empowerment

Koos Neefjes's chapter has a practical focus – how to bring into alignment (i) participation and its goal of empowerment, (ii) the alleviation of poverty, and (iii) environmental improvement. A further problem is how to reconcile the goal of empowerment as an end in itself with the external interventions usually associated with the development agenda. For, as Mary Mellor and Roy Ellen have already pointed out, there is a tendency for grass-roots potential to be taken up and given a wholly instrumental role in the global development agenda.

Neefjes first raises the question, also discussed in this volume by Dobson and Sagoff, of whether the poor can be blamed for environmental degradation. He finds the idea far too simplistic, pointing out that the very poor do not usually have access to chainsaws, dynamite and leather-processing equipment, and that often they have little or no impact either way. He then presents an analysis of poor people's environments, framed in terms of the concept of a (sustainable) 'livelihood', which comprises the capabilities, assets and activities that are required for a means of living. Neefjes observes that the concept makes room for both local and global concerns, and facilitates dialogue between outsider development professionals and the poor themselves. Even though opportunities are limited, livelihood strategies are at least determined by the people themselves, who both carry responsibility and live with the outcome. Participation then seems attainable; less so the empowerment that is its goal, since this requires the redistribution of power. Participation also provides a context in which people are able to look for creative alternatives to their current situation, but it is a further question again whether it can provide any sort of guarantee of environmental improvement; in any event, it seems unlikely to be able to prevent conflicts over resources.

Neefjes closes with a review of trends. Some trends are encouraging. Neefjes singles out the development of civil society, and new and practical manifestations of democracy aided by development agencies, NGOs and the spread of the Internet. He observes too that when the poor are able to participate in decisions and start to feel some benefit from economic growth, then environments tend to improve. Other trends are less hopeful. Here,

Neefjes singles out weaknesses in governance, a lack of 'social' capital, especially education, and serious grounds for doubting the capacity of the environment to cope with both the existing aspirations of the wealthy and the emerging aspirations of the poor.

~ O ~

# 11 PEOPLE DEFINING THEIR ENVIRONMENTS: A FUTURE OF CHANGE

## *Koos Neefjes*

### – INTRODUCTION –

It has been stressed in many discussions that 'participation' is central to putting into practice the concept of 'sustainable development.' However, who is to participate, how, why, and in what, are as contested as the concept of sustainable development itself. The objective of participation is sometimes described as 'empowerment' or as 'strengthening social capital.' But thus understood, it appears to be incompatible with development aid interventions, be these through financial transfers, technical assistance or Freirean attempts at working with local people on their own terms. The difficulties of involving citizens and lower-level officials in development initiatives are highlighted by many publications and in documents internal to development organisations. Critics have also expressed doubts about the compatibility of economic growth with poverty alleviation and environmental improvements, as well as the presumed synergy between environmental sustainability and the alleviation of poverty.

This chapter addresses three questions that are closely linked. These are: (a) whether practical approaches can overcome the apparent contradiction between external interventions and their objective of empowering the poorest and most marginalised people; (b) whether participation and its goal of empowerment would automatically lead to environmental sustainability; and (c) whether alleviation of poverty and environmental improvements are synergistic. The essay is grounded in practice rather than theory – practice of influencing policies, and practice of trying to meet the goals of poverty eradication and environmental sustainability. It is also grounded in the real achievements and impacts of that practice and not just based on plans for future projects. The experiences are drawn mainly, though not exclusively, from the rural South.

The three questions are approached in conjunction, and from different angles. The first section below assesses whether poor and vulnerable people are primarily the perpetrators of environmental degradation; the next looks at poor people's own images of their environments and of their relationships to their livelihoods. This is followed by an analytical framework compatible with poor people's discourses on sustainable development. The further two sections discuss, respectively, aspects of 'participation' and people power, and different views regarding environmentalism and the risks of resource conflicts. Alternatives will also be presented, suggesting promising future opportunities. However, the chapter will conclude that even genuine participation and empowerment of poor and marginalised people cannot be expected to solve the global environmental crisis, and that actual eradication of poverty will not necessarily solve the crisis either, because of the limitations of technological developments, threats of resource conflicts, enormous educational gaps between the poorer and the better-off, weaknesses in governance and lack of social capital, and ever-increasing aspirations towards consumption. There are many things that can be done, but real improvements in poor people's livelihoods and environments have proven to be difficult to achieve, slow, and often rooted in social movements rather than in developmental interventions.

## – SUSTAINABLE DEVELOPMENT AND POVERTY ERADICATION: BLAMING THE VICTIM? –

'Sustainable development' has become one of the most contested subjects in development discourse in the last decade or so. The Brundtland Report defines it as 'development that meets the needs of the present without compromising the ability of future generations to meet their own needs (Brundtland 1987, p. 43).' It also says:

> The concept of sustainable development does imply limits - not absolute limits but limitations imposed by the present state of technology and social organisation on environmental resources and by the ability of the biosphere to absorb the effects of human activities. But technology and social organisation can be both managed and improved to make way for a new era of economic growth. The Commission believes that widespread poverty is no longer inevitable. Poverty is not only an evil in itself, but sustainable development requires meeting the basic needs of all and extending to all the opportunity to fulfil their aspirations for a better life. A world in which poverty is endemic will always be prone to ecological and other catastrophes. (Brundtland 1987, p. 8)

The Report (a) implies that sustainable development is a normative concept with the over-arching goal of meeting the basic needs of the poor; (b) acknowledges that there are limitations on technology, social organisation and environmental resources, and that these limitations are not static; (c) recognises that endemic poverty and ecological catastrophes are causally linked; and (d) holds that economic growth is possible if technology and social organisation are well-managed.

Ekins (1993) has argued that the assumptions behind the Report and subsequent discussions and publications about the potential of technology development, as a panacea for enabling the poor to consume at a level similar to that of the better-off (such as the industrialised nations or high-consumption elites elsewhere), are utopian unless the better-off elite radically reduces its excessive consumption (which is already undermining the integrity of the biosphere). Policies of governments and the international community to reduce the impact of consumption, to develop ecologically less-destructive technology, in order to make it more possible for poorer people to consume more, include fiscal policies which provide incentives for reduced resource consumption instead of taxing labour, tougher (internationally agreed) standards for energy consumption and pollution, and policies to encourage the transfer of 'clean' technologies from industrialised nations to developing countries (Le Quesne, 'Ecological footprints').

However, such policies and the 'solutions' they imply do not necessarily help all poor people and all environments. Sachs (1992) has pointed out that sustainable development, following Brundtland, simply incorporates 'environment' within the otherwise unchanged goal of GNP growth. This leads to 'blaming the victim': 'the poor were quickly identified as agents of destruction' and 'the environment could only be protected through a new era of growth' (Sachs 1992, p. 29). Williams (1998) offers a framework of 'environmental victimology' and a range of case studies, regarding, in particular, health hazards associated with pollution; and Ho (1998) presents the dangers of genetic engineering for (poor) people's health and livelihoods. Analysis of the causes of global warming and climate change and other global environmental degradation shows that the poor or poorer nations cannot seriously be blamed for such degradation. National or regional environmental problems such as urban pollution, deforestation, land degradation (including desertification), wildlife extinction, and reduced fish stocks can rarely be blamed on the poorest and by no means always on a larger group of 'the poor.' A smaller subset of poor people – those, for example, with the means to fell trees on a relatively extensive scale, fish with dynamite and destroy coral, or process leather and pollute locally – may be blamed for some degradation; but they do so to serve high-level consumers whom they reach through (international) markets. Large-scale deforestation, mining, and fishing are usually in the hands of big enterprises, controlled by the rich and often the more powerful from industrialised nations, serving the world's affluent elites.

Peet and Watts (1996) conclude that work on political ecology 'has affirmed the centrality of *poverty* as a major cause of ecological deterioration . . . [although it is] at best only a *proximate* cause of environmental deterioration' (p. 7). Guha and Martinez-Alier (1997) argue that wealth is a greater threat to the environment than poverty is; however, poverty can be a cause of local environmental degradation, for example when poor people who cannot afford fossil fuels use dung and trees instead, thereby causing land degradation, in particular in arid regions. Chambers (1997, pp. 24-9) reports that increased densities of trees are associated with increased densities of people in parts of Kenya, and refers to several findings challenging myths regarding poor people and their population growth as the main causes of environmental degradation. Comparatively poor (traditional) people who created patches of forest in the savannah of Guinée in West Africa are reported by Fairhead and Leach (1996), effectively undermining the orthodoxy that deserts encroached upon forests because of poor people's activities. Furthermore, it may also be true that the poorest are neither the agents of ecological degradation nor the agents of improvement. In a rural community in Vietnam, for example, 'the very poorest families, women and men, in Lung Vai commune did not take much part in the environmental change, whether negative or positive, and whether as culprit, victim or restorer of degraded environments' (Neefjes 1998b, p. 29).

'Nature' also destroys in the absence of anthropogenic causes, and usually with grave effects, on poorer people in particular. Several authors have struggled with the notion of 'environmental refugees' because people are rarely on the move solely for environmental reasons. Renner, for example, describes a range of environmental reasons that contribute to the displacement of people:

> People are turned into environmental refugees either by sudden 'unnatural' disasters, such as the 1986 Chernobyl nuclear accident . . . or by the more gradual worsening of environmental conditions . . . land degradation, water scarcity and the threat of famine . . . In Ethiopia massive deforestation and soil erosion combined with population growth, inequitable land tenure systems and inefficient agricultural practices to force large numbers of peasants out of the highland farming areas. (Renner 1996, pp. 105-6)

Environmental degradation and shocks no doubt play a role in extreme human suffering, including that which leads to large-scale displacement, but credible explanations usually go well beyond neo-Malthusian and other similarly simplistic models. The political economy of wars and 'complex emergencies' has been studied and theorised by authors such as Macrae and Zwi (1994).

## – Poor people's environments –

Poor people's environments are primarily local environments – the forests, seas, rivers and streets where poor people live and usually work. They and their environments are obviously affected by global and national processes of change, economically and environmentally. Poor rural and urban people in Bangladesh are affected by increased river flooding caused by deforestation in watersheds and canalisation of the rivers which carry water from neighbouring countries. And the threats to lives, livelihoods and environments posed by sea-level rise associated with global warming, and the expected increase in the frequency and severity of cyclones and tidal surges following changes in climatic patterns, can best be illustrated by the 400,000–500,000 deaths in coastal parts of Bangladesh since 1970.[1]

The people living in coastal communities in Bangladesh are not all similarly poor; in fact, many of the landless Bangladeshis are strongly dependent on powerful elites who control most of the productive land and also the agri-business sector. Analysis of power differences and social differentiation along economic, class, gender, religious and ethnic axes is important for understanding the effects of environmental disasters, and the impact of poor as well as better-off people on their environments. This was obvious for the participants in a meeting of representatives of NGOs and community organisations from Mexico and Central America in 1992, who discussed 'sustainable development' and defined the term 'environment.' They concluded that 'sustainable development must promote equality and solidarity; to overcome gender problems is essential.' Furthermore, they concluded, one must grasp that:

> environment is both Nature and Society, which relate to each other and co-exist. In the environment we find forests, human beings, land, mountains, water, air, animals, etc. The relationship between human beings and the other components can be good or bad. It is good when human beings can make adequate use of other environmental components, like water, forest and air. It is bad when humankind has destroyed them (for example deforestation), or when some people appropriate resources and thus endanger our survival and reproduction. That is

why we need conservation, harmony and equality between human beings, and between human beings and Nature.[2]

What stands out is that these participants' interpretations of the terms are normative too. But unlike Brundtland, the authors do not stress (economic) growth – they stress equality instead. They also talk of 'harmony' between people and nature, and importantly, of a whole and of connections between the parts which make up that whole – their talk emphasises connections between social development and natural resource conservation.

This holistic understanding of what is important is consistent with what citizens, groups, slum dwellers and the rural poor around the world, whenever given the opportunity, would communicate about environments, livelihoods and sustainabilities. Small farmers in marginal areas of Kenya, in particular women farmers, are adopting 'conservation farming' techniques with the primary motivation of increasing and sustaining the productivity of their fields and increasing their income (Neefjes et al. 1997). In a mountainous region of Vietnam, poor farmers equated 'environment' with tree planting, soil conservation and integrated pest management, primarily to ensure future, sustained production and income. In north-eastern Sudan, nomadic Beja men identified, with ease, wild plants which have multiple uses particularly in times of drought. They recognised the threat to their survival posed by the spread of the exotic and invasive mesquite tree, *Prosopis juliflora* (Neefjes 1998c). The Zabbaleen in Cairo, garbage collectors who recycle a large percentage of the city's waste, defined as their main environmental concerns those related to their personal health, which included the lack of a supply of safe drinking water, hygenic sewerage disposal, the risks (run primarily by girls and women) of getting their hands cut by sharp objects in refuse bins, and smoke from self-igniting plastic bags (the main un-recyclable type of garbage) in the alleyways of the community (Neefjes and Sabri 1996).

It is worth stressing that poor people and many development organisations often look positively at their environments and environmental productivity. This contrasts with much Northern-based environmentalism, alarmism, and statutory regulation which is predominantly about minimising negative impacts.[3]

## – Analysing people's livelihood environments –

A useful framework for analysing the relationships of poor and vulnerable people with their diverse environments has grown out of the work, amongst others, of Sen (1982), Chambers and Conway (1992), and Leach, Mearns and Scoones (1997), and is accessibly presented by Scoones (1998) and Carney (1998). Such work describes what constitutes livelihoods, what factors determine and improve the sustainability of livelihoods, and to some extent, how they relate to one another. It is a framework which puts people and their claims over resources at the centre, combines a holistic view with discourses of ordinary people, and permits an examination of the macro global issues of policy and environmental change without displacing the micro issues of livelihoods and their goals, or the local environmental matters which affect such livelihoods. The framework has normative aspects, such as endorsing the values of participation and equality. Although the definition of its terms and interpretations of its aspects may not be over-tight, it is, nevertheless, grounded in theory. For example, Sen's theoretical approach helps explain the occurrence of famine, showing that it occurs more as a result of a failure in people's entitlements than as a result of shortage of food at a national level. This frameworkd also bears many of the characteristics of political ecology, which attempts to establish causal links between ecological change and economic growth.[4]

A framework of sustainable livelihoods – following the work of Carney, Scoones, Chambers and Conway cited above – may be said to include the following elements:

1. Definition of sustainable livelihoods. 'A livelihood comprises the capabilities, assets (including both material and social resources) and activities required for a means of living. A livelihood is sustainable when it can cope with and recover from stresses and shocks and maintain or enhance its capabilities and assets both now and in the future, while not undermining the natural resource base' (Carney 1998 after Chambers and Conway 1997).
2. Identification of sustainabilities. Environmental, economic, social and institutional sustainabilities are identified. These should also be analysed at local, national and international levels.
3. Social disaggregation. The livelihoods that are targeted or studied should be those of individuals, households, groups of men and of women, and whole communities, and analysis should combine trends observed at these different levels.
4. Livelihood strategies. Individual women and men, households and communities usually pursue multiple livelihood strategies which, in one way or another, depend on natural resources and markets, and may include migration.
5. Livelihood outcomes. Outcomes of livelihood strategies include, for example, increased food security or income, and greater environmental sustainability, particularly of local environmental resources.
6. Assets and capitals. What people may or may not have at their immediate disposal for pursuing their livelihood strategies includes tangible and intan-

gible assets, which can be expressed as 'capital': human, social, technological/ physical, natural and financial. They thus include actual rights and claims to resources as well as capabilities to use, maintain and improve them.

7. Institutions and policies. Government structures, markets, laws, cultural practices and institutions, at local and and higher levels, define rights and duties which people can influence in more or less direct, more or less effective, ways. These rights and duties are often decisive factors in creating livelihood opportunities and strategies.

8. Contexts. Contextual factors are outside the immediate control or influence of people pursuing their livelihoods. They include natural disasters such as volcanic eruptions, effects of global climate change, sudden changes in world market prices of commodities, and war-related and technological developments beyond the influence of local people.

These elements need to be taken as no more than a checklist of what an analyst should consider before arriving at overall judgements of degradation or improvement in livelihoods and sustainabilities. Many, though not all, are in practice considered by local, poor and vulnerable people when making assessments of their problems and opportunities; however, policies and issues beyond the local level are not always in the forefront of their consciousness. It is important to note that both the theoretical grounding of this framework and its application in development practice have a strongly rural bias. However, there are no obvious ways in which the framework contradicts urban realities of poor and vulnerable people, although the difference in context requires adjusting the relative importance of some of its elements.

The framework has proved helpful in dialogues and shared analysis between outsider development professionals and insider and marginalised people, as it provides the former with a language that is compatible with what the latter is trying to communicate. The examples mentioned of people's views of 'environment' in the previous section bears this out; the examples cited in the rest of this chapter will refer back to several of the framework's elements in a further attempt to show its practical usefulness.

## – Participation and people power –

The sustainable livelihoods framework is so constructed as to highlight that women, men, families and communities are the agents which determine what their livelihood strategies are. Although their opportunities and decisions are constrained by various factors (of which some are necessarily beyond their control), it remains true that they alone bear responsibility for change in their environments and that they must live with the consequences. Of course, there are processes of environmental change happening without human interference, but as Blaikie and Brookfield (1987) point out, change only becomes 'degradation' in relation to possible or actual (human) uses of the environmental resource concerned.

As humans are at the centre of environmental change, certain key issues must be addressed: how they change their environments and value those changes, how power differences and relationships between people affect environmental change, whether it is possible objectively to determine that an environmental change amounts to environmental degradation, and whether those causing such degradation should be allowed to get away with it. The sustainable livelihoods framework does not offer simplistic answers to these questions; however, by identifying certain key elements, it helps to clarify an assessment of, and thereby influence, environmental changes which are taking place and the processes involved.

People power, and people's participation in social-political processes and development activities, have been analysed and various typologies have been derived. Adnan et al. (1992) have come up with a useful typology of participation as a result of research into the influence of Bangladeshi citizens on a large range of projects and planning exercises to combat the negative effects of floods – see figure 11.1.

Information Processes
  1. Unilateral announcement
  2. Listening
  3. Consultation
  4. Data collection
Project-related Activities
  5. Instrumental involvement
  6. Functional involvement
  7. Negotiation
  8. Externally initiated organisation
  9. Conflict resolution
People's Initiatives
  10. Self-mobilisation
  11. Empowerment

Figure 11.1 Typology of 'participation' (Source: Adnan et al. 1992)

Many of the forms of participation identified by Adnan et al. are top-down or externally initiated, and only the last two are types which could be classified as activism, where local people themselves take control of their resources, environments and livelihood opportunities. 'Empowerment' uniquely expresses the idea that disadvantaged and poor people improve their bargaining power *apropos* more powerful groups. Development agencies, and in particular NGOs, usually declare empowerment as their aim, but often do not practice or achieve more than a few of the information- or project- related forms of participation.

Participation in the sense of activism is different; the agenda is set by local people, although social movements are often dominated by individuals or small elite groups, too. The motivation for participation may be related to ecological conditions or to an attempt to find an alternative path of development, but does not necessarily oppose economic development. Rangan, writing about activism in India (including the well-known Chipko movement), says:

> Chipko's ecological successes resulted in new environmental regulations that compounded the lack of economic opportunities and development in the region . . . I challenge some contemporary views that see new social movements in the Third World as grassroots agents seeking alternatives *to* development . . . social movements in India are, contrary to these views, centrally concerned with access to development. (Rangan 1996, p. 206)[5]

Through a number of case studies of large projects in developing countries funded by the World Bank, the EU and the UK Government, Feeney (1998) shows that development interventionists, in direct collaboration with national governments, often fail to involve affected people in development projects, in particular in the earlier stages when important decisions are made. Participation, intervention and lobbying by local, national and international development NGOs have influenced legislation and project-management procedures, and have attracted and sparked off people's movements, but it is obviously difficult to turn around large projects towards real empowerment of local people.

There are many different participatory methods and approaches, currently practised in projects funded by the World Bank and NGOs alike; the most popular is commonly known as Participatory Rural Appraisal (PRA). Its authors and promoters speak of three main aspects: (a) reversals in the behaviour and attitudes of 'uppers' towards listening, enabling and respecting the ability of 'lowers' to speak and analyse, (b) methods which are often diagrammatic tools through which 'lowers' can show and discuss preferences, opinions and facts, and (c) sharing of knowledge and analysis, in particular between 'lowers' (Chambers 1997, p. 105).

One of the most complex and practically most difficult areas is making sure the 'sharing' becomes shared analysis between 'lowers' and 'uppers', outsiders and insiders, people with local knowledge and those with scientific and/or global perspectives. The framework of sustainable livelihoods has provided a basis for such dialogue and shared analysis in several cases (Neefjes 1998a; Neefjes and Sabri 1996), but not always successfully. It is a checklist for the outsider ('upper'), not a particularly useful dictionary for insiders ('lowers'). A review of conservation farming projects in Kenya, in which a range of 'stakeholders' participated, showed how outsiders' macro policy interests were accepted by all as important for increasing impact (Neefjes et al. 1997). In such a situation, a near-consensus between different stakeholders could be arrived at, unlike situations where conflict is rife, and in which people and projects continue to struggle for survival and improvements in livelihood opportunities (Neefjes 1999a).

Criticism of PRA and other methodologies of participation has been voiced, in particular regarding the exclusion of certain people, including women, from participatory processes,[6] and also regarding lack of understanding on the part of development practitioners of the complexity of facilitating processes of shared learning. Such criticism focuses on the less than ideal implementation of participatory approaches and methodologies, and does not imply that full participation of all important stakeholders and real empowerment of poor and marginalised people is actually impossible. Although Chambers (1997) claims that PRA has often been used as a mere label, instead of helping to reverse roles and empower marginalised people, and that 'the sudden popularity of PRA has generated huge problems and widespread bad practice . . . quality assurance has become a massive concern' (p. 115), his book, nevertheless, documents abundant evidence of good practice and enthusiasm in development and academic circles.[7]

The trend, suggested by development practice, is one of increased self-determination and involvement of stakeholders, including the more marginalised and poor, and in more general terms one of increasing 'social capital.' The trend is not visible everywhere, as weak government, weak civil society, violence and social destruction are predominant in many parts of the world (Neefjes 1999b). Some even argue that the 'bads' of globalisation could outweigh this trend. But if it were to continue, the future could belong to poor people.

However, the question remains whether this increase in people power provokes improvements in the environment, locally and globally. The example of conservation farming in Kenya suggests that poor and marginalised people can find ways of improving their livelihoods via environmentally benign practices, which could be enhanced through collective and participatory learning processes seeking to influence technology development and policy making (Neefjes et al. 1997). Similarly, people's movements in Brazil[8] and India[9] have achieved ecological, as well as social, benefits. Local, national and international NGOs in Mindanao in the Philippines, collaborating with local leaders of ethnic minorities, have made important legislative gains regarding recognition of rights over ancestral domains in the face of the expanding mining activities of large and international companies (SEAMEO 1997). However, these and other anecdotes and case studies do not prove automatic synergy between environmental gains at local level and poor people's empowerment. Furthermore, when aggregated, these positive effects are unlikely to counterbalance the global and local impacts of high consumption. The participation of poor and vulnerable people does not necessarily mean that global responsibilities are taken, nor that all non-participants' interests are looked after, including those of future generations and neighbouring countries and communities. It seems that environmental improvements at all levels happen, in particular, when different stakeholders work together and decisions and actions are informed by more than the local perspective alone.

## – ENVIRONMENTALISMS AND RESOURCE CONFLICTS –

There are obviously real differences in culture and political analysis between the North and the South, and between different social groups, about what constitutes a global and local environmental crisis and what action is necessary to cope with it. Guha and Martinez-Alier (1997) have drawn attention to this set of problems, contrasting the 'environmentalism of the poor' with 'First-World environmentalism', the former being characterised by 'nature-based conflicts' as well as by an 'environmentally destructive process of development', and the latter by 'the car which, more than anything else, opens up a new world, of the wild, which is refreshingly different from the worlds of the city and the factory' (pp. 16–17).' Within both the North and the South, other big differences also exist, including the opposition between movements involving direct action or appealing to spiritual or traditional values, and those associated with Enlightment philosophy and based on dualism, reductionism and rationality (Shiva 1988). Hayward (1994) writes with lucidity about such differences and argues that, at a fundamental level, it is possible to unite Enlightenment approaches with those associated with several forms of more radical environmentalism, such as holism. Also, forms of ecofeminism, in North and South, object to environmentalisms derived from the Western technocratic worldview on grounds of patriarchy and blindness to gender-based power differences.[10]

However, in spite of such deep-seated differences, the political processes which bear them out usually remain non-violent. Peaceful negotiations take place between industrialised and developing countries over issues such as the emission of greenhouse gases, climate change, biodiversity, intellectual property rights regarding crop seeds, and the environmental impacts of freeing up global trade (Watkins 1995). However, protests and people's movements sometimes elicit a violent reaction from governments, enterprises or local elites; these confrontations often concern a mixture of local issues, such as exclusion from economic development, unequal access to environmental resources, different views regarding the valuation of environmental resources, and the effects on human and animal health of environmental degradation. There are also conflicts, near-conflicts and potential conflicts between peoples and states over regional resources. Intense international negotiations as well as military confrontation also occur, in particular regarding international rivers such as the Nile, the Euphrates, the Rhine, the Ganges, and the Mekong, and the management of their watersheds.

Resource-related conflicts always threaten or actually affect the poorer and most vulnerable much more than others, which is what national and international NGOs address in lobby efforts. Global climate change, global warming and sea-level rise are a threat to people in unprotected deltas such as that on the coast of Bangladesh (especially those who cannot flee before floods hit), and smallholders who survive through rain-fed farming in much of semi-arid or semi-humid Africa. People displaced by storage dam construction and wildlife parks and their related commercial interests, or affected by mining and deforestation, suffer in order that the better-off can be supplied with electricity, gold or timber, or in the general name of industrialisation.[11] Furthermore, competition for natural resources can fuel war. Neo-Malthusian thinking, which argues that population increases of poor people in poor nations is the main cause of competition over resources and of environmental degradation, is too simplistic, and should be resisted as already observed. The genocide in Rwanda was about competition for land but, significantly, in the absence of non-land-based alternative livelihood opportunities (Neefjes 1999b).

## – A future of alternatives –

People develop alternative technologies, social arrangements and livelihoods in the face of (local) crises, environmental or otherwise. Many of these alternatives are creative and have potential for widespread adoption. Across the world, smallholder farmers are developing and adopting forms of 'sustainable agriculture' which enable them to increase their productivity, reduce their dependency on external inputs like pesticides and fertilisers, improve the sustainability of their environments, and protect or indeed even improve their own health and that of the consumers of their products (Reijntjes et al. 1992). Conway (1997) argues powerfully, on the basis of the failures of what became known as the Green Revolution, that a 'doubly green revolution' is happening, which will solve the multiple problems of poverty, food insecurity, and (rural) environmental degradation. He promotes participatory approaches to technology development and partnerships between scientists and farmers, in sharp contrast to the aggressive claims made by transnational companies that their genetically modified crops are the solution to world hunger.[12] Many development NGOs are seeking to support the development of such partnerships and agricultural alternatives. Oxfam and other international agencies have long supported Philippine NGOs, scientists and community groups in their action against destructive industrial fishing, and in the development of techniques that help regenerate coral and fishing grounds (Magsanoc Ferrer et al. 1996).

In urban areas, creative alternatives and solutions are found by governments, citizens' groups and NGOs alike. A much-quoted success story is the transport system in the Brazilian town of Curitiba (Davidson and Myers 1992) and also the collection and recycling of urban waste by the Zabbaleen in Cairo (Dem and Hart 1996). Grass-roots groups and NGOs such as the NGO PREDES near Lima in Peru take action against recurrent floods and mudslides that threaten the lives of urban dwellers (Davidson and Myers 1992, pp. 115–17), and initiate building and improving sewerage, transport and housing systems, such as the Orangi Pilot Project in Karachi (Gibson 1996, pp. 159–65). Local Exchange and Trade Systems (LETS) are developing in the USA, UK and other industrialised countries as ways to share resources and tap and provide skills and services from, and to, nearby people and create new forms of community. Gibson also describes a participatory approach to neighbourhood planning and improvement with the name 'planning for real' which began in the UK and has found applications in the rest of Europe, Africa, Asia and America, besides a plethora of successful people's initiatives to change their lives, neighbourhoods and indeed environments.

People-centred development alternatives are not new; E. F. Schumacher's *Small is Beautiful* (1973) is a well-known precursor to current work. Today, numerous types and examples of documented alternatives are available which have already been cited. They are all strongly rooted in people's own initiatives and participation and they are often led by enthusiastic activists, or 'moving spirits', as Gibson calls them. Governments, and other bodies such as international development (and funding) agencies, also play supporting roles. Success is often rooted in approaches, behaviour and lessons from process management (Chambers 1997, and Gibson 1996). Pye-Smith and Feyerabend (1994, pp. 171–82) describe factors for the success of people-centred sustainable development, including decentralisation of resource management and the importance of local leadership, and especially the growing alliances between non-governmental organisations, academics, (health) professionals and local peasants and residents.

## – Issues in the twenty-first century –

Predicting the future is the domain of fortune-tellers, and is not usually what development practitioners and scientists engage in. Some environmentalists do, and they tend to predict doom and gloom. This chapter merely confines itself to examining current trends to see if it is possible to outline what needs addressing in order to create better conditions for the survival and flourishing of poor and marginalised people in the near future.

Some current trends are promising. In many parts of the industrialised and industrialising worlds, deepening participation, with new, more complex and more practical manifestations of democracy and people's power, is appearing. Civil society is developing, supported by development agencies, the free press and the spread of the internet. Methodologies are evolving which enable developmental interventions to be transformed into empowering processes; they combine experience in participatory processes (such as PRA) with analytical frameworks (such as that regarding sustainable livelihoods), accommodating the discourses of both 'uppers' and 'lowers.' Practice suggests that there is no necessary contradiction between the existence of external agencies and indeed of 'interventions' on the one hand, and the objective of empowerment on the other. Experience also indicates that when popular movements grow in strength and genuine participation occurs, (local) environments tend to improve and regenerate while destructive developments are stopped. Furthermore, there are ample claims from development professionals and academics alike that where poor people can start benefiting from economic growth, their environments, urban or rural, benefit, although synergy does not always exist (Neefjes 1998b). Also, success is often achieved when wider (stakeholder) participation helps address concerns that go beyond the local level. However, it must also be borne in mind that people's empowerment and self-determination do not necessarily imply abjuring technological innovations which may turn out to have relatively severe ecological costs – Bebbington (1996) discusses a peasant movement in Ecuador where people were liberated from their past domination through adopting Green Revolution technology, while successfully preserving their identity. In general, however, poor people do look positively upon their environments as something to maintain, improve, respect and nurture.

On the downside, there are enormous pressures on resources from high-level consumers, which implies more potential for conflict at all levels, from local to international. There are huge educational gaps (and thus gaps in 'human capital') between the better-off and the poorer and more vulnerable groups in societies, as well as weaknesses in governance and a lack of 'social capital' in many developing countries. Furthermore, it is unlikely that technological improvements in resource-use efficiency will be able to keep up with the ever-increasing consumption aspirations of the affluent and the emerging middle classes in developing countries. The twin problems of poverty and environmental degradation are currently worsening by many accounts, at a global level and in many individual countries. In both North and South, the participation of local people – the poorer and also the better-off – in local initiatives can definitely make a difference, but for the eradication of poverty and environmental degradation in the twenty-first century, several requirements can be identified. These include the following:

1. More deeper a deepened collaboration between states and citizen groups is required to prevent conflicts and ensure a type of sustainable development that is people-driven, people-oriented, and understood as much as a social issue as an environmental or economic one. Governments must make resources accessible to their peoples, for example through land reform, and, more generally, must decentralise control over natural resources and the management of urban (environmental) services.
2. Collaboration between governments is also important in order to prevent resource competition from spilling over into trade wars or military conflict. National and international legislation and agreement must be developed further and adhered to consistently. Environmental resources must be shared between groups and countries.
3. Equality between social groups needs to be pursued much more vigorously, for example through redistributive efforts by governments to enable the poorest· to start benefiting from economic development. A case in point comes from Vietnam, where the very poorest, unlike the somewhat less poor, could not engage in tree-planting and terracing until the government intervened to alleviate their poverty by providing them with improved seeds (Bebbington 1996). Evidence also shows that national economic growth is positively supported by limited inequality (Watkins 1998).
4. High-level consumption of resources by affluent people needs to be urgently addressed. The poorest people cannot help the world out of its environmental

crisis, but those who ultimately cause it can and should. Extreme poverty does mean that poor people cannot contribute to environmental care and regeneration. Neither can they contribute to the economic activity beyond survival and subsistence level, nor much to the economic and institutional sustainability of their society. Reduction of resource consumption by the affluent depends on technological advances that need to be achieved by government regulations, fiscal incentives and subsidies, complemented by major behaviour changes of consumers, ranging from re-use and recycling of waste to severe reduction in energy and transport use.

5. People's power, participation and the building of social capital must be further encouraged and strengthened. Although democratic formations remain fragile, or non-existent, in many parts of the world, there are also many democratic gains. So much is happening, but so much more needs to be supported by governments, NGOs and also businesses.

6. People's power is also developing with regard to technology and environmental resources, which should prove to be a countervailing force to the increasing size and power of technocratic, narrowly scientific, and profit-greedy businesses. Activists are in the forefront of some of these initiatives, but they are not necessarily the implementers of them on a large scale. Innovation, technological and social alternatives are more likely to arise with good, appropriate and widespread education, something which is missing in much of the developing South, although industrial and rich countries, such as the UK, are not necessarily exempt from this criticism. We must be aware of the absence of an automatic synergy between these alternatives on the one hand, and regeneration of the local as well as global environments which are important for future generations on the other.

This essay cannot but end with the formulation of an aspiration rather than an assertion. At all levels, in all types of economies, the priority must be to promote policies which ensure poverty alleviation and economic growth with more equity, which bring about more effective use and regeneration of natural resources, which discourage and curb resource consumption by urban elites, which reduce urban pollution, and which secure a healthy environment for everybody, everywhere.

## – ACKNOWLEDGEMENTS –

This chapter has benefited from the work of, and collaboration with, many people in developing countries, rural and urban, women and men. Colleagues of Oxfam in national programmes were always helpful and took part in much of this work, as did staff members of Oxfam's partner organisations. Particular appreciation goes to Ian Scoones and Diana Carney, and many thanks also go to Ines Smyth and Sophie Bond for comments on the draft of this paper.

## – NOTES –

1. See Adnan et al. 1992; Davidson and Myers 1992.
2. Unpublished and translated by the author from the original Spanish text of an exchange meeting under Oxfam's South-South Environment Linking Project, on 10–11 September 1992.
3. This 'negative' approach of governments to the environment in the North and also in the South may be best grasped in terms of the standards which they set to limit pollution, and in terms of the requirement to do Environment Impact Assessments as an important part of planning procedures. Such exercises usually produce different (more or less negative) scenarios of environmental impact; decision-makers choose between these, weighing their negativities against projections of economic gains.
4. See Blaikie and Brookfield 1987; Hayward 1994; Peet and Watts 1966.
5. NGOs, working with poor people in participatory ways, commonly find that poor people are first and foremost interested in moving out of poverty through economic improvements in productivity, not merely in sustainability. See Neefjes 1998b.
6. Mosse 1995; Guijt and Shah 1998.
7. For more about participatory approaches and PRA (in particular, the latter's weaknesses, achievements and potential), see Guijt and Shah 1998; Estrella and Gaventa 1997. On the actual methodologies for empowerment and action research, see Pretty et al. 1995.
8. See, for example, Feeney (1998), who mentions the 'Movimento dos Trabalhadores Rurais Sem Terra' (MST), a landless people's movement.
9. See Rangan on the Chipko movement.
10. See, for example, Guijt and Shah 1998; Joekes et al. 1995.
11. See Oxfam (UK & Ireland) 1996 on the Masai and their land struggle, and Smyth 1997 on the implications of industrialisation in Java, Indonesia.
12. See also Moore-Lappé et al. (1998) who highlight lessons from the Green Revolution, challenging the idea that 'nature' is a main cause of poverty and famine and that feeding the world's poor would necessarily be environmentally problematic.

## – BIBLIOGRAPHY –

Adnan, Shapan, Alison Barrett, S. M. Nurul Alam, and Angelika Brustinow (1992), *People's Participation, NGOs and the Flood Action Plan – An Independent Review*, Dhaka: Research & Advisory Services (commissioned by Oxfam-Bangladesh).

Bebbington, Anthony (1996), 'Movements, modernisations and markets: indigenous organisations and agrarian strategies in Ecuador', in Richard Peet and Michael Watts (eds), *Liberation Ecologies: Environment, Development and Social Movements*, London and New York: Routledge.

Blaikie, Piers, and Harold Brookfield (1987), *Land Degradation and Society*, London and New York: Methuen.

The Brundtland Report (World Commission on Environment and Development) (1987), *Our Common Future*, Oxford: Oxford University Press.

Carney, Diana (1998) ed., *Sustainable Rural Livelihoods – What Contribution Can We Make?*, London: Department for International Development.

Chambers, Robert (1997), *Whose Reality Counts? Putting the First Last*, London: Intermediate Technology Publications.

Chambers, R., and G. Conway (1992), *Sustainable Rural Livelihoods: Practical Concepts for the twenty-first Century*, Brighton: Institute for Development Studies (Discussion Paper 296).

Conway, Gordon (1997), *The Doubly Green Revolution – Food for All in the Twenty-first Century*, London and New York: Penguin Books.

Davidson, Joan, and Dorothy Myers, with Manab Chakraborty (1992), *No Time to Waste*, Oxford: Oxfam.

Dem, M., and R. Hart (1996), 'Examples of urban development work from Senegal and Egypt', in Nicolas Hall, Rob Hart, and Diana Mitlin (eds), *The Urban Opportunity – The Work of NGOs in Cities of the South*, London: Intermediate Technology Publications.

Ekins, Paul (1993), 'Making development sustainable', in Wolfgang Sachs (ed.), *Global Ecology: A New Arena of Political Conflict*, London: Zed Books.

Estrella, Marisol, and John Gaventa (1997), *Who Counts Reality? – Participatory Monitoring and Evaluation*, Brighton: Institute for Development Studies.

Fairhead, James, and Melissa Leach (1996), 'Rethinking the forest-savannah mosaic – colonial science and its relics in West Africa', in Leach, Melissa and Robin Mearns (eds), *The Lie of the Land – Challenging Received Wisdom on the African Environment*, London and Oxford: The International African Institute/Heinemann.

Feeney, Patricia (1998), *Accountable Aid: Local Participation in Major Projects*, Oxford: Oxfam.

Gibson, Tony (1996), *The Power in Our Hands: Neighbourhood Based World Shaking*, Charlbury: John Carpenter.

Guha, Ramachandra, and Juan Martinez-Alier (1997), *Varieties of Environmentalism: Essays North and South*, London: Earthscan.

Guijt, Irene, and Meera Kaul Shah (1998), *The Myth of Community: Gender Issues in Participatory Development*, London: Intermediate Technology Publications.

Hall, Nicolas, Rob Hart, and Diana Mitlin (1996) eds, *The Urban Opportunity – The Work of NGOs in Cities of the South*, London: Intermediate Technology Publications.

Hayward, Tim (1994), *Ecological Thought: An Introduction*, Cambridge and Oxford: Polity Press/Blackwell Publishers.

Ho, Mae-Wan (1998), *Genetic Engineering: Dream or Nightmare? The Brave New World of Bad Science and Big Business*, Bath: Gateway Books.

Joekes, Susan, Melissa Leach, and Cathy Green (1995) eds, *Gender Relations and Environmental Change*, Brighton: Institute for Development Studies.

Leach, M., R. Mearns, and I. Scoones (1997) eds, *Community-Based Sustainable Development: Consensus or Conflict?*, Brighton: Institute for Development Studies.

Le Quesne, Carolyn (1995), 'Ecological footprints', in Kevin Watkins (ed.), *The Oxfam Poverty Report*, Oxford: Oxfam.

Macrae, Joanna, and Anthony Zwi, with Mark Duffield and Hugo Slim (1994), *War and Hunger – Rethinking International Responses to Complex Emergencies*, London: Zed Books.

Magsanoc Ferrer, Elmer, Lenore Polotan dela Cruz, and Marife Agoncillo Domingo (1996) eds, *Seeds of Hope: A Collection of Case Studies on Community-Based Coastal Resources Management in the Philippines*, Quezon City: University of the Philippines.

Moore-Lappé, Frances, Joseph Collins, and Peter Rosset, with Luis Esparza (1998), *World Hunger – 12 Myths*, London: Earthscan.

Mosse, David (1995), 'Authority, gender and knowledge: theoretical reflections on participatory rural appraisal' ODI Network Paper No. 44, London: ODI.

Neefjes, Koos (1998a), *Food Security in Southern Niassa – A Mid-term Review of the Impact of Oxfam's Programme in Nipepe, Metarica and Maua Districts* (Unpublished Oxfam mimeo).

Neefjes, Koos (1998b), *Oxfam's Impact on Livelihoods in Lung Vai: A Study of Change in a Commune in Lao Cai Province, Vietnam* (Unpublished Oxfam mimeo).

Neefjes, Koos (1998c), 'Ecological needs of communities during and after dryland crises', in H. D. V. Prendergast, N. L. Etkin, D. R. Harris and P. J. Houghton (eds), *Plants for Food and Medicine*, Kew: Royal Botanic Gardens.

Neefjes, Koos (1999a), *Participatory Review in Chronic Instability: The Experience of the 'Ikafe' Refugee Settlement Programme, Uganda*, London: ODI.

Neefjes, Koos (1999b), 'Ecological degradation: a cause for conflict, a concern for survival', in A. Dobson (ed.), *Fairness and Futurity*, Oxford: Oxford University Press.

Neefjes, Koos, Paramu Mafongoya, and Muthoni Mwangi, with Eliud Ngunjiri and Esther Mugure (1997), *Conservation Farming, Food Security and Social Justice – A Sectoral Review of Agricultural Work with Small NGOs and National Networking by Oxfam-Kenya* (Unpublished Oxfam mimeo).

Neefjes, Nicolaas, and Amal Sabri (1996), *Community and Environmental Health in the Moqattam – Report on Training in Participatory Learning and Action, and Assessment of Environmental Health and Project Impact* (Unpublished Oxfam mimeo).

Oxfam UK & Ireland (1996), *Land Tenure and Claims in Ololosokwan, Ngorongoro District in Tanzania.* (Unpublished Oxfam mimeo).

Peet, Richard, and Michael Watts (1996) eds, *Liberation Ecologies: Environment, Development, Social Movements*, London and New York: Routledge.

Pretty, Jules N., Irene Guijt, John Thompson, and Ian Scoones (1995), *A Trainer's Guide for Participatory Learning and Action*, London: IIED.

Pye-Smith, Charlie, and Grazia Borrini Feyerabend, with Richard Sandbrook (1994), *The Wealth of Communities: Stories of Success in Local Environmental Management*, London: Earthscan.

Rahnema, Majid (1992), 'Participation', in Wolfgang Sachs (ed.), *The Development Dictionary: A Guide to Knowledge as Power*, London: Zed Books.

Rangan, Haripriya (1996), 'From Chipko to Uttaranchal: development, environment and social protest in the Garhwal Himalayas, India', in R. Peet and M. Watts (eds), *Liberation Ecologies: Environment, Development, Social Movements*, London and New York: Routledge.

Reijntjes, C., B. Haverkort, and A Waters-Bayer (1992), *Farming for the Future – An Introduction to Low-external-input and Sustainable Agriculture*, London and Leusden: MacMillan/ILEIA.

Renner, Michael (1996), *Fighting for Survival – Environmental Decline, Social Conflict, and the New Age of Insecurity*, New York and London: Norton.

Sachs, Wolfgang (1992) ed., *The Development Dictionary: A Guide to Knowledge as Power*, London: Zed Books.

Sachs, Wolfgang (1993) ed., *Global Ecology: A New Arena of Political Conflict*, London: Zed Books.

Schumacher, E. F. (1973), *Small is Beautiful: A Study of Economics as if People Mattered*, London: Sphere Books.

Scoones, Ian (1998), *Sustainable Rural Livelihoods: A Framework for Analysis*, Brighton: Institute for Development Studies Working Paper No. 72.

SEAMEO (1997), *Policy Consultation – Workshop of Oxfam (UK & I) and Partners on Sustainable Resource Management of Indigenous People's Ancestral Domain* (Summary documentation, unpublished mimeo, SEAMEO Innotech, Diliman, Quezon City, Philippines).

Sen, Amartya (1982), *Poverty and Famines: An Essay on Entitlements and Deprivation*, Oxford: Clarendon Press.

Shiva, Vandana (1988), *Staying Alive: Women, Ecology and Development*, London: Zed Books.

Smyth, Ines (1997), *Industrialisation and Natural Resources: Household Adaptive Strategies in Java, Indonesia*, Bandung: Akatiga.

Wackernagel, Mathis, and William Rees (1996), *Our Ecological Footprint: Reducing Human Impact on the Earth*, Gabriola Island, BC: New Society Publishers.

Watkins, Kevin (1995), *The Oxfam Poverty Report*, Oxford: Oxfam.

Watkins, Kevin (1998) *Economic Growth with Equity: Lessons from East Asia*, Oxford: Oxfam.

Williams, Christopher (1998) ed., *Environmental Victims: New Risks, New Injustice*, London: Earthscan.

# Notes on the Contributors

JOERI BERTELS graduated in environmental biology at the University of Amsterdam. After that, he did a Master's degree in Environmental Management. He has worked at the Institute for Environmental Studies of the Free University, Amsterdam, where he also contributed to a multi-disciplinary textbook about the environment. More recently, he partici-pated in projects on the interface between environmental issues and spatial developments, sponsored by the Dutch Council for the Environment at the Centre of Environmental Science in Leiden State University. He is pre-sently employed at the Dutch Ministry of Housing, Spatial Planning and the Environment.

JAN BOERSEMA is Senior Lecturer in Environmental Science and Philosophy at Leiden University and project director at the Ministry of Housing, Spatial Planning and the Environment. Educated as an biologist, majoring in ethology, at the University of Groningen, he graduated on a thesis entitled: 'Thora and the Stoics on Man and Nature.' His publications cover a wide range of subjects in the environmental field. He is editor-in-chief of a textbook on environmental science, *Basisboek Milieukunde* (Boom, Amsterdam) and of *Milieu*, a scientific journal. With Wim Zweers he edited *Ecology, Technology and Culture* (White Horse Press).

AVNER DE-SHALIT (D.Phil., Oxford) is Senior Lecturer at the Hebrew University of Jerusalem and associate fellow at the Oxford Centre for Environment, Ethics and Society. He the author of *Why Posterity Matters* (Routledge, 1995), and co-editor of *Communitarianism and Individualism* (Oxford University Press, 1992) and of *Liberalism and Its Practice* (Routledge, 1998). His monograph entitled *The Environment: Between Theory and Practice* is forthcoming.

ANDREW DOBSON is Professor of Politics at Keele University. His publications include *An Introduction to the Politics and Philosophy of José Ortega y Gasset* (Cambridge University Press, 1989), *Green Political Thought* (Unwin Hyman, 1990; second edition, 1995, Routledge), *The Green Reader* (ed.) (André Deutsch, 1991), *Jean-Paul Sartre and the Politics of Reason* (Cambridge University Press, 1993), *The Politics of Nature* (co-edited with Paul Lucardie) (Routledge, 1993), *Justice and the Environment* (Oxford University Press, 1998), *Fairness and Futurity* (ed.) (Oxford University Press, 1999). He is presently working on the idea of ecological citizenship.

ROY ELLEN is Professor of Anthropology and Human Ecology at the University of Kent at Canterbury. He has published widely on ethnobiological classification and the ecology of small-scale subsistence producers in the tropics, mainly in connection with long-term fieldwork in eastern Indonesia. His recent books include *The Cultural Relations of Classification: An Analysis of Nuaulu Animal Categories from Central Seram* (Cambridge University Press, 1993) and (edited with Katsuyoshi Fukui, 1996) *Redefining Nature: Culture, Ecology and Domestication* (Berg, 1996).

ALAN HOLLAND is Professor of Applied Philosophy at the University of Lancaster. He is the founding editor of the interdisciplinary journal *Environmental Values* and was formerly Director of the MA Programme in Values and the Environment at Lancaster. His recent publications include a co-edited volume on *Animal Biotechnology and Ethics* (Chapman and Hall, 1998), and several articles on policy-related themes in applied philosophy, including sustainability, environmental decision-making and genetic handicap. He is currently working on a critique of the use of information models in biology.

KEEKOK LEE is now with the Department of Philosophy, the University of Lancaster in a research capacity. Environmental philosophy is one of her main areas of research, especially with regard to the implications of science and technology for environmental philosophy. As such she attempts to tie up her interests in the philosophy and history of science and the philosophy and history of technology with environmental philosophy itself. But she also has a long-standing interest in social philosophy. Her involvement with this volume stems from this preoccupation as well as that with environmental concerns. Her latest major publication is *The Natural and the Artefactual: The Implications of Deep Science and Deep Technology for Environmental Philosophy* (Lexington Books/Rowman & Littlefield, 1999).

ENRIQUE LEFF is co-ordinator of the Environmental Training Network for Latin America and the Caribbean (United Nations Environment Programme), and Professor of Political Ecology at the National University of Mexico. He is the author of several books and articles. Among the more recent ones are: *Green Production: Towards an Environmental Rationality* (Guilford Publications, 1995); and *Saber Ambiental: Sustentabilidad, Racionalidad, Complejidad, Poder* (Siglo XXI Editores-UNAM-PNUMA, 1998).

DESMOND MCNEILL is Director of the Centre of Development and the Environment, University of Oslo. He has worked as an adviser and consultant in more than fifteen developing countries, mostly in Africa and Asia, for various aid agencies including the World Bank, UNDP, NORAD, ODA, USAID, and the Asian Development Bank. He is the author of *The Contradictions of Foreign Aid* (Croom Helm, 1981). His current research interests include foreign aid policy, sustainable development, consumption patterns and the relationship between research and policy.

MARY MELLOR is Professor of Sociology and Chair of the Sustainable Cities Research Institute at the University of Northumbria at Newcastle. Her previous books include *Breaking Boundaries: Towards a Feminist Green Socialism* (Virago, 1992) and *Feminism and Ecology* (Polity and New York University Press, 1997).

KOOS NEEFJES has been a policy adviser on environment and development for the past eight years at Oxfam UK's Policy Department. Previous to that, he worked extensively in Africa, Asia and Latin America on development projects and acted as a consultant to various projects and missions. He is currently working on a book entitled *Poor Peoples' Environments: A Professional Development Guide to Improving the Sustainability of Livelihoods* (Oxfam UK, 2000).

MICHAEL REDCLIFT is currently Professor of International Environmental Policy at Keele University, where he is head of the Department of Environmental Social Sciences. He was formerly Director of the Global Environmental Change programme of the ESRC (1990–1995) and has researched and worked in Spain, Mexico and the United States of America.

MARK SAGOFF is Senior Research Scholar at the Institute for Philosophy and Public Policy in the School of Public Affairs, University of Maryland. He is the author of *The Economy of the Earth* (Cambridge University Press, 1988), and was named a Pew Scholar in Conservation and the Environment in 1991. From 1994–1997, he served as President of the International Society for Environmental Ethics. He has an A.B. from Harvard and a

Ph.D (Philosophy) from the University of Rochester, and has taught at Princeton, the University of Pennsylvania, the University of Wisconsin (Madison), and Cornell. He has published widely on philosophical issues in law, economics, technology and the environment.

# Index

Abortion, 149, 193
Absorption capacity, 66
Academic field, 18
  research, 17
Academicians, 66
Academics, 9-13, 15, 23, 155, 188, 214
Accumulation of capital, 34, 103, 148,
  155
  of wealth, 132
Achuar, 66
Acid rain, 1
Activism, 24, 209
Activist(s), 9, 10-13, 25, 38, 56, 150-1,
  155-6, 188, 213, 216
Adriatic Sea, 80
Affluence, 44, 64, 90, 126, 130
Africa, 106-7, 115, 121, 147, 150, 191,
  203, 212-13, 223
*Agathis*, 176
Agenda, 21, 63, 80, 100, 156, 179
Agriculture, 7, 81, 89, 121, 135, 147-8,
  158, 173-6, 178, 213
Agro-ecology, 69-70
Agro-forestry, 70
Aid, 18, 106, 129, 200, 223
Air travel, 196
Allocative resources, 100
Aluminium, 118, 127
Amazon, 66
Ambergris, 176
Amenity value, 35
Amino acids, 40
Amphibian species, 89
Andes, 171
Animal rights, 22
Animal(s), 40, 50, 57, 80, 123, 133-4, 152,
  177, 195, 204, 212
Anthropocentrism, 35, 59
Anthropologist(s), 9, 15, 17, 21, 25, 100,
  116, 168, 174, 204
Anthropology, 18, 172
Antigua, 115

Aquaculture, 114, 122
Asia, 89, 103, 106, 150, 213, 223
  economic crisis, 178
  'tigers', 101
Atlantic coast, 66
Atmosphere, 99, 101, 124
Authoritarianism, 68
Automobiles, 84, 119

Bacteria, 39, 118, 121
Baduy, 175
Bali, 178
Bananas, 129
Bangalore, 150
Bangladesh, 109, 204, 208, 212
Barriers to trade, 126
Basic needs, 42-3, 70, 116, 130, 132, 150,
  201-2
Bauxite, 127
Beja, 205
Biodiversity Convention, 1, 5, 16, 35, 39,
  48, 50-2, 56-8, 66, 77, 85-7, 89, 101,
  151, 175-6, 179, 212
Biofuels, 125
Biologist(s), 117, 133-4
Biomass, 65
Bioregionalism, 68
Biosphere, 57, 134, 201-2
  reserves, 65
Biospheric imperative, 100
Biotech, 122
Biotechnologists, 121
Biotechnology, 39, 121, 123, 151, 179
  firm 122, 128
Bird-nests, 176
Birmingham, 52
Birth control, 149-50
Blueprints, 170
Borneo, 177
Brazil, 23, 67, 126, 131, 211
Brazilian Women's Coalition, 155
Bretton Woods, 106-7, 109